Praise for the Kiss, Bow, or Shake Hands

"In this global economy, ANYONE who leaves the U.S. is a fool if they don't read up on their destination's customs. *Kiss, Bow, or Shake Hands* is THE definitive authority on how to conduct yourself around the world. You can easily offend your prospects and there is no faster way to kill the most lucrative business deal. *Kiss, Bow, or Shake Hands* has been immeasurably helpful over the years."

—Louis Altman, President, New Hampshire International
Trade Association (NHITA), and President, GlobaFone

"*Kiss, Bow, or Shake Hands* has been an invaluable resource for international businesspeople for years. Don't leave home without it."

—Joe Douress, Vice President,
LexisNexis Martindale-Hubbell

"*Kiss, Bow, or Shake Hands* is a great resource of cultural and business-related information. The material is concise and easy to read. The cultural information is unique, educational, and fun! It's a book that can be enjoyed by a great number of people, from a student, to a leisure traveler, to the most sophisticated

1/08

ent,
hia

"In my wo   o
manage the   v,
or Shake H   i-
viduals in   ss
internation

s,
L

"To help a   s,
there are cr   y
phone, and

s,

It is possible to consider the loci of decision-making as a series of concentric circles. In the center, in the smallest circle, is the individual. The next circle, slightly larger, is usually the family. Many cultures expect each individual to consider "What is best for my family?" prior to making any decisions. The next circle represents a larger group. It could be an ethnic group, a religion, or even the individual's country. Some cultures expect individuals to consider the best interests of the entire, expansive group.

Of course, when a person is acting as representative for a company, the best interests of the company may be paramount.

Sources of Anxiety Reduction

Every human being on this planet is subject to stress. How do we handle it? How do we reduce anxiety?

We can identify four basic sources of security and stability that people turn to: interpersonal relationships, religion, technology, and the law. Frequently, a combination of sources is used.

A person who must decide on an important business deal is under stress. If this person is your client, it may help you to know where he or she will turn for help and advice. This is especially true when the person turns to interpersonal relationships. If an executive is going to ask his or her spouse for advice, you had better make sure that you have made a good impression on that spouse.

Issues of Equality/Inequality

An important characteristic of all cultures is the division of power. Who controls the government, and who controls the business resources?

"All men are created equal" is a sacred tenet of the United States. Despite this, prejudice against many groups still exists in the United States.

All cultures have disadvantaged groups. This section identifies some sectors that have unequal status. These can be defined by economic status as well as by race or gender. Only the most industrialized nations tend to have a large, stable middle class. Many countries have a small, rich elite and a huge, poverty-stricken underclass.

is overwhelmingly advantageous simply because they want their own people to do it. It doesn't matter that you can provide a better-quality product at a much lower price; they believe it is better that their fellow citizens produce the product, even if they produce an inferior product at a higher cost. Presenting facts to such a person is a waste of time. His or her faith operates independently from facts.

Clearly, people who believe in facts want to see evidence to support your position. They can be the most predictable to work with. If you offer the low bid, you get the job.

People who believe in feelings are the most common throughout the world. These are the people who "go with their gut instincts." They need to like you in order to do business with you. It can take a long time to build up a relationship with them. However, once that relationship is established, it is very strong. They aren't going to run to the first company that undercuts your offer.

▶ VALUE SYSTEMS: THE BASIS FOR BEHAVIOR

Each culture has a system for dividing right from wrong, or good from evil. After a general statement concerning the values of the culture, this section identifies the culture's three value systems (Locus of Decision-Making, Sources of Anxiety Reduction, and Issues of Equality/Inequality). These following three sections identify the Value Systems in the predominant culture of each country.

Locus of Decision-Making

This section explores how much a culture prizes individualism as opposed to collectivism. Some countries, such as the United States, are very individualistic, while others, such as Chile, are more collectivistic. A person in the United States may consider only himself or herself when making a decision, while a person in Chile may need to determine how a decision might reflect on his or her group or extended family.

Pure individualism and collectivism are rare. In most countries people consider more than just themselves, but are not bound by the desires of the group.

to extrapolate data and consider hypothetical situations ("I've never experienced X, but I've read about how such things might occur").

Obviously, no country has more than its share of smart (or dull) people. However, some cultures have come to value abstractive thinking, whereas others encourage associative patterns. Much of this has to do with the educational system. A system that teaches by rote tends to produce associative thinkers. An educational system that teaches problem-solving develops abstractive thinking. The scientific method is very much a product of abstractive thinking. Both northern Europe and North America produce a lot of abstractive thinkers.

Particular or Universal Thinking?

One final category has to do with how thinking and behavior are focused. People are divided into *particular* versus *universal* thinkers. The particularistic person feels that a personal relationship is more important than obeying rules or laws. On the other hand, the universalistic person tends to obey regulations and laws; relationships are less important than an individual's duty to the company, society, and authority in general.

Not surprisingly, the previous categories tend to go together in certain patterns. Abstractive thinkers often display universalistic behavior: It requires abstractive thought to see beyond one's personal relationships and consider "the good of society" (which is a very abstract concept).

▶ NEGOTIATION STRATEGIES: WHAT WE ACCEPT AS EVIDENCE

In general, let us assume that everyone acts on the basis of his or her own best interests. The question becomes: How do I decide if this is a good deal or not? Or, in a broader sense, what is the truth?

Different cultures arrive at truth in different ways. These ways can be distilled into *faith*, *facts*, and *feelings*.

The person who acts on the basis of faith is using a belief system, which can be a religious or political ideology. For example, many small nations believe in self-sufficiency. They may reject a deal that of the most sacred precepts established by the founding fathers of the United States.

That North American is being closed-minded. He or she is refusing to even consider the Muslim's reasoning. A truly open-minded person would consider the proposition. He or she might reject the possibility after due thought, but not without a complete evaluation.

In fact, a person who wants to study cultural orientation should consider such questions. Granted, most businesspeople would probably decide that the United States should not become a theocracy. But considering the topic can lead to some useful insights. Perhaps most important is the concept that much of the world does not share the United States' predilection for the separation of church and state. This separation is a specifically Western notion, which evolved out of the hundreds of years of European religious wars that followed the Protestant Reformation.

In point of fact, most cultures tend to produce closed-minded citizens as long as things are working fairly well. It often takes a major disaster to make people open-minded. For example, the citizens of many former Communist nations are now becoming open-minded. Their old Communist ideology has fallen apart, and they realize they need new answers.

Associative or Abstractive Thinking?

Another aspect of cognitive styles is how people process information. We divide such processing into *associative* and *abstractive* characteristics.

A person who thinks associatively is filtering new data through the screen of personal experience. New data (we'll call it X) can only be understood in relation to similar past experiences (Is this new X more like A, or maybe B?). What if X is not like anything ever encountered before? The associative thinker is still going to pigeonhole that new data in with something else (X is just another B). On the other hand, the abstractive thinker can deal with something genuinely new. When the abstractive person encounters new data, he or she doesn't have to lump it in with past experiences (It's not A, it's not B or C—it's new! It's X!). The abstractive person is more able

Cognitive Styles: How We Organize and Process Information

The word "cognitive" refers to thought, so "cognitive styles" refers to thought patterns. We take in data every conscious moment. Some of it is just noise, and we ignore it. Some of it is of no interest, and we forget it as soon as we see/hear/feel/smell/taste it. Some data, however, we choose to accept.

Open-minded or Closed-minded?

Studies of cognitive styles suggest that people fall into *open-minded* and *closed-minded* categories. The open-minded person seeks out more information before making a decision. The closed-minded person has tunnel vision—he or she sees only a narrow range of data and ignores the rest.

Something that might surprise you is that most experts in cultural orientation consider the citizens of the United States and Canada to be closed-minded.

Open-minded people are more apt to see the relativity of issues. They admit that they don't have all the answers, and that they need to learn before they can come to a proper conclusion. Frankly, there are not many cultures like that. Most cultures produce closed-minded citizens.

Here's an example: Most theocratic (governed by religious leaders) cultures are closed-minded. That's one of the characteristics of such a culture: God tells you what is important. Anything outside of those parameters can be ignored. From a business point of view, that can be a weakness. For example, Islam prohibits charging interest on a loan. There can be no argument and no appeal: Charging interest is wrong. Obviously, running a modern banking system without charging interest is challenging.

So why are Canada and the United States closed-minded?

Assume that someone from an Islamic country tells a North American that the United States is evil and should become a theocracy. The North American is likely to scoff. The United States a theocracy? Nonsense! Why, the separation of church and state is one

Cultural Orientation

FOR EACH OF THE COUNTRIES in *Kiss, Bow, or Shake Hands: Europe* there is a Cultural Orientation section. The study of cultural orientation gives us a model for understanding and predicting the results of intercultural encounters. It is, however, a model—a theory. New discoveries continue to be made about why we act the way we do.

Furthermore, communication always takes place between individuals, not cultures. Few individuals are perfect representations of their culture. Citizens of the United States are generally known for addressing one another by first names, a habit that most of the world does not follow. However, there are many U.S. citizens who are more comfortable with formality, and prefer to use last names and titles. This does not make them any less like U.S. citizens. It just makes them individuals.

Many global executives adopt the manners of their targeted countries, so why do U.S. executives need to study foreign ways? There are a variety of reasons. First of all, many foreign businesspeople often cannot or will not imitate U.S. mannerisms. Can you afford to leave them out of your business plans? Second, you might wish to sell to the general public in a foreign market. The average foreign consumer is certainly not going to have the same habits or tastes as consumers in the United States. Third, although your business counterpart in Spain may act or speak like an American or Canadian or Australian at times, he isn't. He probably is not even thinking in English; he is thinking in Spanish. Knowing how Spanish people tend to arrive at decisions gives you an edge. And don't we all need every business advantage we can get?

Here is a breakdown of the information in the cultural orientation section.

KISS, BOW, OR SHAKE HANDS: EUROPE

How to Do Business in
25 European Countries

- CULTURAL OVERVIEWS
- TIPS FOR DOING BUSINESS • KNOW BEFORE YOU GO
- NEGOTIATING STRATEGIES
- PROTOCOL

TERRI MORRISON AND WAYNE A. CONAWAY

BUSINESS

AVON, MASSACHUSETTS

A Antonio
Il mio cuore.
And to Nica, Brendan, and Alex
Forever Wise, Forever True, Forever Loved
—Terri Morrison

To my Parents
I hope I was a good long-term investment.
—Wayne A. Conaway

And to the late George A. Borden, Ph.D.,
a gifted friend.

Published by Adams Media, an F+W Publications Company
57 Littlefield Street
Avon, MA 02322
www.adamsmedia.com

ISBN 10: 1-59869-218-6
ISBN 13: 978-1-59869-218-1

Printed in Canada.

J I H G F E D C B A

Library of Congress Cataloging-in-Publication Data
is available from the publisher.

Contents

Preface

IN THE DOZEN YEARS since *Kiss, Bow, or Shake Hands* was originally published, the world has changed in remarkable ways. Several countries have dissolved (such as the Soviet Union), others have been absorbed (East Germany), and some have emerged (Azerbaijan). Trade barriers have been lifted (South Africa and Vietnam were added to the large edition of *Kiss, Bow*) and economies have radically shifted (Ireland and India).

The interesting thing is that over twelve years—throughout all of the massive political and economic changes—the cultures, values, and belief systems of major ethnic groups have remained constant.

For example, many European executives are fully aware of international business practices, yet they clearly appreciate it when others show some knowledge of their own negotiating styles and cultural values. Just understanding that Germans generally keep a slightly larger personal space around themselves than most British or North Americans may give you an advantage over other executives who do no research, or ignore protocol. As Johann Wolfgang von Goethe said, "There is nothing more terrible than ignorance in action" (*Es ist nichts schrecklicher als eine tätige Unwissenheit.*).

During my life, I have seen world war, reconstruction, terrorism, and tremendous advances in technology. On this increasingly interconnected planet, businesses need to acknowledge that people are not alike all over the world—the more you respect local attitudes toward families, work, and religion, the more successful you will be in those locales. Priorities in Lisbon are not equivalent to those in Los Angeles.

Once again, it is a pleasure to introduce you to this important book. Review it before you embark on your international trips. Gain the information you need on business practices, cognitive styles, negotiation techniques, and social customs. Give the right gift; make the right gesture. Read *Kiss, Bow, or Shake Hands: Europe.*

—HANS H.B. KOEHLER,
Former Director of the Wharton Export Network

"*Audi alteram partem.*"
"Hear the other side."

Introduction

WHAT WILL YOU NEED TO KNOW in 2010 or 2020 to work in Europe? As Hans Koehler pointed out in his Preface, we live in changing times. But many of the cultural tenets presented here in *Kiss, Bow, or Shake Hands: Europe* took hundreds or thousands of years to develop. These stable precepts help us understand why people behave differently around the world, and they will help you to avoid committing global marketing faux pas like these:

> *In July 2006, after eight years of investment, the U.S. retail giant Wal-Mart relinquished all its German stores to a competitor and wrote off a loss of over $1 billion. While cultural conflicts were not the sole cause of the failure, they definitely contributed to the meltdown. Besides annoying German customers by bagging all their purchases (German consumers do not like strangers to touch their food), Wal-Mart management tried to impose the following U.S. employment practices on their staff:*
>
> * *Wal-Mart employees were prohibited from dating colleagues in senior positions.*
> * *Flirting at work was* verboten.
> * *And . . . if flirting or dating was detected, employees were instructed to use a phone hotline to inform on each other's transgressions. (A German court ruled against the last procedure.)*
>
> *The disgruntled employees and customers, combined with the high cost of labor, were significant factors in Wal-Mart Germany's demise.*

McDonald's Corporation settled a group of lawsuits for $10 million in 2002. Why were they sued? Because of their French fries and hash browns. After 1990, McDonald's stated that only pure vegetable oil was used to cook their fries, implying that they were prepared in a "vegetarian" manner. However, the oil contained the essence of beef flavor, which is an anathema to Hindus and vegetarians worldwide. Most of the money from the lawsuit was donated to Hindu and other vegetarian causes.

As these examples show, an unintentional misstep can threaten or destroy your costly international marketing efforts.

Kiss, Bow, or Shake Hands: Europe is organized in a clear, consistent manner to help you easily find the data you need to avoid many of the errors others have made before you.

The work to develop this volume resulted in not only this book, but much additional information that is available on our Web site *www.kissboworshakehands.com.* The Web site also contains information on official world holidays, recommendations for learning foreign languages, gift-giving suggestions, legal data, and hundreds of articles like "Subtle Gestures," and "Lie To Me." *Kiss, Bow* is now part of a larger electronic database—*Kiss, Bow, or Shake Hands: Expanded Edition.* You are also welcome to contact us at 610-725-1040 or e-mail *TerriMorrison@getcustoms.com* with your questions or comments.

Each chapter in this book focuses on a single country, and all are organized into sections, such as in the following example for Switzerland:

What's Your Cultural IQ?	Three quick questions to gauge your knowledge
Tips on Doing Business in Switzerland	Three business-related highlights
Country Background	History, Type of Government, Language, and The Swiss View (perspectives from the country's viewpoint)

Know Before You Go   Natural and human hazards

Cultural Orientation   A cultural anthropologist's view. This section is
                                described in detail in the introductory chapter.

Business Practices   Including sections on Punctuality, Appointments,
                                and Local Time; Negotiating; and Business
                                Entertaining

Protocol   With discussions of Greetings, Titles/Forms of
                                Address*, Gestures, Gifts, and Dress

As in the previous edition, many Cultural Notes are also scattered throughout the chapters.

Please remember that you will work with individuals, and there are always exceptions to every rule. For example, *Kiss, Bow: Europe* suggests that many Spaniards have a strong sense of personal honor, have an exceedingly strong network of family and friends, and are sensitive to being reprimanded in public. This is reflected in the proverb *"Quién a uno castiga, a ciento hostiga"*—"He that chastens one, harasses one hundred."

Now, somewhere there is probably a reserved, quiet, and emotionless Spanish manager, without any family or friends, who never takes umbrage at a punishing tone in public. Just because we haven't met him (or her) doesn't mean that no such person exists.

The process of communication is fluid, not static. The success of your intercultural interactions depends upon you, and the quality of your information. *Kiss, Bow, or Shake Hands: Europe* provides you with the best and most current data possible on what foreign business and social practices to expect in your efforts at globalization.

> "The most universal quality is diversity."
> —MICHEL DE MONTAIGNE, 1580

*For more details on Titles/Forms of Address, Mailing Addresses, etc., we also recommend an excellent book called *Merriam-Webster's Guide to International Business Communications*, by Toby D. Atkinson.

Issues of male-female equality are also analyzed in this section. It is useful for a female business executive to know how women are regarded in a foreign country.

Never forget that this model represents cultural patterns that may or may not apply to each individual you contact and get to know. Utilize this information as a guideline and remain open to the new experiences we all encounter abroad.

> *"Vérité en-deca des Pyrénées, erreur au-dela."*
> —BLAISE PASCAL, 1623–1662

> "There are truths on this side of the Pyrenees
> which are falsehoods on the other."
> —TRANSLATION: GEERT HOFSTEDE

MAP OF EUROPE

North Atlantic Ocean

Ireland
PAGE 120

United Kingdom
PAGE 293

Denmark
PAGE XX

Norway
PAGE 162

Sweden
PAGE 242

Finland
PAGE 60

Russia
PAGE 206

Netherlands
PAGE 148

Belgium
PAGE 26

Germany
PAGE 83

Poland
PAGE 173

Belarus
PAGE 13

Ukraine
PAGE 280

Spain
PAGE 231

France
PAGE 71

Czech Republic
PAGE 36

Slovak Republic
PAGE 219

Switzerland
PAGE 254

Austria
PAGE 1

Hungary
PAGE 109

Romania
PAGE 195

Italy
PAGE 132

Turkey
PAGE 266

Portugal
PAGE 186

Vatican City
PAGE 144

Greece
PAGE 99

Austria

Republic of Austria
Local short form: Öesterreich
Local long form: Republik Öesterreich

Cultural Note

Learn to enjoy Austria's coffeehouses, but don't expect to be able to get a hurried cup of coffee in one. Austrians give specific instructions on how they want their coffee, and then may make that single cup last their entire visit.

▶ WHAT'S YOUR CULTURAL IQ?

1. Which of the following Austrian emperors ruled for an astonishing sixty-eight years?
   a. Francis I
   b. Ferdinand I
   c. Francis Joseph I
   d. Charles I

   ANSWER: c. Francis Joseph I—also known as Franz Joseph—ruled from 1848 to 1916. He died during the First World War, to be succeeded by Charles I, the final emperor.

2. Austria has a glorious musical heritage. In addition to Mozart and Haydn, there were multiple composers named Strauss. Which one of the following people was *not* an Austrian composer?
   a. Oscar Straus
   b. Eduard Strauss
   c. Johann Strauss
   d. Richard Strauss

   ANSWER: d. Richard Strauss was German; his work is unfortunately associated with Nazi Germany, although after the war he was cleared of charges of collaboration with the Nazis.

The Austrian Strauss family included two men named Johann (traditionally called "the Elder" and "the Younger"), plus Josef Strauss and Eduard Strauss. Oscar Straus (note the single s at the end of the name) was also Viennese but unrelated to the Strauss family.

3. Literature is also very important to Austrians, although most Austrian writers are not well-known outside the German-speaking world. TRUE or FALSE? The classic Walt Disney cartoon *Bambi* was based on the work of an Austrian writer.
   ANSWER: TRUE. It is from a short 1923 novel written by Felix Salten (real name Siegmund Salzmann) (1869–1954) titled *Bambi, ein Leben im Walde* ("Bambi, a Life in the Woods"). He coined the name "Bambi" from the Italian word for "baby," *bambino*.

▶ TIPS ON DOING BUSINESS IN AUSTRIA

- Once the center of the huge Austro-Hungarian Empire, modern Austria has been drastically diminished in size and power. However, this has not diminished its cultural richness. Austrians expect foreigners to appreciate their achievements in music, architecture, and literature.
- Austrian management style emphasizes consensus-building and sophisticated "people skills." Confrontation is usually avoided, even if rules must be bent to do so.
- Austrians are animal lovers, and the government has passed one of the toughest animal rights laws in the European Union (EU). Chickens must be free-range (not caged), dog ears cannot be cropped, and "invisible fences" are illegal. Ask about their beloved Lipizzaner stallions.

▶ COUNTRY BACKGROUND

History

The written history of Austria dates back to 14 B.C., when the Romans marched north to the Danube River, conquering a Celtic kingdom known as Noricum. Thereafter, Austria's history paralleled that of Germany and France. Eight centuries later, Austria became part of Charlemagne's empire. Like the French and the Germans, the Austrians consider Charlemagne a forefather of their nation.

Rudolph of Habsburg was elected emperor of the Holy Roman Empire in 1273. He seized Austria (among other territories), marking the beginning of Habsburg rule of Austria.

In 1477, Maximilian of Habsburg married Mary of Burgundy, initiating the tradition of Habsburg rulers gaining territory through marriage rather than conquest. When Maximilian died in 1519, his grandson Charles V inherited a dominion ranging from Austria to the Netherlands to Spain. In 1521, he split the Habsburg domains. His brother Ferdinand I became ruler of Austria and its nearby territories, which included parts of northern Italy. Ferdinand later added Hungary and Bohemia to his holdings. Both Charles and Ferdinand kept their lands Catholic in the face of the Protestant Reformation; Austria remains Catholic to this day.

In a watershed event for all Europe, the Ottoman Turks laid siege to Vienna in 1683. Thanks to help from the Polish and German armies, the Turks were swept back—not just from Austria, but from Hungary as well.

In reaction to Napoleon's annexation of various Habsburg lands, Francis II renounced his title of Holy Roman emperor and declared himself hereditary emperor of Austria (this made him Francis I of Austria). In 1806, the Holy Roman Empire ceased to exist, replaced by Napoleon's Confederation of the Rhine.

Metternich became foreign minister of Austria in 1809, and for the next thirty-nine years, he cleverly manipulated the politics of Europe. Following Napoleon's defeat in 1814, Metternich presided over the Congress of Vienna, a gathering of the victorious powers. Metternich assured Austrian supremacy over Germany by making Austria the president of the new German Confederation.

Orchestrated by Otto von Bismarck, Prussia defeated Austria in the Seven Weeks War (or Austro-Prussian War) of 1866. Henceforth Prussia (later Germany), not Austria, was the supreme German-speaking nation.

In 1867, the crowns of Austria and Hungary were granted to a single monarch, who was emperor in Austria and king in Hungary.

This empire became known as Austria-Hungary and was popularly referred to as the dual monarchy. They were separate states, each with its own constitution, government, parliament, and language. The Magyars had a privileged position in Hungary while the Germans predominated in Austria.

The First World War was sparked in 1914 by the assassination of Archduke Francis Ferdinand and his wife in the Bosnian capital of Sarajevo.

Austria-Hungary fought as one of the Central Powers alongside Germany and the Ottoman Empire—which was the losing side in the war.

After the war, Austria-Hungary was carved up into separate nations. Austria itself became an independent republic in 1918.

In 1938, German troops entered Austria, and Anschluss (annexation) was declared. Austria, renamed the Ostmark (Eastern March), was divided into seven administrative districts under the central authority of the German Third Reich.

The Austrian Republic was restored after World War II. Allied forces—including those of the USSR—remained for ten years. Austria narrowly escaped becoming a Soviet satellite like its Eastern European neighbors. The occupying troops left only after Austria promised to remain neutral, allied with neither East nor West.

Austria became a member of the European Union on January 1, 1995.

Type of Government
The Republic of Austria is a federal multiparty republic with two legislative houses, the Federal Council and the National Council. The president is the chief of state; the chancellor is the head of the government.

Suffrage is universal at eighteen years of age and is compulsory for presidential elections.

Austria has a high standard of living, but this cannot be maintained as its population ages. The country has two choices: to allow increased immigration or to encourage its elderly to re-enter the work force (probably by cutting social entitlements). Both of these are controversial political issues.

For current government data, check with the Embassy of Austria: *www.austria.org.*

Language
The official language of Austria is German. When Austrians study foreign languages, they usually learn those of their neighbors, especially the French and Italians. English speakers can usually be found in major cities and in multinational corporations.

The Austrian View
The Austro-Hungarian Empire was staunchly Catholic, but modern Austria has no official religion. The majority of Austrians remain Roman Catholic (78 percent). Nonreligious and atheists make up the next largest group at 8.6 percent, followed by Lutherans (4.8 percent), and Muslims (2.0 percent). Today, Jews constitute only 0.2 percent of Austria's population.

Austria's birth and death rates are almost equal. Thanks to immigration, Austria now exhibits a miniscule growth rate of 0.22 percent. Since the immigrants are usually Turkish, this is a concern for Austrians, who see their cultural traditions under siege. Whether or not to limit immigration is a constant political issue.

Almost all Austrians avow a love of nature. In addition to skiing, many Austrians enjoy hiking and camping. They also enjoy long vacations to take advantage of their country's scenic landmarks.

Some Austrians believe that their country's best days are past. Because change has been bad for Austria, there is substantial resistance to change and technology.

One exception to this is in the field of medical technology. Austria ranks near the top of countries with the best medical care for its citizens. For example, Austria ranks in the top five for the number of MRI machines per population.

The preoccupation with Austria's glorious past weighs less heavily upon the younger generation. Some are far more optimistic about Austria's future. Younger executives are also much less likely to be technophobes. However, power is heavily concentrated in the hands of senior executives and politicians.

☑ Know Before You Go

The greatest hazards to visitors tend to be exposure to cold and sunburn. Because of Austria's high altitude, there is less protection from the sun.

Avalanches and landslides are also hazards. Earthquakes occasionally occur in Austria.

Almost 75 percent of Austria's land surface is more than 1,700 feet above sea level. Altitude sickness is a danger for visitors to the mountains, but not for travelers in the cities. Altitude sickness can strike anyone, even if you have never experienced it before. There is no sure prevention except gradual acclimation to high elevation. Alcohol consumption tends to make the symptoms worse.

Austria has an active Green Party, which believes Austrians are in danger from aging nuclear power plants in neighboring Slovenia and the Czech Republic.

▶ CULTURAL ORIENTATION

Cognitive Styles: How Austrians Organize and Process Information

Austrians traditionally have a structured approach to absorbing and processing information. They are most comfortable with a linear approach to data, and feel concern about taking action in a premature manner.

Negotiation Strategies: What Austrians Accept as Evidence

Scientific data, or facts, are the most important component of any decision. Feelings sometimes influence the process, because of the number of people who are usually consulted prior to large decisions. However, if there is a conflict between an individual's feelings, faith, and scientific evidence, the facts will outweigh any other factor.

Value Systems: The Basis for Behavior

The following three sections identify the Value Systems in the predominant culture—their methods of dividing right from wrong, good from evil, and so forth.

Locus of Decision-Making

A desire to seek consensus and a widespread respect for order are Austrian characteristics, as evidenced by the fact that there have been almost no labor strikes in the postwar era. Every Austrian has a responsibility to support the social order. Actions that disrupt this social order are seen as inherently wrong.

Sources of Anxiety Reduction

Some sociologists believe that Austrians have a high index of uncertainty avoidance. As a result, Austrians use laws and morality to give structure to their worldview. Certainly, Austrians tend to be extremely averse to risk.

In 1955, the USSR demanded that Austria adopt permanent neutrality in exchange for agreeing to remove its troops from Austria. Official neutrality (while remaining economically engaged with the West) seems to have suited the Austrian character. The fall of the Iron Curtain and Austria's entry into the European Union has required some redefinition of neutrality.

Issues of Equality/Inequality

Although titles of nobility were abolished after the First World War, Austria still has a rigid class system. Business leaders tend to come from the upper class.

Historically, Austria's ornate Catholic churches were the only place where all citizens, whatever their status, could enjoy the sort of environments found in the palaces of the nobility. Today, church attendance has plummeted, but Austrian laws protect all citizens equally. Even legally employed noncitizens (of any nationality) belong to a legal body designed to protect their interests. For most workers, this is the Arbeiterkammern (Workers' Chambers), which provides legal representation without regard for a worker's ability to pay. In fact, when it loses a case, the Arbeiterkammern usually pays the opponent's legal fees.

▷ BUSINESS PRACTICES

Punctuality, Appointments, and Local Time

- In business meetings between equals, Austrians are very punctual, expecting to begin at the exact time specified. They expect the same from visitors.
- As in every country, rank has its privileges: a higher-ranking person can make a subordinate wait. However, a subordinate who makes his boss wait even five minutes is in trouble.
- Social events in Austria (such as the start time of the opera) also begin on time.
- Lateness is not just impolite in Austria; it is believed that an inability to use time wisely is indicative of deficiencies in other areas. Failure to be prompt will eliminate you from consideration as a prospective business partner.
- Austrian executives have their schedule planned weeks in advance (or longer). Make your appointments as far in advance as possible, and try and give plenty of advance notice if you must reschedule.
- The residents of Austria, like most Europeans, write the day first, then the month, then the year (e.g., December 3, 2010, is written 3.12.10 or 3/12/10).
- Many Austrian businesspeople take just thirty minutes for lunch.
- Do not expect to catch Austrian executives at work after business hours. Many Austrians believe that people who work excessively late are using their time inefficiently.
- Austrians typically take long summer vacations (often the entire month of August) and long December holidays. Check on Austrian official holidays at *www.kissboworshakehands.com*.
- Austria is one hour ahead of Greenwich Mean Time (G.M.T. + 1). This makes it six hours ahead of U.S. Eastern Standard Time (E.S.T. + 6).

Cultural Note

Listen for reports of "good snow" at the many ski resorts. Many Austrians ski, and they may take off from work to take advantage of excellent skiing weather.

Negotiating

- Business meetings typically begin with small talk. Expect to be asked about your journey, what scenic Austrian sights you have visited, and so on. You may also be asked your opinion about current events. Although this conversation seems inconsequential, you are being judged by the Austrians, so be ready with intelligent commentary.
- All meeting attendees are expected to be fully prepared. Facts and figures must be provided—if not in the body of your presentation, then in supplementary materials.
- Unless a presentation is being made, the senior person present sets the agenda. Expect discussions to be linear and to follow the agenda point by point.
- When the final item is addressed, the meeting may end abruptly. Austrian concepts of time management do not call for meetings to "wind down." If additional matters not on the agenda require discussion, those will be dealt with in subsequent meetings.
- Austrians tend to negotiate in a direct, linear fashion. Anything that upsets the natural order of things tends to throw off the entire process.
- Decision-making is generally slow in Austria. Although consensus is sought, the top of the hierarchy, which tends to be very traditional and averse to risk, makes final decisions.
- There are still relatively few female executives at the upper levels of Austrian management. Foreign businesswomen should not be offended if Austrian men are more formal and courteous around them.

Business Entertaining

- Austrians keep a strict division between work and play. While you may invite your Austrian counterparts to a dinner or a party, do not be surprised if they decline. You might never see them outside the office until the close of successful negotiations, when they will invite you to a meal.
- Breakfast is usually eaten at home; business breakfasts are still rather uncommon.

- Midmorning breaks often include a sandwich; midafternoon breaks usually involve coffee and cake.
- While the typical Austrian lunch is often as brief as thirty minutes, it can nevertheless be a heavy meal. A business lunch will probably last longer.
- Invitations to dine will usually be at a restaurant. Austrians rarely entertain business associates at home.
- If you are invited into an Austrian home, consider it an honor. Dress well and bring gifts.
- Keep your hands above the table during the meal.
- Good topics of conversation include Austria's culture, cuisine, history, and beautiful landscape.
- The Austrians take coffee and wine quite seriously.
- Except for traditional winter sports such as skiing, Austrians do not tend to be sports fanatics. Even football (soccer) did not become an important sport in Austria until after the Second World War. Snowboarding has become popular.

⊙ PROTOCOL

Greetings

- If possible, find someone to introduce you. Austrians do not feel it is appropriate to introduce yourself to strangers.
- The usual greeting between men is a brief but firm handshake. (Most Austrians will have excellent posture—no hands in your pockets, etc.) While it is not traditional for men to shake hands with women, Austrian men will do so if a woman offers her hand first. Austrian women do not traditionally shake hands with each other, but may choose to do so in a business setting.
- Never put your hand in your pocket for longer than it takes to retrieve an object. Austrians find it insulting when someone speaks to them with his hands in his pockets.
- Carry a good supply of business cards. If your company is an old one, include the year it was founded on your card.

- Extended, direct eye contact is expected when conversing. Failure to meet an Austrian's gaze will give the impression that you are untrustworthy.

Titles/Forms of Address
- In business settings, Austrians address each other by titles and surnames. Do not address an Austrian by his or her first name unless requested to do so.
- Even when an adult Austrian is not present, it is considered ill-mannered to refer to him or her by surname alone. The title or honorific must be used at all times.

Gifts
- Gift giving is not traditionally an integral part of doing business in Austria. When given, gifts tend to be well-chosen but modest in value.
- It is wise to carry several small presents with you, so if you are presented with a gift you can reciprocate immediately.
- Preferred gifts are manufactured in your home country. An illustrated book of your home city or region is a good choice. If the recipient drinks alcohol, wine or spirits produced in your home region is also a good choice.
- In business settings, Austrians open gifts immediately.
- Once a close business relationship is established, Austrians give business colleagues gifts at holidays (especially Christmas) and to celebrate the completion of a successful business deal.

Dress
- Conservative, formal dress is expected in Austria. Shoes must be recently shined. Clothes must be clean and recently pressed.
- Dark, sober colors are preferred. Flashy, bright clothing is inappropriate for a business setting.

Cultural Note

Austria has a hierarchical culture, in which age is respected. Your company should send senior executives to important meetings in Austria. If younger people (such as technicians) must be sent, they should be accompanied by an older executive—even if he or she has no real function other than to provide gravitas.

When speaking to Austrian executives, do not make jokes. Austrians do not believe that jokes and humor have any place in business. Never open a speech or presentation with a joke or humorous anecdote.

On the other hand, in social settings, Austrians are great admirers of wit. Many intellectual habitués of Austrian coffeehouses were noted for their cleverness.

Belarus

Republic of Belarus
Local long form: Respublika Byelarus'
Former: Belorussian (Byelorussian) Soviet Socialist Republic

Cultural Note

This nation has been known in the West under several different names: White Russia, Byelorussia, Belorussia, and others. Historians sometimes use the term "Ruthenia," although the Ruthenians are both Belarusians and Ukrainians. Its current official name is the Republic of Belarus.

There is still dispute on the spelling of the adjectival form in English. Both Belarusan (without the *i*) and Belarusian (with the *i*) are currently in use. Some even use Belarussian (two *s*'s and an *i*, as in Russian).

▶ WHAT'S YOUR CULTURAL IQ?

1. TRUE or FALSE? When the United Nations was formed, the Byelorussian Soviet Socialist Republic had a vote in the UN, separate from that of Russia.

   ANSWER: TRUE. The price for the USSR to join the United Nations was that they received three votes in the general assembly, not just one. Russia, Ukraine, and Byelorussia all had a vote. Of course, all three voted the same way.

2. The Radzivil family was the most famous and accomplished house of Belarusian nobles. Match the individual with his or her accomplishments.

   a. Mikalaj Radzivil Corny   1. Fought Calvinism;
   (1515–1565)   wrote travelogues

13

b. Mikalaj Radzivil Sirotka   2. Established first
   (1549–1616)   secular Slavic theater
c. Franciska Ursula Radzivil   3. Governor of Vilnius
   (1705–1753)
   ANSWERS: a. 3; b. 1; c. 2

3. TRUE or FALSE? The Pahonia—a symbol featuring an armored
   knight astride a charging horse—is now the national symbol of
   the Republic of Belarus.
   ANSWER: FALSE. The Pahonia (which can be translated as "the chase") was often used as the
   national symbol of Belarus, including immediately after the collapse of the USSR in 1991.
   However, it was banned as an official symbol in 1995 because it is also associated with the
   Nazi-occupied state of Belarus during the Second World War.

▶TIPS ON DOING BUSINESS IN BELARUS

- While many Russians will assure you that reunification between
  Russia and Belarus is only a matter of time, you should take Belarusian nationalism seriously. Many Belarusians consider themselves ethnically separate from Russians and believe they are fully
  entitled to a separate state. Stating a different opinion may invite a
  lecture on the complex, interlocking history of Ruthenians, Poles,
  Lithuanians, Ukrainians, and Russians. On the other hand, there
  are many citizens of Belarus who would welcome reunification
  with Russia. These are not limited to ethnic Russians.

- Western governments have accused Belarus of all manner of
  crimes, from money laundering to weapons trafficking with Iran
  to human rights violations. Of interest to foreign businesspeople
  is Belarus' habit of confiscating entire shipments and the vehicles
  they came in on if there is the slightest irregularity. A 2005 World
  Bank report lists Belarus as one of the most difficult countries in
  the world in which to do business.

- Despite all the drawbacks, Belarus currently has a growing
  economy and there are business opportunities there. The country
  reminds some intrepid foreigners of Russia in the lawless years
  after the collapse of the USSR.

▶ COUNTRY BACKGROUND

History

Belarus experienced it first modern independence in 1917 and 1918, after the collapse of Czarist Russia and the Brest-Litovsk Treaty, which divided up the Russian Empire. This Belarusian Peoples Republic was short-lived; it was soon absorbed into the new USSR.

Between the wars, Belarus and neighboring Ukraine suffered famine due to purges and the forced collectivization policies of Stalin. Millions of people died, and thousands more were deported to Siberia.

Belarus was occupied by Nazi Germany from 1941 to 1944. Thousands of Jews were executed and deported to concentration camps. As they did in other occupied areas of the USSR, the Nazis raised local troops to fight Moscow.

In 1986, the Chernobyl nuclear accident in neighboring Ukraine spewed radioactive fallout over much of Belarus.

Belarus declared its independence from the USSR on July 27, 1991. It established itself as a parliamentary republic within the Commonwealth of Independent States (CIS).

In 1994, Alexander Lukashenko was elected the first president of Belarus. Thanks to a constitutional referendum in 1996, he extended his presidential term and concentrated almost all government power in the executive branch.

Belarus signed the Belarus-Russian Union Treaty on April 2, 1997. This provided close coordination of military and economic policies between the two countries. Eventual union of the two nations is considered likely, but no date for that has been set.

By 2004, President Lukashenko had been in office for ten years, but he wanted to remain in power despite term limits. He responded angrily to various sanctions against his government. These included the Belarus Democracy Act of 2004 of the United States, an EU travel ban on four top Belarus Ministers, and Greece's refusal to allow the Belarus minister of sport to attend the 2004 Summer Olympic Games in Athens.

Type of Government

The Republic of Belarus is a parliamentary republic. However, since his election in 1994, all power has gravitated to Lukashenko. Sometimes called "the last European dictator," President Lukashenko has ruled Belarus while maintaining a semblance of democracy. Lukashenko's "market socialism" has effectively isolated his country from Western capitalism and trade. Most of Belarus' trade is with Russia and Ukraine.

Belarus was one of three founding members of the Commonwealth of Independent States, a successor organization to the USSR.

For current government data, check with the Embassy of Belarus, which has a Web site at *www.belarusembassy.org*.

Language

The official language of Belarus is Belarusian, which is understood by some 98 percent of the population. Belarusian is written in Cyrillic script. It is a Slavic language, midway between Russian and Ukrainian. Most dialects of Belarusian are more or less intelligible to speakers of both Russian and Ukrainian.

Because of the dominance of Russia in education and the media, most citizens of Belarus can also speak Russian. In fact, many ethnic Belarusians use Russian in everyday life.

Also spoken in Belarus are Polish, Ukrainian, Yiddish, Tatar, Lithuanian, Latvian, and Roma (Gypsy).

The Belarusian View

There is no official religion in Belarus, but at least 60 percent of the population identify themselves as Orthodox. (Some reports indicate as high as 80 percent Orthodox.) Formerly this was the Russian Orthodox Church, but in 1990, Belarus was designated an exarchate.

Religion was discouraged under Communism, so church attendance has experienced a substantial revival since independence. Nineteen different religious denominations have been officially registered.

As with other institutions, churches have historically been under the control of outsiders in Belarus. Some three-quarters of Belarusians once belonged to the Uniate Church, which is a Greek rite church that accepts the authority of the Roman Catholic pope. Moscow outlawed the Uniate Church in 1839, replacing it with the Orthodox faith. More recently, Moscow suppressed the Roman Catholic Church, especially when John Paul II of Poland became pope. Recently, various Protestant groups have experienced rapid growth.

Belarus is considered the slowest ethnically Slav republic to make adjustments to capitalism.

Belarusians generally do not feel in control of their own destiny. They have lived under authoritarian governments their entire lives. Also, the radioactive fallout from the Chernobyl accident in neighboring Ukraine has contaminated much of Belarus, causing increased rates of thyroid cancer—another factor over which they have no control.

While many older citizens of Belarus feel nostalgia for the USSR and would welcome reunion with Russia, these feelings are not necessarily shared by the young, who have grown up in an independent Belarus.

The best and brightest of Belarus have often left their homeland. During the days of the USSR, many left for more prestigious positions in Moscow. Today, some also seek success in the West.

☑ Know Before You Go

Reciprocity, a common tactic in the Cold War, is alive and well in Belarus. If your nation does something that displeases the leaders of Belarus, you may be caught up in the dispute. For example, if your nation refuses entry to an important citizen of Belarus, you may be refused entry into Belarus—even though you had nothing to do with your government's actions.

As in other former republics of the USSR, street crime is present. Corruption is rife; the police are always willing to demand a few dollars from foreigners for some imaginary infraction.

Although the location of Belarus in eastern Europe should make it an important transit point for trade, many of its roads remain in poor condition.

Street demonstrations against the government occur at times, especially in the capital of Minsk. Foreigners should avoid such demonstrations, which risk the possibility of arrest.

Despite recent claims by the Belarusian minister of health that their health care system "is now reaching the world level in terms of using modern equipment and technologies," the U.S. State Department recommends that foreigners who experience medical emergencies in Belarus opt for medical evacuation and seek treatment elsewhere.

Although the 1986 Chernobyl nuclear accident occurred in Ukraine, the prevailing winds blew much of the fallout into neighboring Belarus. The cleanup of this fallout has been haphazard; vast stretches of southern Belarus remain contaminated. There is also soil pollution from heavy pesticide use.

⊚ CULTURAL ORIENTATION

Cognitive Styles: How Belarusians Organize and Process Information

Belarusians have a great desire for independence and autonomy, but they are steeped in tradition and tend to follow powerful leaders without question. Most education is skill-oriented; it is practical rather than conceptual. Belarusians' concerns are generally for the immediate, particular situation.

Negotiation Strategies: What Belarusians Accept as Evidence

Truth is found in the pressing, real-time feelings of the participant. It is often enhanced by faith in an ideology or a strong leader, but not generally by the accumulation of objective facts.

Value Systems: The Basis for Behavior

Although the name of this country means "White Russia," Belarusians are more similar to Ukrainians in their values than they are to Russians. The following three sections identify the Value Systems in the predominant culture—their methods of dividing right from wrong, good from evil, and so forth.

Locus of Decision-Making

There is a continual struggle between individual freedom and obligations to the collective unit. Traditionally, the extended family is the basic unit for decision-making, but this unit includes persons other than blood kin who are accepted into the family. Although all members have a strong need to contribute to the welfare of the collective unit, the head of the family or the family unit makes decisions. In general, Belarusians value stability over freedom, and are willing to cede decision-making to a strong leader as long as he keeps the peace.

Sources of Anxiety Reduction

Because Belarus has historically been dominated by Poland, Lithuania, and Russia, there is considerable national ambiguity stemming from the controversies over its name, language, traditions, and national heritage. Loyalty to an employer or local leader provides a sense of security. This makes the extended family or collective unit essential in avoiding uncertainty.

Religion has experienced a revival since 1990 and helps provide structure and reassurance into the lives of its adherents. However, even here there is uncertainty, with some smaller religions (such as the Uniates, the Old Believers, and some Protestant sects) claiming that they are the true nationalist Church of Belarus, while the two majority religions (Orthodoxy and Roman Catholicism) are controlled by non-Belarusians.

Issues of Equality/Inequality

There is a strong desire for autonomy, individual freedom, and private property, but both tradition and Communism have taught Belarusians to accept and respect collectivism. Power is vested in the leader, and he or she is responsible for the behavior of subordinates. (For example, disobedience among children is considered the fault of the parents.) Men and women have strict sex roles that are not to be confused, but each has an autonomy that is respected by the other. There is a strong sense of equality between husbands and wives, even though men do not usually share the household chores.

⊙ BUSINESS PRACTICES

Punctuality, Appointments, and Local Time
- Belarusians believe that punctuality is a hallmark of foreign business practices. Your image as a business professional depends upon your punctuality.

- Don't be surprised if high-level Belarusians are late. Punctuality is your tradition, not theirs.
- Residents of Belarus write the day first, then the month, then the year (e.g., December 3, 2010, is written 3.12.10 or 3/12/10).
- Before your first meeting, the company's top executive should know who you are, what you are interested in, what your project is, and (most importantly) which other Belarusian bureaucrats have agreed to it or are supportive.
- This data is usually transmitted most effectively through your hired intermediary. Your contact can be a medium-level executive, but he or she should be respected and known by top management.
- At the first meeting, Belarusian managers will appreciate a written, straightforward outline of the project under discussion. Your intermediary should be prepared to expand on details when necessary.
- The intermediary should not only promote your project but follow up as well. A good intermediary verifies that e-mails and faxes are properly prepared, translated, transmitted, and received. Equipment and delivery can be frustratingly inefficient.
- Further meetings should be planned immediately and the dates fixed; the names of people to be involved (plus their contact information) should also be determined. If this meeting is to be a month later, send follow-up messages with copies to your intermediary.
- Belarus is three hours ahead of Greenwich Mean Time (G.M.T. + 3). This makes Belarus eight hours ahead of U.S. Eastern Standard Time (E.S.T. + 8).
- Belarus undergoes a form of daylight-saving time, with the switch usually occurring around the end of March and October. The exact dates of time changes are announced from year to year and generally differ from the schedule used in western Europe.

Negotiating
- Traditionally, bureaucrats tended to answer "no" to a proposal if they had nothing to gain by agreeing. Indeed, the ability to say "no" was historically their only real power.

- More recently, the higher the executive level, the easier it seems to be able to get a "yes." But this does not guarantee an affirmative on lower levels. Remember that Belarus isolated itself from capitalism, so some routine Western business practices may be unfamiliar. Be prepared to explain every aspect of a deal.
- Getting a positive response at every bureaucratic level requires solid groundwork and help from an intermediary.
- At this time there is a dearth of experts in Belarus' ever-changing business and legal regulations. Belarus executives themselves may not have a full grasp of the legal issues. Hire a local lawyer who is an expert in Belarusian law to monitor the entire business environment and report to you independently.
- Belarusian negotiators may walk out of the talks at some juncture. While this tactic is becoming less common, and can alarm westerners, a deal might not be considered well made if its discussion and details went completely smoothly.
- Your Belarusian partners are expecting concessions, so go to the talks with a private list, made in advance, of items on which you are prepared to bargain. Concede one item at a time, so that your partners feel that such benefits are a result of their efforts. Once a deal is final, Belarusians usually consider renegotiation impossible.
- At the appropriate time, make certain that all sides completely understand any legal regulations from your home country that are involved in the deal.

Business Entertaining
- Business breakfasts are not common.
- Belarusians like to invite business partners to restaurants or to their homes. They have a strong tradition of hospitality that was strictly restrained during the Communist years, when every foreigner was considered a spy.
- The people of Belarus have a reputation as being more pleasant than Russians. Visitors report that, when drinking, Belarusians may sing.

- Accept all invitations. Be aware that the food will be rich and the drinks strong. In fact, Belarusians feel that business arrangements go more smoothly when their business partner is more relaxed through convivial drinking. Belarusian men are proudly confident of their own drinking ability, and a man may drink half a liter of vodka in an evening without any obvious effect.
- It is gracious to learn a few toasts. The most common are *na zdo ro vie* (your health) and an ancient Polish toast, *sto-lyat* (a hundred years).
- When hosting a meeting, be certain to use china, not plastic, for serving refreshments. Belarusians usually supply a variety of refreshments when conducting meetings and appreciate reciprocity. Also, have a supply of cigarettes, lighters, calculators, and so forth.
- Traditional Belarusian restaurants have tables designed for four or six people. If your party has only two or three, you may be asked to share a table with strangers when you are seated.
- Once you open one, you must pay for an entire bottle; no matter how little of it you drink. Many restaurants and cafés accept only hard currency.
- Bottles are often left on the tables, along with as much food as the guests can possibly consume, because it is traditional to present an atmosphere of comfortable abundance. Choices of sodas, wines, cocktails, brandy, and "the best Belarus vodka in the world" will be served.
- Dinner invitations at a home are usually for Saturdays at six, but guests take up to an hour to gather. In a home, you will probably find that the children are included.
- Good topics of conversation include the cultural and artistic achievements of Belarus, sightseeing, and (especially) sports. For a small country, Belarus has produced more than its share of Olympic winners.
- Bad topics of conversation include anything that might meet with disapproval from the government of Belarus, such as allegations of corruption, money-laundering, or human rights violations.

- Remember that it is usually to your advantage to look and sound like a foreigner because foreigners get preferential treatment and help almost everywhere. (However, this can also make you more of a target for street crime since you presumably have more valuables.)

⊙ PROTOCOL

Greetings
- Belarusians are not demonstrative in public. Only relatives, very good friends, or well-known business friends of long standing are greeted cheerfully with an embrace and a kiss on each cheek.
- Except at formal or state affairs, Belarusians usually shake hands and state their own last name to a stranger instead of using a phrase like "How do you do?" Respond in the same way.
- Men and women readily shake hands with each other.

Cultural Note
When written in a foreign alphabet, there may be many ways to write a Belarusian name. For example, in English, the president's surname is alternately written as Lukashenko or Lukashenka. His first name may be Anglicized into Alexander, or the more traditional Alyaksander or even Alyaksandr.

Since there is no rule to follow, ask your Belarusian associate how he or she would like the name to be transcribed into your language.

Titles/Forms of Address
- Belarusian names are written in the same order as in the West. The middle name is a patronymic (a name derived from the father's first name). In the example of "Svyatoslav Alesevich Bryl," Svyatoslav is the first name, the patronymic means "son of Ales," and the surname is Bryl.
- Women often add an *a* to their surname.
- Be careful not to confuse the order of names. It is now acceptable to use only the last name for a person of slight acquaintance; for example, Bryl, Gospodin Bryl (the polite method), or even Mr.

Bryl is appropriate. His wife would be Gospozha Bryl or Mrs. Bryl.

- The only title of respect traditionally used in Belarus is "Professor." It is used when addressing a doctor of science, an elderly scientist, or a schoolteacher beyond the elementary level.
- There are few variations of first names and surnames. Some are so often used (e.g., Vasil, Vasilievich, and Vasiliev) that confusion is inevitable. Furthermore, if you are invited to address a person by his or her first name, remember that all first names have diminutives, nicknames, and pet names. Which you will use depends on the depth of your acquaintance. The best advice is to ask; he or she will be happy to explain.

Gestures

- Belarusians have their share of obscene gestures. The North American "okay" sign (thumb and forefinger touching in a circle) and any shaken-fist gestures are interpreted as vulgar.
- It is impolite to sit with your legs spread apart or with your feet propped up on a table.
- The thumb between the forefinger and middle finger means "you'll get nothing."
- Whistling is not a sign of approval at a concert or sporting event; instead, it indicates strong disapproval.
- Whistling inside a building is also inappropriate because of a superstition that it will cause one to lose money.
- Sitting a minute before leaving home brings good luck, as does knocking three times on wood.
- The "thumbs-up" sign means "good" or "okay," as it does in North America.
- *Nyekulturny* is a Russian word that is used the same way in Belarus. It means that something is "just not done," or is ill-mannered. Some *nyekulturny* behaviors include:
  - Wearing an overcoat in a public building, concert hall, or restaurant, and particularly the theater. Leave your coat in the *garderob* (cloakroom). Many office buildings have them, too.

- Sitting on your coat at a concert or restaurant (but it is acceptable at the cinema)
- Standing with your hands in your pockets, raising your voice, or laughing loudly in public buildings, subways, or on the street

Gifts

- Belarusians appreciate small gifts—pens, business card holders, rock or country and western CDs, illustrated books, fine bars of soap, American cigarettes, solar calculators, gold or silver jewelry, or electronic gadgets (digital cameras, iPods, etc.)
- Note that some visitors may give expensive, prestigious watches, pens, lighters, and so forth. You are not expected to compete in gift giving. Flowers are always proper to give to a hostess.
- Exotic food, especially seafood, can be a good gift, but avoid caviar, salmon, sturgeon, and shrimp, all of which are abundant in the area.

Dress

- Belarusians dress conservatively for the office. Even business-people who are familiar with current Western styles rarely wear clothes that draw notice.
- Some buildings may not be well heated in winter, so a layered dress style will be more comfortable.
- Dress for a dinner invitation can be anything from black tie to blue jeans. Hosts may offer slippers, but guests sometimes bring extra footwear, especially in winter, when overshoes are often left at the door.

Cultural Note

Don't forget the effects of the Chernobyl nuclear accident. At least one-quarter of the topsoil in Belarus was contaminated by radioactive fallout, and this is easily transferred onto shoes. If you have reason to walk around in the Belarusian countryside, you might consider disposing of those shoes when you leave Belarus. At the very least, wash them off—otherwise you might risk setting off radiation detectors when you go through an airport security checkpoint.

Belgium

Kingdom of Belgium
Local short form: Belgique/Belgie
Local long form: Royaume de Belgique/Koninkrijk Belgie

Cultural Note
Belgium has the most complex legislation regarding language in Europe. Three languages are recognized by the constitution: French, Dutch, and German. Brussels is officially bilingual (French and Dutch). The northern part of the country (called Flanders) speaks Dutch, while the southern part (called Wallonia) speaks French. Business is conducted in both. You will hear German most in the eastern part of Belgium.

▶ WHAT'S YOUR CULTURAL IQ?

1. The Benelux countries have a tradition of religious tolerance and took in substantial numbers of Jews who fled from other countries (especially from Spain and Portugal during the Inquisition). But during the Nazi occupation during the Second World War, the Jewish communities were destroyed. TRUE or FALSE? Thanks to the Belgian Resistance Movement, almost half of Belgium's Jews escaped from occupied Europe.
   ANSWER: TRUE. Sadly, most of the remainder were killed in the Nazi death camps.

2. Some familiarity with Belgium's impressive artistic history is expected of visitors. This includes such world famous artists as Peter Paul Rubens, Peter Bruegel (the Elder), Jan van Eyck, and the surrealist painter René Magritte. Magritte's painting "L'Oiseau de Ciel" (Sky Bird) sold for 3.4 million euros (approximately U.S.$2.7 million) in 2004. TRUE or FALSE? The money went to charity.

ANSWER: TRUE. "L'Oiseau de Ciel" was originally commissioned by the former Belgian airline, Sabena (which went bankrupt in 2001). Profits were donated to help the 12,000 ex-Sabena employees.

3. Belgium is often used as a test market. What is the primary reason for this?
   a. Statistically, Belgians reflect the average population of the European Union.
   b. Belgians are notoriously difficult to sell to; if they'll buy a product, most other consumers will.
   c. The Belgians are the wealthiest of the Benelux people—they've got the money to buy products.
   d. All of the above.

ANSWER: a. The Belgians are not a hard sell, nor are they the wealthiest. They simply mirror the average EU member in age, income, and education.

▶ TIPS ON DOING BUSINESS IN BELGIUM

- Belgium has three main linguistic groups. Most Belgians speak at least two languages, and are native French or Dutch speakers. There is a small German-speaking population.
- Belgians value privacy, so open-plan offices are uncommon. Expect high-ranking executives to have traditional offices. Office doors are kept closed—knock and wait to be admitted. When you enter, close the door after you.
- Executives who work with both the Dutch and the Belgians usually find the Belgians friendlier and more flexible. Belgians also tend to be more comfortable with multitasking.

▶ COUNTRY BACKGROUND

History
Julius Caesar conquered what is now Belgium in 50 B.C. Roman rule faded, and Belgium came under the domination of the Franks in the fifth century. After Charlemagne's empire fragmented, Belgium was attached to one duchy after another.

In 1516, through marriage and inheritance, Belgium and the Netherlands came under the rule of Spain (the whole area was then called the Spanish Netherlands). The Protestant Dutch resented being ruled by the Catholic Spanish king. With some help from Protestant England, the Dutch successfully broke away and formed the Dutch Republic. Catholic Belgium did not revolt, but it was hard-pressed to survive, trapped between two aggressive nations—the Dutch in the north and the French in the south.

After the War of the Spanish Succession, the Treaty of Utrecht gave control of Belgium to Austria in 1713. Religious repression continued, and Belgium became more Catholic as many of its Protestants emigrated north into the Netherlands.

With France in the grip of the French Revolution, the Austrians and Prussians decided to invade France in 1792. This was a mistake; the French army not only defeated them but also occupied the Austrian Netherlands. Belgium would remain a part of France until the final defeat of Napoleon I in 1815.

When the Congress of Vienna redrew the map of Europe in 1815, control of Belgium was given to the Netherlands. The Belgians successfully broke away from the Netherlands (with help from Britain and France) in 1830. The independent Kingdom of Belgium dates from this revolt.

When, in 1879, the Belgian Parliament declined to establish an African colony, King Leopold II put together a private company to exploit the resources of the Congo. International censure over the treatment of the people of the Congo led to the colony's annexation by the Belgian government in 1908, when the name of the country was changed to the Belgian Congo. After the First World War, Germany's African colonies of Ruanda and Urundi (now called Rwanda and Burundi) were given to Belgium by the League of Nations. This marked the extent of the Belgian Colonial Empire. After the Second World War, Belgium's African colonies gained their independence.

Belgium remained neutral in the Franco-Prussian War of 1870. Unfortunately, for the Belgians, German armies would occupy their country in both world wars, marching through Belgium on the way to invading France.

In 1957, Belgium became a founding member of the European Economic Community, which evolved into today's European Union.

In 1995, Belgium completed a constitutional realignment from a centralist to a federal form of government. This has granted more power to the regions, but failed to satisfy demands for regional autonomy. Further devolution of power to the regions was undertaken in 2002.

Type of Government

Belgium is a constitutional monarchy with two legislative houses. The king is the chief of state, and the prime minister is the head of the government. Elections to Parliament occur every four years, and voting is compulsory. There is a Senate and a House of Representatives. Local communities and regions have been granted the authority to make decisions regarding education, welfare, public works, and investment.

Brussels is not only the capital of Belgium, but is also the headquarters of the European Union and the North Atlantic Treaty Organization (NATO).

Belgium has a high standard of living, supported in part by the politicians of the European Union who meet in Brussels. It also has very high taxes.

For current government data, check with the Embassy of Belgium, at *www.diplobel.us*.

Language

The Kingdom of Belgium recognizes three official languages: French, Dutch, and German.

Linguists have identified eight languages spoken in Belgium. One of them is an artificial language called Europanto; as an invented tongue, it is a second language with no native speakers.

English is the common language of choice for the politicians of the European Union in Brussels.

The Belgian View

Although all the major world religions are represented in Belgium, the country is overwhelmingly Roman Catholic. Holidays and cultural festivals are determined by the Catholic Church calendar.

Belgium's northern region, called Flanders, is populated primarily by Dutch speakers. In the southern region (Wallonia), Belgians usually speak French. The north and the south are almost separate, rival countries. Historically, the economic center of Belgium has fluctuated between the two regions. Before the Second World War, the mines and heavy industry in the south made Wallonia the wealthier region. Since the war, Wallonia's industries proved unable to fight off global competition, but Flanders prospered. Today, the Dutch speakers suggest that the Walloons are an economic drag on the economy.

To foreigners, Belgians can seem extremely private and unwilling to discuss their interests with visitors. One of their saving graces is their absurdist sense of humor—which compliments their most important artistic movement—surrealism.

☑ Know Before You Go

Belgium is a very safe and peaceful country. Some wits claim that the greatest hazard to visitors are the high prices in Brussels.

Belgium is one of the "Low Countries." Flooding is always a hazard during long spells of rain. Land has been reclaimed from the sea via dikes (although not as much as in the Netherlands). A failure in the dike system would cause catastrophic property damage and perhaps loss of life.

Belgium (like Luxembourg) is a European banking haven, where illegal funds are sometimes laundered.

In response to high taxation, Belgium has a large underground economy, which may be as large as 20 percent of Belgium's GNP.

⊙ CULTURAL ORIENTATION

Cognitive Styles: How Belgians Organize and Process Information

In general, the Belgians are open-minded to outside information and will engage anyone in a discussion of facts, principles, ideas, or theories. Information is generally processed from a conceptual perspective. They are proud of their intellectual heritage. The German speakers tend to follow abstract codes of behavior while the Dutch and French speakers are more apt to emphasize interpersonal relationships. In all three groups, friendships tend to run particular and deep.

Negotiation Strategies: What Belgians Accept as Evidence

Although facts are the most valid form of evidence, the Belgians' strong humanitarian perspective makes feelings important in any negotiation situation. Belgians also have a strong faith in the perspectives of their religious ideologies.

Value Systems: The Basis for Behavior

There are three major cultural value systems in Belgium: Dutch, French, and German. Knowing the cultural orientations of these three cultures may help someone who goes to Belgium. The following three sections identify the Value Systems in the predominant culture—their methods of dividing right from wrong, good from evil, and so forth.

Locus of Decision-Making

The individual is responsible for his or her decisions. Although ethnocentric values are adhered to, the relationship between the participants is a major variable in the decision-making process. Decision-making is slow and involved, as all peripheral concerns must be taken care of in the process. Belgians hold to the principles of common sense and compromise.

Sources of Anxiety Reduction

Some sociologists believe that the Belgians have an extraordinarily high index of uncertainty avoidance. Presumably, this is the result of being twice occupied by German armies in the twentieth century—not even as a goal in itself, but more as a convenient transit to invading France. As a result, Belgians are highly risk-averse and use laws and morality to give structure to their worldview.

The nuclear family remains the basic unit, but the extended family is the primary focus all through life, bringing structure and stability. One of three social units shapes a person's life: A person is born into the Catholic, socialist, or liberal group. This then supplies the agencies in which the person participates socially. Belgians are usually joiners, so there is an organization for every kind of need.

Issues of Equality/Inequality

Although most Belgians are Catholic and bi- or trilingual, they have not come to terms with their religious and linguistic cleavages. There is still considerable group and ethnic bias. Class distinctions remain.

Cultural Note

The Belgians often cope with adversity through a self-deprecating sense of humor. Even King Leopold II put down his nation with the comment *"petit pays, petites gens"* ("small country, small-minded people"). However, such comments are only allowed by the Belgians themselves. Foreigners who make negative comments about Belgium or its people will quickly find themselves on the defensive.

▶ BUSINESS PRACTICES

Punctuality, Appointments, and Local Time

- Always be punctual for business appointments in Belgium.
- Belgians write the day first, then the month, then the year (e.g., December 3, 2010, is written 3.12.10 or 3/12/10).
- At 35.8 hours, the Belgian work week is one of the shortest in the world.
- Most Belgians take a one-month vacation each year.
- Phone, e-mail, or write for an appointment at least a week in advance.
- The Belgian company will set the time of your appointment. An 11:30 A.M. appointment is a lunch appointment.
- Expect the first appointment to be social. Most Belgians must get to know you before they decide whether they want to do business with you.

- For Belgium's official holidays, visit *www.kissboworshakehands.com.*
- Belgium is one hour ahead of Greenwich Mean Time (G.M.T. + 1). This makes it six hours ahead of U.S. Eastern Standard Time (E.S.T. + 6).

Negotiating
- With two distinct business cultures, business practices naturally vary. Meetings may begin with socializing, or may immediately get down to business. If Belgians want to engage in small talk, do so. Although such conversation may seem inconsequential, your Belgian counterparts are judging you.
- Be modest about talents and about wealth.
- Mutual trust is highly valued by Belgian businesspeople.
- Senior executives arrive at the office later than subordinates do. Don't try to "get in good" with the staff by going early, because Belgians are very aware of status and will feel uncomfortable.
- The Belgians respect privacy; knock and wait for an answer, and keep doors closed in the office.
- It is important to reply promptly to any request from a Belgian office.
- Assure clients that you will be available and will meet all deadlines.
- Exchanging business cards is standard practice.
- It is good to have your business card translated; one side can be in English and the other in French or Dutch, depending on the dominant language in your region.
- Present the card with the language of your colleague facing him or her.
- The cultural and linguistic divisions of the country are sensitive subjects. Do not confuse the major cultural groups and their languages.
- In general, Belgians do not discuss personal subjects. At a social event, the question "What do you do?" is considered too intrusive.

- Religion is not a good topic of conversation. Unless they are in the news, it is better not to bring up Belgium's former African colonies. Belgium's colonial era did not reflect well upon its rulers.
- Belgians prize visual stimuli. Your presentation should include high-end graphics.

⊚ PROTOCOL

Greetings
- Belgians shake hands with everyone in the room or office upon meeting and departure.
- Among friends, Belgians touch cheeks and kiss the air, alternating cheeks. Men will do this as well.
- Never converse with a Belgian while you have your hand in your pockets—Belgians find this very rude.
- Belgians do not use toothpicks in public.
- It is rude to point with the index finger.
- Snapping the fingers of both hands is ill-mannered in Belgium.

Titles/Forms of Address
- Remember that there are three linguistic groups in Belgium; each has its own customs.
- With German or Dutch speakers, you should use the English terms "Mr." and "Miss," "Mrs.," or "Ms." before the surname.
- With French speakers, use "Monsieur" and "Madame" or "Mademoiselle" before the surname.
- As in much of Europe, the use of first names is inappropriate with the older generation, except among close friends. Younger Belgian executives may invite you to use their first name—but when in doubt, err on the side of formality.
- The order of names is the same as in most of Europe: first name followed by surname. However, Belgians often introduce themselves by saying their surname first. If you are unsure as to which is the given name and which is the surname, ask.

Gifts

- Gift giving is not normally a part of business relationships in Belgium.
- When gifts are given, they are opened immediately in the presence of the giver.
- If you wish to give a gift to a close business associate, do not include your business card with it, and do not give a gift that is a vehicle for your company logo.
- If you are invited to a Belgian home, bring flowers (not chrysanthemums, which signify death) or chocolates for the host. Do not bring thirteen of any flower. Red roses are only for lovers.
- Present your gift before, not after, the meal.
- Some Belgian businesspeople follow the French tradition of sending holiday cards at the New Year. You are welcome to do the same.

Dress

- Conservative, formal dress is expected in Belgium. Clothes must be clean and recently pressed.
- Shoes should be recently shined. Slip-on shoes (such as loafers) are not appropriate for men, except when going through security checkpoints where shoes must be removed.
- Belgians dress in their finest clothes on Sundays, whether they intend to go visiting or just take a stroll.

Cultural Note

In 2003, Belgium passed legislation banning the construction of new nuclear reactors. They also committed to closing their existing seven nuclear reactors by 2025. The government will be exploring and investing in alternative energy resources, such as renewable energy products and gas reserves.

Czech Republic

Local short form: Cesko
Local long form: Ceska Republika

Cultural Note

The Czech Republic has undergone two radical but nonviolent changes in recent years: the "Velvet Revolution" that removed the USSR-backed Communists from power and the "Velvet Divorce" that separated Czechoslovakia into two independent nations, the Czech and Slovak Republics. Even at their most angry moment, when protesters jammed Prague's Wenceslas Square demanding the removal of the Communists, the protesters admonished one another not to trample on the flower beds!

▶ WHAT'S YOUR CULTURAL IQ?

1. The Czech Republic has frequently been ruled by outsiders. Which of the following was *not* a former foreign ruler?
   a. Austro-Hungarian Empire
   b. Kingdom of Bohemia
   c. Holy Roman Empire
   d. Nazi Germany
   ANSWER: b. Bohemia is another name for most of the Czech Republic (the westernmost portion is known as Moravia).

2. TRUE or FALSE: The 1618 Defenestration of Prague refers to an incident that marked the revolt of Bohemia against the Emperor Ferdinand of the Holy Roman Empire.
   ANSWER: TRUE. "Defenestration" is a fancy term for throwing something or someone out of a window. The Bohemian nobility became so angry with Ferdinand's viceroys that they threw them both out of a window of a Prague castle. The viceroys survived the fall, and the incident sparked the Thirty Years' War (1618–1648).

3. Under Communist rule, many of Czechoslovakia's greatest modern writers fled to the west. Which of the following stayed in Czechoslovakia:
   a. Václav Havel
   b. Milan Kundera
   c. Josef Škvorecký
   ANSWER: a. Václav Havel endured years of repression to become the first president of post-Communist Czechoslovakia (and later the Czech Republic). Kundera, author of *The Unbearable Lightness of Being*, fled to Paris; Škvorecký, author of *The Engineer of Human Souls*, immigrated to Canada.

▶ TIPS ON DOING BUSINESS IN THE CZECH REPUBLIC

- Prague has become a magnet for young Western expatriates. Czechs have become used to dealing with English speakers.
- During the Communist era (1945–1989), industrial pollution was seen as a sign of industrial progress. Since then, pollution control and environmental stewardship has become very important to Czechs.
- Even if you do not drink beer, you should express admiration for the breweries of the Czech Republic. Many Czechs can expound on the subtleties of beer for hours.

▶ COUNTRY BACKGROUND

History

The Czech Republic represents the westernmost migration of Slavic tribes into Europe. During the fifth century A.D., these tribes arrived in what would eventually become Czechoslovakia. Two distinct Slavic groups emerged: the Czechs, who settled in the west, and the Slovaks, who took the east. By 900 A.D. the Slovak tribes were conquered by the Magyars (Hungarians). In the west, the city of Prague was developing into one of the most important cultural and political centers of the Holy Roman Empire.

In the fifteenth century, Prague became a focal point for the Protestant Reformation. Protestant leader Jan Hus, burned at the stake in

1415, is still a national hero to the Czechs. But the Battle on the White Mountain in 1620 put an end to Czech resistance, and both Czechs and Slovaks came to be ruled by the Austrian Habsburg dynasty until the twentieth century.

While all of Czechoslovakia spent centuries under the control of the Austro-Hungarian Empire, these two ethnic areas developed independently of each other. The western Czech provinces (Bohemia and Moravia) were industrialized; they prospered under direct Austrian control.

After its defeat in World War I, the Austro-Hungarian Empire was broken up into smaller states in accordance with Woodrow Wilson's principles of self-determination. The Czechs and the Slovenes found themselves lumped together in the newly independent state of Czechoslovakia. The aggressive, educated, and more numerous Czechs quickly took charge, and the Slovenes felt excluded from their own government. The existence of other minorities within the Czechoslovakian borders, notably the ethnic Germans in the Sudetenland, also caused friction. Nevertheless, Czechoslovakia managed to remain a democracy until it was overrun by Nazi Germany in 1938–1939.

Liberated by the Red Army in 1945, Czechoslovakia became a Soviet satellite. Despite repressive measures, the Communist leadership in Prague was unable to keep protests from periodically erupting, notably in 1968 and 1977. Finally, the tide of reform that washed over Eastern Europe in 1989 allowed the Czechoslovak people to elect a truly popular, non-Communist government. Dissident writer Václav Havel was elected the country's president.

Czechoslovakia became a parliamentary democracy and remained so until 1992, when political and social events resulted initially in the establishment of a multiparty republic of two equal states, and eventually in two separate countries—the Czech and Slovak Republics.

As an independent state, the new Czech Republic came into being on January 1, 1993. The Czech Republic also joined NATO in 1999 and the European Union in 2004.

Type of Government

The Czech Republic is a multiparty parliamentary democracy. The president is the chief of state—a largely ceremonial office. The prime minister is the head of the government. There are two legislative houses, an upper Senate and a lower Chamber of Deputies.

For current government data, check with the Embassy of the Czech Republic at *www.mzv.cz/washington*.

Language

The official language is Czech, which is a West Slavic language related to Polish. Although the Czechs and the Slovaks have gone to great lengths to differentiate their languages, the Czech and Slovak languages are actually quite similar and are mutually intelligible.

Czech is considered a difficult language for English speakers to master. Although it is written in the Latin alphabet (with diacritical marks), its pronunciation includes several sounds which are not present in English.

The Czech View

There is no official religion in the Czech Republic. Religion was actively discouraged under the former Communist regime. More Czechs identify themselves as nondenominational (39.9 percent) than as members of the dominant religion, the Roman Catholic Church (39.0 percent). Most other religions are represented in the Czech Republic. Some local Protestant variations include Czechoslovak Brethren Reformed (2.0 percent), Czechoslovak Hussite (1.7 percent), and Silesian Evangelical (0.3 percent).

Avoidance of violence is an important part of Czech philosophy. Czechs are proud of the way they endured two wrenching changes without violence: the 1989 Velvet Revolution in which the Communist regime gave way to democracy, and the peaceful separation of Czechoslovakia into the separate Czech and Slovak Republics in 1993.

Egalitarianism is a priority in Czech thinking. In fact, one of the disappointments Czechs have with the market economy is that everyone is no longer equal. Under Communism, most Czechs lived under similar conditions.

Czechs tend toward modesty and informality. Ostentation is seen only on old buildings from the days of the Austro-Hungarian Empire. However, some younger Czechs are adopting a more opulent style, at least in matters of dress.

The Czech populace is well educated, with a 99 percent literacy rate. Emphasis has been placed on scientific research, and the educated elite is the equal of any in the world.

☑ Know Before You Go

The greatest hazard to travelers to the Czech Republic is probably vehicular accidents. Czechs tend to be erratic drivers.

There is also a substantial amount of petty crime, mostly pickpocketing.

Tobacco smoke is also omnipresent. Czechs even smoke in places meant primarily for children, such as ice-cream parlors. This adds to the heavy pollution in many Czech cities.

The Czech Republic still operates mainly on cash. Credit cards and checks are accepted only in a limited number of venues.

While bribery is not omnipresent, the Czech police have a reputation for needlessly stopping foreign drivers, then accepting small bribes in lieu of a ticket.

▶ CULTURAL ORIENTATION

Cognitive Styles: How Czechs Organize and Process Information

The Czechs have always been open to information on most issues. They tend to be more analytic than associative, but they value relationships more than obedience to abstract rules of behavior.

Negotiation Strategies: What Czechs Accept as Evidence

Czechs find truth through a mixture of subjective feelings and objective facts. Their faith in the ideologies of humanitarianism and democracy will influence the truth in nearly every situation.

Value Systems: The Basis for Behavior

The amicable separation of Czechoslovakia into the Czech and Slovak Republics is an example of the humanitarian value systems of both cultures. The following three sections identify the Value Systems in the predominant culture—their methods of dividing right from wrong, good from evil, and so forth.

Locus of Decision-Making

The responsibility for decision-making rests on the shoulders of the individual. Individualism has always been encouraged, and individual achievement is more important than family in determining status. Czechs feel that they have a right to a private life; their friends are few and specific to their needs. Czechs feel that the same values should apply to all members of their culture.

Sources of Anxiety Reduction

With the demise of Communist rule, the guarantee of full employment ended. This produces considerable day-to-day anxiety. Although the traditional role of the family as the basic educating and socializing unit has been weakened, the family unit is still recognized as a stabilizing force. Religion seems to be regaining its influence on family life and social structure, and with this comes more security for both the individual and the family.

Issues of Equality/Inequality

The homogeneity of the Czech culture has eliminated most of the ethnic bias that existed before the breakup of Czechoslovakia. There is keen competition for status, but when a person is recognized for his or her accomplishments, that individual gains prominence among equals. The desire for power may undercut the humanitarian need for equality. This drive for power can yield strong, hierarchical structures in government, business, and society.

The husband is the titular head of the home. However, because most women work outside the home, husbands take some responsibility for raising the children.

Although women have legal equality with men, sexual harassment is still widespread in the workplace.

Cultural Note

There is a general feeling among Czechs that Communism cheated them out of forty years of profits. Consequently, many Czechs want to earn years of profits in a single business transaction. They may make inordinate financial demands upon foreigners.

▶ BUSINESS PRACTICES

Punctuality, Appointments, and Local Time

- Punctuality is important; be on time for business and social engagements.
- Czechs, like most Europeans, write the day first, then the month, then the year (e.g., December 3, 2010, is written 3.12.10 or 3/12/10).
- For many years, Russian was the foreign language most frequently studied in schools. Since the Velvet Revolution of 1989, Western languages like English and German have become the most popular. English speakers should expect to hire a translator, especially if their destination is outside of Prague itself.
- Appointments should be made well in advance. Allow one to two weeks' notice for an appointment made by telephone or e-mail.
- Business letters may be written in English, although your counterpart will be favorably impressed if you take the trouble to translate the letter into Czech.
- As the business day begins early and ends in midafternoon, expect to schedule your appointments between 9:00 A.M. and 12 noon or between 1:00 and 3:00 P.M.
- Most Czechs receive four weeks of vacation per year. The traditional vacation time runs from mid-July to mid-August, so do not expect to be able to conduct business during this period.
- The National Holiday is Czech Founding Day, 28 October. For further official holidays, visit *www.kissboworshakehands.com*.
- The Czech Republic is one hour ahead of Greenwich Mean Time (G.M.T. + 1), or six hours ahead of U.S. Eastern Standard Time (E.S.T. + 6).

Negotiating

- Expect the decision-making process to operate at a fairly slow pace. Czechs do not necessarily believe that "time is money."
- Many Czechs have adopted the German propensity for slow, methodical planning. Every aspect of the deal you propose will be pored over. Do not anticipate being able to speed up this process.
- Only a few entrepreneurs are ready to move more quickly. However, you should move cautiously with the ones who offer you a partnership, since you will be the one putting hard currency into the enterprise.
- The change from a communist to a capitalist society has resulted in a tangle of regulation. Don't depend on a Czech joint-venture partner to understand the law. Hire a Czech business lawyer.
- While Czechs are known for their hospitality, they may take a lot of time to establish a close business relationship.
- Executives usually understand enough English to decipher a business card, so it is not necessary to have a card in English translated. However, it is preferable to have promotional materials and instruction manuals translated into Czech.
- Bring plenty of cards; quite a few Czechs may wish to exchange them with you.
- If your company has been around for many years, the date of its founding should be on your card. Education is highly respected, so be sure to include any degree above the bachelor's level as well.
- Do not get down to business too quickly. Czechs typically converse before talking business. Expect to be asked about your flight, your accommodations, where you are from, your impressions of the country, and so forth.
- Your counterparts may not mind asking or being asked personal questions. You may want to ask about an executive's family. Part of establishing a relationship is expressing an interest in each other's family, although it may be a while before you actually meet them.
- While political discussions cannot be avoided, don't ask embarrassing political questions. Many of the people with enough money to conduct business are former Communists or black

marketeers. Also, do your best to avoid siding with Czechs against Slovaks, or vice versa.

- Czechs tend to be well informed about politics and to have firm political opinions. They are also honest, and may tell you their opinions. While they dislike what Communism has done to their country, they may not be as approving of the West as you might expect.
- Sports are a good topic for conversation; soccer, ice hockey, hiking, and cycling are popular sports. Music is a good topic as well, as are dogs—Czechs are inordinately fond of their dogs.
- Czechs make some excellent beers. The pilsner style of beer was developed here. The town of Budweis (now renamed Ceské Budéjovice), after which "Budweiser" was named, is in the Czech Republic. A beer drinker will be happy to explain about Czech beer.
- Coffee is usually served during business meetings. Taste it before you add sugar; it may already be sweetened. The coffee is Turkish, and will probably have grounds at the bottom.

Business Entertaining
- Breakfast meetings are not as common as in North America.
- Historically, business meetings were confined to offices. Business lunches were rare; the only meal people shared with a business associate was a celebratory dinner. However, this segregation was due in part to restrictive government regulations—fraternization with westerners was actively discouraged. Czechs are now accustomed to Western business practices, including business lunches.
- At a lunch, business may be discussed before and (sometimes) after the meal, but rarely during the meal itself. If you are invited out to a luncheon, you may offer to pay, but expect your host to decline your offer. Insist on paying only when you have made the invitation.
- Restaurants tend to be very busy. Always make a reservation. It may be easier to ask your counterpart to choose a restaurant; just make sure to explain that you intend to pay for the meal.

- Do not anticipate good service in all restaurants. Under the Communists, restaurant workers got the same pay no matter how busy they were. Additional customers were simply an inconvenience. These attitudes take time to change.
- The one category of customer to get immediate attention in restaurants is dogs! Like the French, the Czechs allow people to bring their dogs into their restaurants.
- You may be invited to eat lunch in the company cafeteria.
- Czechs do not often entertain business associates in their homes. If you are invited into a home, consider it a great honor. Do not be surprised if the living quarters are crowded. You may be asked to remove your shoes when you enter a private home.
- A host will invite you to eat additional portions. It is traditional to turn down the first invitation.
- When eating, always use utensils; very few items are eaten with the hands. Place your utensils together on one side of the plate when you have finished eating. If you just wish to pause between courses, cross your utensils on the plate.

Cultural Note

If you happen to be inside a Czech home just before Christmas, you might see a large live fish swimming in the bathtub! It is a Czech tradition to serve a meal of carp on December 24; so many Czechs buy a live carp before Christmas and store it in their bathtub.

⊙ PROTOCOL

Greetings

- Always shake hands, firmly but briefly, when introduced. When introduced to a Czech woman or an elderly person, wait to see if he or she extends a hand before offering to shake.
- In both business and social situations, always shake hands upon arriving and upon departing from any meeting.
- When several people are being introduced, take turns shaking hands. It is impolite to reach over someone else's handshake.

- Never keep your left hand in your pocket while shaking hands with your right.
- In formal situations, it is better to be introduced by a third person than to introduce yourself. However, in informal situations, it is appropriate to introduce yourself.
- When you are the third person making an introduction between two parties, give the name of the younger (or lower-ranking) person first.

Titles/Forms of Address
- The order of names is the same as in most of Europe: first name followed by a surname.
- Traditionally, only family members and close friends address each other by their first names. While young people are using first names more frequently, most businesspeople you meet will prefer to be called by their title or surname.
- When speaking to persons who do not have professional titles, use "Mr.," "Mrs.," or "Miss" and the surname:
    Mr. = Pan (pronounced "Pahn")
    Mrs. (or Ms.) = Pani ("PAH-nee")
    Miss = Slecna ("SLEH-chnah")
- Use professional titles. Attorneys, architects, engineers, and other professionals will expect you to address them as "Pan" or "Pani" plus their title. This goes for anyone with a Ph.D. as well.

Gestures
- To get someone's attention, raise your hand, palm facing out, with only the index finger extended. Avoid waving or beckoning.
- When sitting, cross one knee over the other, rather than resting your ankle on the other knee. Do not prop your feet up on anything other than a footstool.
- The eldest or highest-ranking person enters a room first. If their age and status are the same, men enter before women.
- Do not talk to someone with your hands in your pockets or while chewing gum.

Gifts

- Under the Communist regime, the frequent shortages made gift giving simple: You gave whatever was in short supply in Czechoslovakia. Now that consumer items are freely available (albeit expensive), gift giving is more of a problem.
- By and large, businesspeople do not give or expect to receive expensive gifts. A gift should be of good quality, but not exorbitant.
- Appropriate gifts include good-quality pens, small electronics (such as MP3 players), cigarette lighters, and imported wine or liquor, especially Scotch, bourbon or cognac.
- When invited to dinner at a Czech home, bring a bouquet of unwrapped flowers for your hostess. The bouquet should have an uneven number of flowers, but not thirteen. Red roses are reserved for romantic situations, and calla lilies are for funerals.

Dress

- Czech clothing is modest and unassuming; whether in business or casualwear. Ostentation is looked at askance, as are bright clothing or loud patterns.
- Generally, businessmen wear dark suits, ties, and white shirts. Businesswomen also dress conservatively, in dark suits or dresses and white blouses.
- Follow the lead of your colleagues with regard to removing jackets or ties in hot weather.
- There are many social events in the Czech Republic, and Czechs often dress up for them. Business wear is also appropriate for most formal social events: parties, dinners, and the theater.
- Formal wear is expected for the opening night of an opera, concert, or play. Men are expected to wear their best dark suit or tuxedo, and women a long evening gown. Virtually every Czech institution, including business associations and libraries, hosts a formal ball sometime during February, and formal wear is required for them.
- Casualwear is essentially the same as in the United States. Jeans are ubiquitous, but they should not be worn, torn, or dirty.

Denmark

Kingdom of Denmark
Local short form: Danmark
Local long form: Kongeriget Danmark

▶ WHAT'S YOUR CULTURAL IQ?

1. Which of the following are true about "The Little Mermaid"—the famous statue in Copenhagen's harbor?
   a. She has been blown off her granite stone by explosives.
   b. She has been decapitated.
   c. Her right arm was cut off.
   d. All of the above.
   ANSWER: d. This beautiful statue is one of the most-often photographed pieces of art worldwide. It is also one of the most abused. A Danish brewer, Carl Jacobsen, commissioned the statue after attending a performance of *The Little Mermaid* in 1909. The Danish sculptor was Edward Eriksen.

2. Match these famous Danes with their areas of accomplishment
   a. Vitus Jonassen Bering (1681–1741)   1. Astronomy
   b. Niels Bohr (1885–1962)   2. Exploration
   c. Tycho Brahe (1546–1601)   3. Quantum physics

ANSWER: a. 2; b. 3; c. 1. Of the three, only physicist Niels Bohr died in Denmark. Brahe died in Prague, and Bering died on an island in what is now called the Bering Sea.

3. Which of the following Danes did *not* win the Nobel Prize for literature?
   a. Karen Blixen, writing as Isak Dinesen (1885–1962)
   b. Karl Adolph Gjellerup (1857–1919)
   c. Johannes V. Jensen (1873–1950)
   d. Henrik Pontoppidan (1857–1943)
   ANSWER: a. Ironically, Blixen is the best known of these authors outside of Denmark (in part because of the Hollywood film version of *Out of Africa*). She wrote in English, then translated her work into Danish. Isak Dinesen was just one of her pseudonyms.

▶ TIPS ON DOING BUSINESS IN DENMARK

- Danes try to maintain a strict divide between their public and private lives. Most do not like working overtime and are unwilling to discuss business matters outside of the office. Similarly, they do not like to discuss their personal lives with casual business acquaintances.
- Danes are very individualistic, and leading a Danish company requires skill at consensus building. There is a great deal of give-and-take among all levels of a Danish company. Strong negative input from even a minor member of a company could sink your proposal.
- Danes are both slow to decide and independent, so a hard sell is the worst technique one can take. Present your pitch, supply all the follow-up data requested (no matter how extraneous this data may seem to you), and wait. The Danes cannot be rushed.

▶ COUNTRY BACKGROUND

History
During the Middle Ages, the Viking raiders and conquerors were largely Danes. For a time, the Danish realm included most of Scandinavia and England.

In 1389, the Danish queen Margaret I acquired the vacant crown of Sweden. Denmark and Sweden were formally united under the Union of Kalmar. Denmark already ruled Norway, Iceland, and the Faroe Islands. Sweden did not permanently break away from Danish rule until 1523.

Christian III became king in 1534. During his twenty-five-year reign, he consolidated Danish power and established the Lutheran Church as the official Church of Denmark.

In the eighteenth century, Denmark colonized Greenland. Danish traders sailed to the West Indies and East Asia.

Denmark supported Napoleon during the Napoleonic Wars. As punishment, the Congress of Vienna took Norway away from Denmark in 1814 and gave it to Sweden.

In 1849, Denmark became a constitutional monarchy.

Denmark lost additional territory in 1864, when it fought both Austria and Prussia for control of Schleswig (along the border of present-day Germany). As a result, Denmark lost 40 percent of its land and over a third of its people. However, what was left was an extremely homogenous population. Denmark's borders have been more-or-less stable since then.

Although Denmark has existed since around 750, it became a constitutional monarchy in 1849. By the 1880s, Denmark experienced both economic growth and a population explosion. Many Danes immigrated to North America.

Despite signing a nonaggression pact with Germany in 1939, the Nazis invaded Denmark in 1940. With Denmark under German control, Iceland severed ties with Denmark in 1944. The United States built military bases on both Iceland and Greenland. At the end of the war, Greenland returned to Danish control, but Iceland remained independent.

Denmark became a founding member of NATO in 1949. The country joined the European Community (now known as the European Union) in 1972.

Almost fifty years of Social Democratic Party control changed after September 11, 2001. Since then, a right-wing coalition, which promised tighter controls on immigration, has held power.

Cultural Note

In 2000, a tunnel and bridge, which connects Denmark with Sweden, was completed.

The Øresundsbron is approximately 16 kilometers long and features a motorway and railway line. Travelers can go from Copenhagen to Malmo over the Øresund fixed link, the world's largest cable-stayed bridge.

Type of Government

The Kingdom of Denmark is today a constitutional monarchy. The symbolic chief of state is the queen or king. The prime minister is the head of the government and is chosen by the Parliament. The legislative body, is called the *Folketing*.

For current government data, check with the Embassy of Denmark at *www.denmarkemb.org*.

Language

The official language is Danish. English starts to be taught at the elementary level; it is the predominant second language, and a majority of Danes speak it with a high level of competency. Most are eager to use their English with visitors from English-speaking countries.

The Danish View

The official religion of Denmark is Evangelical Lutheran. The vast majority (around 97 percent) of Danes belong to this religion, although less than 14 percent attend church regularly.

Denmark observes a National Prayer Day, or Common Prayer Day, called Store Bededag, on the fourth Friday after Easter. Most Danes use it as a long weekend to enjoy the spring.

Other Christian denominations account for about 1.6 percent of the overall population; Muslims make up 1.4. percent. Other religions and persons categorized as nonreligious number 9.6 percent.

Danes have been seafarers for centuries—as you would expect in a country made up of 482 islands.

Their maritime tradition remains strong, as does their merchant tradition. But Danes also have a strong agricultural heritage, and the country is a net exporter of food.

☑ Know Before You Go

Denmark is a remarkably safe county, with little violent crime or accidental death.

Flooding is the major hazard in Denmark, especially in those parts protected from the sea by a system of dikes.

Denmark has various territorial disputes with other countries over fishing rights and ownership of some remote islands. Also, the Faroe Islands often debate independence.

▶ CULTURAL ORIENTATION

Cognitive Styles: How Danes Organize and Process Information

The Danes are a proud people who tend to be satisfied with their own accomplishments and thus do not need (and are not open to) information or help from others. Their educational system is moving away from rote learning and toward the application of abstractive, conceptual thinking. They tend to follow universalistic rules of behavior rather than react to particular situations.

Negotiation Strategies: What Danes Accept as Evidence

Truth is centered in a faith in the ideology of social welfare, with objective facts used to prove a point. Subjective feelings do not play a part in negotiation processes.

Value Systems: The Basis for Behavior

Denmark is a social welfare state in which the quality of life and environmental issues are given top priority. The Danes put a high value on individualism and personal freedom.

The following three sections identify the Value Systems in the predominant culture—their methods of dividing right from wrong, good from evil, and so forth.

Locus of Decision-Making

Danes have a strong belief in individual decisions within the social welfare system. There is a strong self-orientation, but with an obligation to help those who are not able to help themselves. There is an emphasis on individual initiative and achievement, with one's ability being more important than his or her station in life. The dignity and worth of the individual is emphasized, along with the right to a private life and opinions.

Sources of Anxiety Reduction

Sociologists have found that Danes have a low index of uncertainty avoidance. This indicates a society with little concern about ambiguity and a high tolerance for divergent opinions. As a result, Danes are not rule-oriented and have a relatively high tolerance for risk.

Danes reduce their anxiety through a strong social welfare system—the government is there to serve the people. Though individualistic, most Danes are resigned to a high-tax social welfare state in which there is little distinction available through individual accomplishment. Danes who wish to become wealthy often seek their fortunes abroad.

Young people are encouraged to mature early and to take risks to develop a strong self-image.

Issues of Equality/Inequality

Denmark has a middle-class society, with family needs as the central issue of social policy and governmental intervention. Danes strive to minimize social differences, so there is very little evidence of poverty or wealth, although they exist.

Danes have been charted as having the lowest power distance index in all of Scandinavia. Such a society minimizes the differences between the power and wealth of each citizen.

A largely homogeneous population minimizes ethnic differences. In this society, upper-class husbands and wives share the responsibilities of child care.

▶ BUSINESS PRACTICES

Punctuality, Appointments, and Local Time

- Punctuality is very important; be exactly on time for all business appointments. Tardiness conveys to Danes an impression of incompetence and poor time management.
- Danes expect punctuality for social engagements as well.

- When writing down the date, Danes first write the day, then the month, then the year (e.g., December 3, 2010, is written 3.12.10 or 3/12/10).
- As in the rest of Scandinavia, summer is a time of leisure. It is both difficult and inconsiderate to try to conduct serious business during July and August. Many firms close for extended periods during these two months to allow their employees to take summer vacations. Danes have five weeks of paid vacation per year.
- There is no designated national holiday in Denmark, but June 5, Constitution Day, is generally viewed as the national day. For further information on official holidays, see *www.kissboworshake hands.com*.
- Local time is one hour ahead of Greenwich Mean Time (G.M.T. + 1), or six hours ahead of U.S. Eastern Standard Time (E.S.T. + 6).

Cultural Note

If your firm is an old one, have the date your company was established printed on your business card. Danes respect tradition.

Negotiating

- The Danes tend to get down to business right away, with a minimum of small talk.
- For Scandinavians, Danes are relatively informal. As long as he or she is expecting you, you can introduce yourself to an executive, rather than wait for his secretary to introduce you.
- Be prepared to give detailed briefings, because Danes are rather meticulous.
- Danes are often quite frank in their manner of speaking. Statements are often direct but are not meant to be insulting in any way.
- Avoid making any comments that could be regarded as personal. Even complimenting someone on his or her clothes can be taken as too invasive!

- Like most Scandinavians, Danes have a dry sense of humor that can be opaque to foreigners. Don't expect your jokes to translate well, either. In fact, humor has little place in Danish business.
- Although Danes are not as reserved as most Scandinavians, Danes rarely speak to strangers (except when they are anxious to practice a foreign tongue). Don't be surprised or insulted if an unfamiliar Dane is not responsive if you attempt to make small talk with him or her.
- Danes are very tolerant; it is not advisable to criticize other people or political systems.

Business Entertaining

- Danes prefer to eat breakfast at home; business breakfasts are not common.
- Business lunches are held between noon and 2:00 P.M. A typical lunch fare is an open-faced sandwich called a *smorrebord*. This is eaten with a knife and fork, not with the hands.
- The main meal of the day is dinner, which is eaten between 6:00 and 8:00 P.M. This meal usually includes alcohol—either beer or wine.
- Do not discuss business during a meal unless your Danish host does so first.
- Good topics of conversation include sports, Danish culture, and your hometown.
- The smorgasbord, a cold buffet, is very popular.
- Toasts in Denmark can be quite formal. Never toast your host or anyone senior to you in rank or age until he or she has toasted you first. Never taste your drink until the host has said the traditional toasting word, *skoal*.
- If you are toasting someone, or someone is toasting you, be sure to maintain eye contact with that person during the entire toast.
- Toasts are given both standing and sitting. If your host stands when he makes a toast, so should you when you give your toast. Only the person proposing the toast stands.

- A traditional Danish drink, *aquavit* (literally, "water of life"), is quite potent. Be forewarned, as Danes often like to share this alcoholic beverage with their guests.
- In a Danish home, assume very proper manners. For example, your host will suggest where you should sit. (At the table, the host and hostess usually sit at opposite ends, with the guest of honor next to the host.)
- Expect to be at the table for a long time. Danish dinners can take as long as four hours. You should not rise from the table before your hostess does.
- It is impolite to leave a host's home too soon after dinner. Again, cocktails are offered after dinner, not before. These may be at the table or in the main room. It is not unusual for a dinner party to last until 1 A.M., especially in the summer.
- If the weather is pleasant, the dinner party may end with a late-night walk around the neighborhood. This is especially true in the summer, when it stays light very late.
- Danes hold their fork in their left hand, while their knife remains in the right.
- Danes have a traditional way of signaling when they have had enough to eat. To indicate that you have finished eating, place the knife and fork side by side on the plate, pointed away from you. On the other hand, if you want another serving, point the fork's tines down toward you.
- Unlike many Europeans, Danes have a tradition of inviting foreign guests into their homes for a meal. If you are invited to a Danish home for dinner, be prompt. There is often no predinner cocktail, so you may be led straight to the dinner table. Danes usually serve cocktails after the meal, not before.

⊙ PROTOCOL

Greetings
- It is common to rise when being introduced to someone, and to shake hands with both men and women. Handshakes are firm but

brief. When greeting a couple, it is customary to shake hands with the woman first.

- Your colleague will usually shake your hand when leaving as well.
- Danes like plenty of personal space around them. Stand about two arm's length away from a Dane.
- Danes say the traditional greeting *heij*, which sounds exactly like the English "hi," when both greeting and departing.
- The common North American greeting "Hi, how are you?" will lead a Dane to think you really want to know how he or she is doing. A preferable greeting would be "Hi, it's a pleasure to meet you."

Cultural Note

Danes (and other Scandinavians) sometimes use a person's initials and surname instead of using the entire name. For example, the writer Hans Christian Andersen is known as H. C. Andersen in Denmark. That is how you would search for his name in a Danish database. There is no pattern to this, just the personal preferences of the individual.

Titles/Forms of Address

- The order of Danish names is the same as in most of Europe: first name followed by surname.
- It is appropriate to use a person's title and surname until the use of first names is suggested. The use of first names in business environments is currently in vogue in Denmark.

Gestures

- Danes are rather reserved in public. Avoid talking loudly or gesticulating wildly.
- The gesture North Americans use to indicate that someone is crazy (index finger circling while pointed at one's temple) is used to insult other drivers while on the road.
- The North American "okay" gesture (thumb and forefinger forming a circle) can be taken as an insult in Denmark.
- When ascending a flight of stairs, men precede women. When descending, women precede men.

- At the theater, enter a row with your back to the stage (so that you face people seated in the row). It is considered insulting to squeeze past seated people with your backside facing them.

Gifts

- Gifts are not required in a business relationship. If a gift is given, it should be modest so it won't be mistaken for a bribe.
- If and when a gift is given, it can be unwrapped immediately in front of the giver.
- It is quite acceptable to bring a bouquet of flowers or chocolates to a host's home.
- You may bring roses to your hostess in Denmark as long as they are not white (which are associated with mourning). Flowers should be presented wrapped.
- Send your flowers before the dinner, so the hostess does not have to arrange them when you arrive.
- An illustrated book from your home region makes an appropriate gift. So do spirits or wine produced in your home country. Technological gadgets are appreciated as well.
- For further gift-giving guidelines, visit *www.kissboworshakehands .com.*

Cultural Note

The Danish alphabet has three additional letters that are placed at the end of the alphabet. They are:

  27th letter: æ/Æ (pronounced like the *e* in "pet")

  28th letter: ø/Ø (pronounced like the *e* in "err")

  29th letter: å/Å (pronounced like the *o* in "core")

If you have no way of printing these characters, substitute "ae" for æ, "oe" for ø, and "aa" for å.

There are pronunciation differences even in the letters shared by Danish and English. The most notable peculiarity is the Danish "soft *d*," which foreigners—even other Nordics—find difficult to duplicate.

There is also a guttural *r* sound that English speakers have trouble imitating.

Dress

- Sometimes high-ranking Danish executives host formal dinners. Male executives should consider bringing a tuxedo along; female executives may need an evening gown.
- Conservative dress will generally be expected in every business situation.
- Danish casual attire is still conservative, although jeans that are clean and pressed are not uncommon. At the beach, some women wear topless bathing suits.

Finland

Republic of Finland
Local short form: Suomi
Local long form: Suomen Tasavalta

Cultural Note

The Finns are incorruptible—at least they were in 2003. The annual Corruption Perception Index (by Transparency International) rated Finland number 1 out of 102 countries ranked worldwide. Transparency International compiles reports on corruption and bribery around the world. For more information on this nongovernmental organization, headquartered in Germany, see *www.transparency.org*. And leave the bribes at home.

⊳ WHAT'S YOUR CULTURAL IQ?

1. Which of the following languages is mutually intelligible with Finnish?
   a. Estonian
   b. Hungarian (Magyar)
   c. Swedish
   ANSWER: a. Finnish, Estonian, and Hungarian are all members of the Finno-Ugric linguistic family, but only Finnish and Estonian are mutually intelligible. Hungarian has diverged too much for Finns and Hungarians to understand each other. Swedish, Danish, and Norwegian (or English, for that matter) are all Indo-European languages.

2. Finland did not become an independent nation until the twentieth century. TRUE or FALSE? The Russians ruled Finland for almost 600 years.
   ANSWER: FALSE. Although Russia occupied Finland off and on throughout recorded history, it only subjugated Finland for one extended period, from 1809 to 1917. The Swedes ruled Finland for some 600 years.

3. TRUE or FALSE? Although ice hockey and football (soccer) are extremely popular, the Finnish national sport is a variation of baseball.
ANSWER: TRUE. Since its introduction in 1922, Finnish baseball, known as *pesäpallo* (a.k.a., *pesis*), is played by Finnish schoolchildren.

▶ TIPS ON DOING BUSINESS IN FINLAND

• At the present time, Finland boasts the highest Internet and mobile phone penetration rates in the world. However, Finnish business is not all silicon-based. The country is still a leader in the paper and shipbuilding industries. Every fourth cruise ship is constructed in Finland.

• Finland is the closest Nordic nation to the former USSR. This makes it ideally located to conduct business with Russia and the Baltic Sates of Lithuania, Latvia, and Estonia. Currently, more than 40 percent of the European Union's shipments via truck to Russia travel across Finnish roads. When Scandinavia is added to Northwestern Russia and the Baltic States, there are 80 million prospective customers surrounding Finland!

• Unlike the other major Scandinavian (and European) languages, Finnish is not an Indo-European language. Finnish is in the Finno-Ugric linguistic group. Recognize the differences, and be particularly careful to avoid blunders in translations.

▶ COUNTRY BACKGROUND

History
The Finnish people have maintained their separate cultural identity throughout recorded history, despite centuries of domination by either their fellow Scandinavians or the Russians. Swedish involvement in Finland began in 1172, when Pope Alexander III charged the Swedes to protect Catholic missionaries in Finland. The Swedes eventually established control over the Finns, and converted them to Catholicism. This lasted until 1397, when Queen Margaret I of Denmark established the Kalmar Union. This temporarily united all of

Scandinavia under the Danish crown. Eventually, control of Finland returned to Sweden.

Gustavus Vasa, king of Sweden, replaced Catholicism with Lutheranism in Sweden and Finland in 1527.

Twice during the eighteenth century the Russians occupied Finland, causing great destruction. The first occupation lasted for eight years, a period the Finns refer to as the Great Wrath. The Russians later returned for a two-year occupation (the Small Wrath), and again many Finns were slain.

Russia overran Finland in 1808 during the Napoleonic Wars. Sweden was forced to cede Finland to Russia. The Russians insisted that Finland's capital be moved to Helsinki from its traditional site of Turku.

During the tumult of the Russian Revolution, a newly elected Finnish Parliament assumed all powers formerly held by the czar in 1917. Finland was soon declared an independent republic.

From January to May of 1918, Finland was torn by a civil war. The government was supported by the Whites, who largely represented the anti-Communist, middle-to-upper class, Swedish-speaking Finns. The Whites received aid from Germany and used German-trained Finns, called the Jägers. The Reds tended to be poor, rural, Finnish-speaking Communists; they were assisted by the Russian troops. The civil war ended in a White victory. At the start of the Second World War, Finland declared its neutrality. However, the USSR wanted to secure the approaches to Leningrad, and demanded that Finland cede certain territory in return for parts of Soviet-controlled Karelia. When the Finns refused, Soviet armies invaded Finland on November 30, 1939, initiating the Winter War. Finnish troops fought bravely, but were eventually overwhelmed. Russia annexed Finnish land, and some 400,000 Finns moved, rather than live under Soviet rule.

When Nazi Germany attacked the USSR in 1941, the Finns again proclaimed their neutrality. But German use of Finnish territory led the Russians to bomb Finnish cities. Finland then declared war against the USSR, emphasizing that the Finns were not allies of Germany but merely co-belligerents. This conflict is referred to by the Finns as the Continuation War.

After a prolonged standstill, Marshal Carl Mannerheim (Finland's greatest war hero) was installed as president of Finland in August of 1944, with a mandate to secure peace. An armistice with the USSR was signed on September 19.

Finland (along with Austria and Sweden) became a member of the European Union on January 1, 1995.

Cultural Note

Helsinki is the northernmost national capital on the European continent.

Type of Government

Finland is a multiparty republic. In the executive branch, the president is the head of state and shares power with the prime minister, who is chief of government. The president is elected and serves for six years. The prime minister and other members of the cabinet, or Council of State, are appointed by the president. They are not necessarily affiliated with a certain party. There is a legislative house. Many coalition governments have existed over the last century; rarely does a single party have a majority.

Women are totally accepted in high levels of government and business. In 1906, Finland was the first country to grant women the right to vote. Many women hold seats in Parliament, and have served as Cabinet ministers.

Finland's social welfare system is highly developed, and includes health and child care allowances.

For current government data, check with the Embassy of Finland, at *www.finland.org*.

Language

Finland has two official languages: Finnish and Swedish.

English is the most popular third language, and business may be conducted in English.

During the last century, Finns who grew up speaking Finnish were required to study Swedish in school, while Swedish-speaking Finns had to study Finnish. This has changed, but many Finns are multilingual.

Finnish is written in the Roman alphabet. The Finnish language does not utilize the sounds we associate with the letters *b, c, f, w, x,* and *z.* Consequently, these letters are not used in traditional Finnish words. (Of course, they do appear in words borrowed from other languages.) There are many double letters; this indicates that the sound is twice as long when spoken. About half of the words in Finnish begin with the letters *k, t, p, r,* and *v.* Two vowels—*a* and *o*—may use umlauts. The *å* and the *ø,* which are found in other Scandinavian languages, do not appear in Finnish. For foreigners who want to learn Finnish, Finnish words are almost always pronounced exactly as spelled.

J.R.R. Tolkien, author of *The Lord of the Rings,* was an amateur linguist. He reportedly based his fictional Elvish language on Finnish.

The Finnish View

There is no official religion in Finland. Most Finns belong to the Evangelical Lutheran Church of Finland, which is part of the worldwide Church of Christ. There is a Finnish Orthodox Church, patterned after the Greek Orthodox Church, which accounts for a small percentage of Finns. Nonreligious Finns make up about 12 percent of the population; the remaining is split between many different denominations. The Evangelical Lutheran Church of Finland maintains a Web site in English at *www.evl.fi/english/.*

Unlike the Kingdoms of Denmark, Norway, and Sweden, Finland is a republic. Furthermore, while Danes, Norwegians, and Swedes all speak similar, mutually intelligible languages, the Finnish tongue is different. Finnish is quite alien to them; a Dane can no more understand Finnish than he could understand Swahili or Chinese.

Finland's isolation and harsh environment has left its mark on the Finnish character. Many Finns attribute their stoic personality traits to their unforgiving environment.

While Finland is well provided with woods, its stone is particularly difficult to work. Whereas other Scandinavian countries built houses of stone, the Finns built their homes out of flammable wood. Time and again Finnish towns and cities have burned to the ground. As they rebuilt their homes over and over, the Finns developed a pessimistic outlook combined with an indomitable will.

Certainly, a willingness to fight the Russians (after losing forty-two wars to them) displays an astonishing degree of determination.

The proliferation of mobile phones in Finland seems to have made Finns more comfortable with small talk, at least among the young. Interestingly, there was a trend toward more (not less) social formality in the 1990s. This involved using the formal form of address, rather than the more egalitarian informal form.

And finally, their language serves to isolate the Finns. Their Finno-Ugric tongue, incomprehensible to all outsiders (except for the approximately 1 million Estonians), puts a distance between the Finns and the rest of the world.

☑ Know Before You Go

The primary hazard to visitors comes from the Finnish weather. Finland's winter is cold and snowy.

Aside from that, Finland is a very safe country. Most visitors to Finland come away from a visit with no more damage than a hangover from trying to keep pace with Finns.

▶ CULTURAL ORIENTATION

Cognitive Styles: How Finns Organize and Process Information

The Finns are generally cautious toward outside information. New products and new ways of doing things are viewed with circumspection. However, once a product is accepted, the Finns enthusiastically make it their own. Finnish higher education has become more conceptual, with information being processed from an analytical perspective rather than a subjective, associative one. Finns tend to follow universalistic laws and rules of behavior rather than considering each situation as a unique problem.

Finns are a very low-context people. The Finns expect people to say what they mean and mean what they say. The Finnish propensity for silence can make them seem opaque to outsiders.

Negotiation Strategies: What Finns Accept as Evidence

The Finns have faith in their own indomitable determination to survive despite a harsh environment. Objective facts are preferred over subjective feelings. The Finns have a very competitive business environment; expect them to be tough negotiators.

Value Systems: The Basis for Behavior
Traditionally, Finns know how to fight, but they also know how to get along. The term *Finlandisation* refers to the acquiescence of a small nation, Finland, to demands of a larger, more powerful, neighbor—the USSR. Finland is also a social welfare state with strong humanitarian and environmental concerns.

The following three sections identify the Value Systems in the predominant culture—their methods of dividing right from wrong, good from evil, and so forth.

Locus of Decision-Making
The individual is expected to make decisions within the boundaries of the social welfare system. There is an emphasis on individual initiative and achievement, with a person's ability being more important than his or her station in life. Although the dignity and worth of the individual is emphasized, there is a strong feeling of obligation to help those who are not able to help themselves. Finns cherish their right to a private life and personal opinions.

Sources of Anxiety Reduction
Finns use laws and morality to give structure to their worldview.

The strong social welfare system and a strong nuclear family give Finns stability and security. This reduces life's uncertainties and the anxiety that comes with them. Finns are highly nationalistic, with a liberal philosophy of tolerance for dissent and deviation.

Issues of Equality/Inequality
Finland has an egalitarian society with a largely homogeneous population. While class differences exist, they are minor compared to many European countries. There is also a belief that hard work should be rewarded.

Finland is basically a middle-class society where the government helps with family needs. The minimizing of social differences also minimizes the evidence of poverty and wealth.

Child care is considered a priority, with husbands and wives sharing the responsibilities. Finland also boasts one of the most gender-neutral societies in the world.

And, of course, the Finnish sauna is a very egalitarian tradition. It is difficult to behave in an elitist manner if one is nude.

▶ BUSINESS PRACTICES

Punctuality, Appointments, and Local Time

- The Finns are one of the most punctual people in the world. Lateness demonstrates an insulting lack of concern.
- The residents of Finland, like most Europeans, write the day first, then the month, then the year (e.g., December 3, 2010, is written 3.12.10 or 3/12/10).
- Finns may take four or five weeks of vacation per year.
- Avoid business travel to Finland in July, August, and early September, when many Finns will be away on vacation.
- Finland's Independence Day is December 6. For more official holidays in Finland, visit *www.kissboworshakehands.com*.
- Finland is two hours ahead of Greenwich Mean Time (G.M.T. + 2) or seven hours ahead of U.S. Eastern Standard Time (E.S.T. + 7).

Negotiating

- As previously noted, the Finns have a highly competitive business culture. Expect them to be tough negotiators.
- A mix of British English and American English may be spoken. Titles reflect the British style (for example, the CEO is the managing director, etc.). While it is considered courteous to have all materials translated into Finnish, it is not strictly required.
- The Finns tend to be more comfortable talking than writing. They prefer to communicate over the telephone or in person, rather than via e-mail or formal correspondence.
- Avoid any attitude of superiority.

• The propensity of Finns to remain silent for extended periods of time confuses some foreign negotiators. The Finns are comfortable being quiet and somewhat unemotional in public—so you should not be put off by long silences.

Cultural Note

Finns do not have a tradition of group cooperation. Managers from the United States and the United Kingdom sometimes complain that the Finns are not good "team players." (Of course, this view is subjective—the Japanese often consider workers from the United States and the United Kingdom to be uncooperative and too individualistic.) The Finnish lack of "team spirit" is not due to an unfamiliarity with team sports; most Finns play several team sports in school.

Business Entertaining

• Finns love coffee—cafés are everywhere, and breakfasts can be quite substantial.

• Lunch is usually eaten sometime between 11:00 A.M. and 1 P.M. In the past, a business lunch included alcohol and could last for as long as three hours. Today, 90 minutes is about average, and alcohol is rarely served.

• Although drinking has diminished somewhat in recent years, Finns may still engage in prodigious bouts of alcohol consumption. Pace yourself—drunk-driving laws are very strict in Finland.

• It is perfectly acceptable to converse about business during a meal. This may be one reason that Finland's businesses are considered among the most competitive in the world.

• In Finland, the guest of honor at a meal has specific duties. He (or she) is seated to the right of the host. He may not eat until everyone has been served, and should not drink until the host proposes a toast. After the meal, the guest of honor may make a short speech, which includes thanking the host for the meal.

• The cold table (buffet) is known as *voileipapoyta*.

• Good topics of conversation include Finnish history, politics, cuisine, sports, technology, hobbies, travel, and the traditions of the sauna. Avoid personal questions.

- The Finns also have a tradition of social dancing, especially their own version of the tango. Comparing the Argentine and Finnish tango is also a topic of interest.
- Most affluent Finns have a summer cabin away from the cities; their activities there make a good topic of conversation. Favorite rural activities include hiking, fishing, and mushroom picking.
- Finns love reading about their country in foreign books and publications. Make note of favorable mention about Finns or Finland in your country's press.

⊛ PROTOCOL

Greetings
- Finns of all ages and genders usually greet each other with a brief, firm handshake. It should be accompanied by eye contact and a nod of the head. Even children are encouraged to shake hands.
- Finns do not often touch in public, and are not particularly comfortable with additions to handshakes that involve touching (such as a hand on the arm or shoulder).
- Embraces are reserved for close friends and relatives.

Titles/Forms of Address
- Names in Finland are written in the same order as those in most of Europe: first name followed by the surname.
- Finns usually introduce themselves with their full name, minus academic or professional titles.
- In a business or academic setting, Finns expect to be addressed by their title and surname. Finns without a title may be addressed with an honorific (Mr./Mrs./Miss) and surname.
- Younger Finns are more comfortable using first names.

Gestures
- It is not appropriate to fold your arms: this signifies arrogance or a close-minded position.
- A toss of the head is a motion for "come here."

- Finns are not generally comfortable with physical contact such as backslapping.
- It is not polite to talk with your hands in your pockets.
- Sitting with the ankle resting on the knee is too casual.
- Look people directly in the eye when conversing.

Gifts
- Gift giving is not normally a part of doing business in Finland. Indeed, the Finnish reputation for honesty makes the giving of gifts problematic; a gift must not be interpreted as a bribe. Never bring a business gift to the first meeting.
- Fiskars scissors (with the orange handles) are a commonly imitated Finnish product. Avoid giving any type of gift that may compete with them.
- Personal gifts at a friend's home can include a good bottle of wine, flowers, books on a topic of interest to your client/friend/host, or something particularly meaningful from your home country.

Dress
- The weather in Finland is the primary determinant of clothing. Visitors should dress to stay warm, but be aware of local styles.
- Weather conditions aside, Finns are not an ostentatious people, and prefer conservative clothing. Businesspeople still generally wear suits.
- If you are asked to be a guest at a Finn's summer cabin, he or she probably has a selection of outdoor gear to lend you, such as boots and rain slickers.

Cultural Note
"The Finns design products
The Swedes build them
The Danes market them
And the Norwegians buy them."
   This is an old Norwegian saying, referring to the relative skills of the Scandinavian peoples. The Finns have often produced striking designs, while the Swedes have Scandinavia's largest manufacturing capacity, and the Danes are known for their salesmanship abilities.

France

French Republic
Local long form: République Française

Cultural Note

French attitudes about time are different from most of those in Northern Europe, the United States, or the United Kingdom. Surprisingly, a French businessperson might give an excuse for being a few minutes late to a meeting, yet say nothing if he is a half-hour late. No insult is intended by tardiness. To the French, life is complex and many things occur which can cause a delay. People and relationships are always more important than a soulless schedule. (Of course, there are exceptions—some executives will be as punctual as their exquisite watches.)

▶ WHAT'S YOUR CULTURAL IQ?

1. The French consider conversation to be an art. Which of the following are characteristic of most French conversations?
   a. Attentive listening
   b. Waiting for the other person to finish
   c. Scrupulous accuracy
   d. None of the above
   ANSWER: d. French conversation tends to be nonlinear. People frequently interrupt each other—even if the speaker has not finished answering a question. Cleverness is considered more important than accuracy.

2. TRUE OR FALSE: It is probably useless to complain to the management about unsatisfactory service in a small French shop.
   ANSWER: TRUE. A store manager feels such loyalty to an employee that he or she usually supports the employee against the customer—even if the employee is in the wrong. "The customer is always right" is not a French aphorism.

3. TRUE OR FALSE: Joan of Arc inspired the French to defeat the English during the conflict that came to be known as the Thirty Years' War.
    ANSWER: FALSE. It was the Hundred Years' War—which actually lasted 116 years, from 1337 to 1453.

▶ TIPS ON DOING BUSINESS IN FRANCE

*   During negotiations, the French may want to express every possible objection. It is not necessary to respond to each and every single statement—French conversational habits encourage all opinions to be voiced, even if they are not critical to the outcome.
*   Before you ask for directions, assistance, or just plain information, apologize for not speaking French! You are in France, and the French will appreciate your acknowledgement that you cannot speak French well—if at all.
*   Learn proper dining etiquette (including the identification of all the utensils) before you attend a formal French dinner. Understand the seven courses in a Parisian restaurant, in what order they arrive (soup, fish, sorbet, meat or fowl, salad, dessert, coffee) and study a bit about the wines of France.

Cultural Note
France has a civil law system, rather than a common law system. Commercial agreements are short because they refer to the legal code. Many businesspeople have studied law and can draw up their own contracts. Parties to an international contract may choose which country's laws will govern it.

▶ COUNTRY BACKGROUND

History
The cultural roots of the French go back to the Celtic Gauls, who were conquered by Julius Caesar in 51 B.C. Five hundred years later,

Clovis extended Frankish rule over much of Europe. Charlemagne is often considered the true founder of France; during his rule (A.D. 768 to 814), he made France the center of the Holy Roman Empire. But under Charlemagne's successors, both France and the Holy Roman Empire fell into disarray.

Some regions of France came under the control of English kings. The Hundred Years' War (1337–1453) ended with the English expelled from France by Charles VII—aided by Joan of Arc.

The Reformation made inroads into Catholic France, primarily in the form of the Huguenots, causing a series of civil wars. Eventually, most Protestants left, and France remained a Catholic nation.

The Thirty Years' War (1562–1698) devastated Central Europe. The great French ministers Richelieu and Mazarin successfully maneuvered to make France the leading power in Europe; France also annexed Alsace.

The French Revolution of 1789 abolished feudalism and absolute monarchy, but failed to establish democracy. France was held together by Napoleon I, who established the First Empire. France was at war for most of his reign, which ended in France's defeat by a European coalition in 1815.

The Bourbon monarchy was restored in 1814 with Louis XVIII. His successor, Charles X, prompted a revolution in 1830 when he tried to seize absolute power. His cousin, Louis Philippe, took the throne, promising to rule as a "citizen-king." He lasted until the revolutionary year 1848, when he was overthrown and the Second Republic was created.

Louis Napoleon, the nephew of Napoleon I, was elected president of France's Second Republic. In 1852, he decided to restore the empire, and took the title of Emperor Napoleon III. His expansionist foreign policy ended in defeat in the Franco-Prussian War and the foundation of the Third Republic. During this period, France colonized Indochina, parts of North Africa, and the South Pacific.

Like most of Europe, France suffered badly in the First World War (1914–1918). Unlike some European countries, France emerged from the war with its democracy intact. The Great Depression brought a radical-socialist-communist Popular Front alliance to power, which introduced many social reforms.

France entered the Second World War in 1939, and was soon overrun by Nazi Germany.

The Germans allowed the extreme right to set up a puppet dictatorship under Marshall Petain in Vichy. Resistance to the occupation was maintained by the Free French under de Gaulle

The Allies landed in France at Normandy in June 1944, and the German occupation force was pushed back. Officials from de Gaulle's organization in Algiers and local Resistance leaders took over the administration. The war ended the following year. Trials of those who collaborated with the Nazis occupied postwar France for years. In 1957, France joined with five other Western European powers to form the EEC (European Economic Community), a common market of 165 million people largely unencumbered by tariff barriers. This eventually evolved into the European Union.

In 1968, students at the University of Paris, protesting police brutality, went on strike and occupied university buildings. Their example set off strikes of students and workers throughout the country, and by the third week of May, the country was virtually paralyzed by a general strike.

President Charles de Gaulle announced a referendum on two constitutional reforms and declared that he would resign if the voters should reject his proposals. In the voting on April 27, 1969, 53 percent of the voters cast negative ballots, and de Gaulle resigned the next day. Georges Pompidou succeeded de Gaulle in the elections held after his resignation.

Georges Pompidou died in 1974 and the Independent Republican candidate, Valéry Giscard d'Estaing, was elected president.

François Mitterrand replaced Giscard as president in 1981, following a Socialist victory at the polls.

The former prime minister, Jacques Chirac, won the French presidency in 1995 with 52.6 percent of the vote.

France refused to participate in the 2002 war against Iraq, and strongly opposed the U.S.–led invasion.

Type of Government

France is a multiparty republic. The head of the government is the prime minister; the president is chief of state. The French people elect the president and the two houses of Parliament. The president, who appoints the prime minister, serves for five years. The president has a large share of the power, including the right to dissolve the lower house of Parliament, the Assemblée Nationale, and call for new elections. According to the constitution, it is the government and not the president that decides on national policy.

For current government data, check with the Embassy of France, at *www.info-france-usa.org*, which can also provide guides on doing business in France.

Language

The French people are very proud of their language, which was the international language of diplomacy for centuries. The ruling classes of countries as distant as Russia and Mexico spoke French in preference to their own indigenous tongues. The fact that English is now the international language of finance, science, and aviation is inconsequential; the French believe their language is still superior. If you do not speak French, it is advisable to apologize for this— because as far as they are concerned, you are in France, and you should know French.

Many French businesspeople speak English but will prefer to conduct their meetings in French.

The French View

There is no official religion. France is principally a Catholic country (70 percent), although new immigrants are raising the percentage of Islam (5–10 percent). Many other religions, including Protestantism and Judaism, are present, and there are also many people unaffiliated with any religion.

Are the French unfriendly? No—but they can be difficult to get to know. The average French citizen develops personal relationships with many people—including local sales clerks. Customers go to the same store, year after year, and get to know everyone in the shop.

So much is accomplished through personal contacts in France that they do not feel any obligation to be deferential to strangers. Historically, the French have considered foreigners who grin and chat with strangers as either condescending or idiotic.

The strong tendency to build long-term networks is reflected in the French mode of communication. Prior to any major meeting, the French will generally talk with their contacts about any delicate issues that may arise on the agenda. They are thoroughly informed by their networks before, during, and after most meetings.

This dedication to maintaining and expanding one's network is vital to sales processes in France. French interviewers actually inquire, "Who do you know?" far more often than "What have you done or sold?" Sales managers care more about your potential network of leads and contacts than your closing ratio. Sales executives will have a variety of major networks—through their parents, their schools, industry contacts, clubs, associations, etc. Employers value that access, and may prefer a candidate with excellent potential networks rather than the one with the largest tax return.

(As an aside, French interviewers may also do handwriting analyses of job candidates! The French use graphology to determine predominant work characteristics.)

Managers often have strong relationships with their employees. They feel responsible for their staff, treat them like family, and will back them in a dispute.

☑ Know Before You Go

The weather can be hazardous—with everything from flooding to drought, windstorms in the winter months to avalanches in the spring. Near the Mediterranean, they are prone to forest fires.

The island of Corsica has been under French rule since they invaded in 1769. In the 1960s, terrorist groups that craved independence became active—primarily utilizing homemade bombs. The bombings became an almost daily feature of life in Corsica—and escalated to as many as 700 a year in the 1980s. Recently, the island's growing Arab community has been the new target of these attacks. Be cautious when planning your visit.

▶ CULTURAL ORIENTATION

Cognitive Styles: How the French Organize and Process Information

The French will readily accept information for the purpose of debate and may change their minds quickly, but strong ethnocentrism will not allow the acceptance of anything contrary to the cultural norm. Ideas are very important to them, and they approach knowledge from an analytical and critical perspective. They look at each situation as a unique problem and bring all their knowledge to bear on it.

Negotiation Strategies: What the French Accept as Evidence

Arguments tend to be made from an analytical, critical perspective with eloquent rhetorical wit and logic. There is a great love for debate, striving for effect rather than detail and image over facts. Feelings and faith in some ideology may become part of the rhetoric.

Value Systems: The Basis for Behavior

Pride in their heritage sometimes makes them appear egotistical in their behavior. The following three sections identify the Value Systems in the predominant culture—their methods of dividing right from wrong, good from evil, and so forth.

Locus of Decision-Making

The French are strongly individualistic and have a centralized authority structure that makes quick decisions possible. The relationship between the participants becomes a major variable in the decision-making process. An individual's self-identity is based on his or her accomplishments in the social realm. Education is the primary variable in social standing. Individual privacy is necessary in all walks of life.

Sources of Anxiety Reduction

The French seem to be preoccupied with status, rank, and formality. Contacts are of utmost importance, and they may have a low tolerance for ambiguity in one's station. They feel comfortable with rules and regulations. If the French are provided with adequate details and assessments, they are more comfortable with business risks. Their attachment to a public figure gives them a sense of security. Yet individuality is preferable to conformity. People are allowed to show both positive and negative emotions in public.

Issues of Equality/Inequality
An informal stratified class system still exists, but most people are middle class. Superiors expect obedience from subordinates in all walks of life. Power is a basic fact of society, and leaders with the ability to unify the country or group are highly prized. Gender roles in society are fluid, and a person's status is more important than his or her sex.

⊙ BUSINESS PRACTICES

Punctuality, Appointments, and Local Time
- Always make appointments for both business and social occasions. Be punctual, although the French are more relaxed about time in the South.
- Most French get four or five weeks of summer vacation, and take it in July and August. Indeed, except for the tourist industry, France virtually shuts down in August. Try to conduct business during other months.
- A law in 2004 created a full working day without salary, which reduced the number of public holidays in France by one day. Called a "solidarity journey," this day can be applied to any official holiday the company's employees select. If they cannot decide on which day should be the working day/holiday, it automatically forfeits to Pentecost Monday.
- Always present your business card. When receiving the cards of others, treat them very carefully.
- It is best to have your business card printed in French upon arrival. One side can be in English, with the translation in French on the

other side. On the French side, include any academic credentials and your school if it is a prestigious one.

- The best times to schedule meetings are around 11:00 A.M. or 3:30 P.M.
- The National Holiday is Bastille Day, July 14 (1789).
- France is one hour ahead of Greenwich Mean Time (G.M.T. + 1). This makes it six hours ahead of U.S. Eastern Standard Time (E.S.T. + 6).

Cultural Note

Most English-speaking French have studied British-style English, which can lead to communication breakdowns with speakers of American-style English. For example, in the United States, a presentation that "bombs" has failed, but in England, it has succeeded.

Words in French and English may have the same roots, but different meanings or connotations. If you don't speak French, don't be offended too easily. For example, a French person might "demand" something, because *demander* simply means "to ask." If you speak some French, don't assume that an English word will have the same connotation in French. For example, if you ask for the bathroom and use the translation *salle de bains*, it will not be understood that you are asking for *la toilette*.

Negotiating

- Eye contact among the French is frequent and intense—so much so that some Asians and North Americans may be intimidated.
- Because of the strong "old-boy network" and lack of merit-based promotions, employees stick to their job descriptions. Know who does what. If you are in charge of a service-oriented company, make it a policy to promote your French nationals based on good service, because your French management may not do so. Be sure to effectively communicate your company's standards for service.
- The French are known for their formal and reserved nature. A casual attitude during business transactions will alienate them.
- During negotiations, the French may make you seem to be the *demandeur* (petitioner), thus putting you in the weaker position.
- Hierarchies are strict. Junior executives will pass a problem on to a superior. Try to cultivate high-level personal contacts.

- Women should not mistake French gallantry for condescension.
- Don't start a conversation by asking personal questions.
- Don't mistake a high-pitched voice and excited gestures for anger; they usually just mean great interest in the subject.

Business Entertaining
- Business can be conducted during any meal, but lunch is best.
- Though the French are familiar with "le power breakfast," they are not enthusiastic about it.
- Business lunches usually last one to one and a half hours. Dinner is late (8:00 or 9:00 P.M.).
- At a business lunch or dinner, show appreciation for the food before beginning a business discussion.
- The business drink should not be held in a café; they are too noisy. Try a quieter venue.
- Whoever initiates the meal or drink is expected to pay.
- Reservations are necessary in most restaurants, except in brasseries and in hotels. In choosing a restaurant, stick to French rather than ethnic ones.
- The French have a great appreciation for good conversationalists.
- When eating, keep both hands on the table at all times. Food comes gradually, so don't fill up too soon. When finished, place your fork and knife parallel across your plate.
- Cheese is served toward the end of the meal.
- Don't drink hard liquor before meals or smoke between courses. The French believe this deadens the taste buds.
- Respect privacy. The French close doors behind them; you should do the same. Knock and wait before entering.

⊙ PROTOCOL

Greetings
- Always shake hands when being introduced or when meeting someone, as well as when leaving. In general, the woman offers her hand first. French handshakes do not usually involve a strong grip.

- In social settings, with friends, expect to do *les bises*, or touching cheeks and kissing the air.

Titles/Forms of Address
- Find out the titles of older French people you meet and address them in that way, both during the introduction and in the course of conversation. Even simple titles like "Madame" should be used as you converse, whether in English or French.
- Use "Madame" for all women except young girls.
- Don't use first names until you are told to do so. Don't be put off by the use of last names; it doesn't mean that the French are unfriendly. If you speak French, use the *vous* form until you are told to use *tú*.
- The French sometimes say their last names first, so that Pierre Robert might introduce himself as "Robert, Pierre." Ask!

Gestures
- The "thumbs-up" sign means "okay"; the North American "okay" sign (forming a circle with thumb and forefinger) means "zero" in France.
- Slapping the open palm over a closed fist is vulgar.
- To call for the check, make a writing gesture.
- Don't chew gum in public!
- Men may still stand up or make a move to stand up when a visitor or a superior enters the room.

Gifts
- Don't give a business gift at your first encounter.
- Avoid gifts that are either too lavish or too skimpy, as well as gifts with your company logo. Good taste is everything.
- You can insert a business card with your gift, along with a small card that states: "with the compliments of Mr./Madame . . ."
- Good gifts include books or music, as they show interest in the intellect. Bring American bestsellers, especially biographies. The thicker and more complex the book, the better; simplicity is not a virtue in France.

- Bring flowers (not roses or chrysanthemums), fine chocolates, or liqueur to the host. Present them before, not after, the party.
- For thank-yous, send (at least) a note the next day.

Dress
- Clothes are very important in France. This is not surprising; the very words used in English to describe fashion—"haute couture," "chic," etc., are from the French language. The term haute couture dates back to 1908.
- Not everyone in France owns an extensive wardrobe, but what they do own is expensive, well made, and fashionable. Affluent executives purchase the best suits and styles possible.
- The French also tend to have excellent posture, which makes their clothes look even better.
- In the north and in the winter, men should wear dark suits.
- North American men should be aware that French suits are cut differently.
- Never be the first to remove your jacket or tie. Let your colleagues make the first move toward a more relaxed look.

Cultural Note

Bringing a bottle of wine is a common gesture when visiting friends around the world—would it be an appropriate gift for dinner at a French client's home?

Probably not. As a citizen of France, your host may be a serious oenophile, and has likely taken great pains to carefully select the correct wines for each course. Unless your charming little vintage is of interest because it is from your home country, it implies that you know more about wine than your host does. Or, by bringing your own bottle, you may inadvertently communicate that you have doubts about the quality of his or her wine cellar.

Germany

Federal Republic of Germany
Local short form: Deutschland
Local long form: Bundesrepublik Deutschland
Former: German Empire, German Republic, German Reich

Cultural Note

Like many things in Germany, advertising is highly regulated. It is illegal in an advertisement to compare your product to that of a competitor's product. You can say that your product is "#1", but you will be required to prove that with objective data. If you cannot, your ad may be pulled from the airwaves by the German government.

▶ WHAT'S YOUR CULTURAL IQ?

1. Ever since Martin Luther, Germany has been divided between Protestants and Roman Catholics. TRUE OR FALSE: Whatever their religious beliefs, most Germans are fond of a Catholic saint named King Gambrinus.
   ANSWER: TRUE. King Gambrinus is the patron saint of beer drinkers and brewers. German legend even credits him with the invention of beer. Many German breweries and taverns display an inscription honoring Gambrinus.

2. German literature is known for profound, serious authors. Which one of the following is the bestselling German author of all time?
   a. Johann Wolfgang von Goethe (1749–1832)
   b. Heinrich Böll (1917–1985)
   c. Günter Grass (1927–)
   d. Herman Hesse (1877–1962)
   e. Thomas Mann (1875–1955)
   f. Karl May (1842–1912)

ANSWER: f. An author of cowboy-and-Indian adventures, Karl May was (and is) very popular in Germany.

3. In 1948, Adi Dassler started a now-famous company. In 1954, Mr. Dassler's company garnered tremendous publicity when Germany's entire soccer team wore his product and won the World Cup for the first time. TRUE OR FALSE: His company made sneakers. ANSWER: TRUE. Adidas does not really stand for "All Day I Dream About Sports" (or Soccer). The brand is a combination of the first three letters of his names.

▶ TIPS ON DOING BUSINESS IN GERMANY

- In business matters, Germans do not like the unexpected. Sudden changes—even if they may improve the outcome—are unwelcome.
- Whether you know German or use your own language, speak in complete sentences. Make it obvious when a sentence is complete; don't let your sentences trail off. In the German language, the most important word in a sentence is usually the final one. Germans are in the habit of listening for the end of a sentence, and can be annoyed if it doesn't materialize.
- The trade fair (aka, trade show) was largely invented in Germany. Germany hosts almost two-thirds of the international trade fairs, so participation in their conferences is key.

▶ COUNTRY BACKGROUND

History
After the fall of the Roman Empire, Germany was unified under Charlemagne, who established a kingdom that encompassed much of western Europe in A.D. 800. Charlemagne divided his holdings among his sons, and the first all-Germanic kingdom dates back to this division.

The first strong German king was Otto I, who defeated invading Danes, Slavs, and Magyars (Hungarians). In A.D. 926, Pope John XII crowned Otto I as the emperor of the Holy Roman Empire, a loosely organized domain that stretched from Germany down into northern Italy. To modern Germans, this Holy Roman Empire was the "First Reich."

The Holy Roman Empire encompassed many semiautonomous principalities that often fought with each other. The internecine warfare increased after Martin Luther's successful Reformation in 1519. Some areas remained Roman Catholic while others adopted Protestant beliefs. This conflict cumulated in the Thirty Years' War (1618–1648).

In 1740, Frederick II ("the Great") became ruler of Prussia. He greatly expanded Prussia's territory by annexing small German principalities (not to mention about a third of Poland). Prussia soon became one of Europe's great powers and began competing with Austria for leadership among the German-speaking peoples.

Napoleon I conquered most of Germany in 1806. This led to the dissolution of the Holy Roman Empire.

By the eighteenth century, two German-speaking kingdoms had come to dominate Central Europe: Prussia and Austria. Austria felt it was in its interest to keep the German principalities separate; Prussia wanted to unite (and rule) them. Austria's Metternich succeeded in replacing the Holy Roman Empire with a loose union called "the German Confederation" (the Bund). But Prussia eventually won out when Prime Minister Otto von Bismarck led his country into war, first against Denmark, then against Austria and the Austrian-allied German kingdoms, then against France.

As a result of Bismarck's efforts, the Prussian King William I was crowned Kaiser (emperor) of all Germany in 1871. The German nation dates its existence from this event. This "Second Reich" was to last until Germany's defeat in the First World War.

After the First World War, Germany became a republic. Burdened with enormous war reparations and the Great Depression, Germany fell into the hands of the "National Socialists," as they are known to Germans—the term "Nazi" was rarely used within Germany. The atrocities of Adolf Hitler's "Third Reich" present a moral dilemma that each new generation of Germans must face.

At the end of World War II, Germany was occupied by England, France, the United States, and the USSR. This resulted in the division of Germany into the capitalist, NATO-allied Federal Republic of Germany (FRG) and the Communist, Warsaw Pact German Democratic Republic (or GDR). Berlin was also divided into West and East. Consequently, Bonn was selected as the capital of West Germany. Only the changed priorities of Mikhail Gorbachev's Soviet Union allowed the two halves of Germany to reunite on October 3, 1990.

As the largest and most populous nation in the European Union, the reunited Germany has developed into a leading power, and one of the strongest members of the EU.

Type of Government

The reunited Federal Republic of Germany is a democratic federal multiparty republic. Voting is done by proportional representation. There are two legislative houses: the Federal Council and the Federal Diet. The president is the chief of state, and the chancellor is the head of the government.

The government's preoccupations include issues pertaining to the former East Germany. One current hot-button issue is the war on terrorism and the invasion of Iraq. In the past a staunch U.S. ally, Germany vigorously opposed the Second Gulf War.

Abjuring from military intervention after the Second World War, Germany influenced the world via "checkbook diplomacy," contributing far more than its share to international organizations. Germany gave much more to the European Union than it gained in return. However, Germany can no longer afford to be so generous.

In 2005, Germany elected its first female chancellor, Angela Merkel. For current government data, check with the Embassy of Germany at *www.germany-info.org*.

Language

The official language of Germany is German, which is called *Deutsch*. German has many dialects. The accepted national dialect is High German (or *Hochdeutsch*). It gained prominence after Martin

Luther translated the Bible into High German in 1534. Low German *(Plattdeutsch)* was spoken in many low-lying northern regions of Germany.

English and French are currently the preferred foreign languages that Germans study. This is especially true among executives. Germans who grew up in the former German Democratic Republic were forced to study Russian in school. This is no longer the case, but you will find fewer English speakers in eastern Germany.

The German View

The population is split almost evenly between Roman Catholics and Protestants (mostly of various Lutheran sects). Many Germans describe themselves as nonreligious. There are small populations of Jews and Muslims.

The majority of immigrants are Turkish Muslims. Although Germany's aging population needs their labor, their presence is of great concern. Many Germans feel that the Turkish immigrants make an insufficient effort to adopt German customs. Violence against Turks occasionally breaks out.

Germany's powerful economy has been in the doldrums since the 1990s. Restrictive labor laws and high taxes made Germany an unwelcome place for foreign investment. Unemployment has remained relatively high. Many observers believe that Germans are unwilling to allow their industry the flexibility to compete in the global market.

German manufacturing has a reputation for high quality, which German consumers demand. Any instances of quality control failure are cause for worry among German society, not just the individual company involved.

Almost all Germans profess a love of nature. Many Germans enjoy outdoor activities, such as hiking, bicycling, camping, and skiing. They also enjoy long vacations to take advantage of their country's scenic landmarks. Most Germans get at least six weeks of paid vacation per year, plus numerous paid holidays and sick days with partial pay.

☑ **Know Before You Go**

The greatest hazards to visitors tend to be vehicular accidents. There is also the danger from exposure to cold during Germany's bitter winters.

Periodic flooding is a serious danger and has caused much destruction in low-lying areas.

Avalanches and landslides are also hazards. Germany has an active Green Party, which maintains that Germans are in danger from the many toxic waste sites in the former East Germany, as well as from Russian-built nuclear power plants throughout eastern Europe.

⏵ CULTURAL ORIENTATION

Cognitive Styles: How Germans Organize and Process Information

Germans have historically been closed to outside information, and they did not freely share data among units of the same organization. However, the younger generation is becoming more open. Germans are analytic and conceptual in their information processing. They are strongly committed to the universal beliefs of their culture. Friendships are not developed quickly, but they are deep and highly selective.

Negotiation Strategies: What Germans Accept as Evidence

Data, data, data: Germans depend upon objective facts. Emotional involvement is unacceptable in negotiations. Once a position is decided upon, Germans rarely budge, which gives them the reputation for being tough negotiators.

A strong faith in their social democratic ideology influences Germans' perceptions of the truth.

Value Systems: The Basis for Behavior

One may find some differences in the value systems between what was once East and West Germany. There are also generational differences: for example, the postwar generation is less burdened by guilt over Nazi atrocities. The following three sections identify the Value

Systems in the predominant culture—their methods of dividing right from wrong, good from evil, and so forth.

Locus of Decision-Making

A desire to seek consensus and a widespread respect for order are German characteristics. This is reflected in the German phrase: *"Ordnung muss sein"* (There must be order!). Every German has a responsibility to follow the rules, both written and unwritten. Actions that disrupt this social order are seen as inherently wrong. Decisions must be made in reference to larger units: society, one's company, and one's family.

Curiously, the ability of Germans to compartmentalize allows for substantial individual freedom. As long as an individual's duties to society and employer are met, Germans have a wide latitude for private individual behavior.

Decision-making is slow and involved, as all peripheral concerns must be taken care of in the process. Once a decision is made, it is unchangeable. Individual privacy is necessary in all walks of life, and personal matters are not discussed in business negotiations.

Sources of Anxiety Reduction

Germans have a fairly high index of uncertainty avoidance. As a result, Germans use laws and morality to give structure to their worldview. Germans tend to be risk-averse and cautious about making decisions. They also buy every conceivable sort of insurance: life insurance, fire insurance, theft insurance, travel insurance, personal liability insurance, and so on.

As the German population ages, it can be expected that Germans will become even more risk-averse.

Universal rules and regulations combined with strong internal discipline give stability to life and reduce uncertainty. There is a high need for social and personal order, and a low tolerance for deviant behavior. There is very little show of emotion because of strong internal structures and control.

Germans are more oriented toward near-term issues. German skepticism about the future (economic, political, and social) can breed anxiety and pessimism. There is a sense of helplessness about humanity's ability to produce a desirable outcome in the long-term

Issues of Equality/Inequality

Titles of nobility were gradually abolished after the First World War, but Germany still has a class system with very little flexibility. Business leaders tend to come from the upper class. Although equality is guaranteed by law, German businessmen sometimes denigrate women as "lacking self-confidence" and "unable to command male subordinates." This is changing, as evidenced by the 2005 election of Angela Merkel, the first female Chancellor of Germany. One thing is clear: Germans respect self-assurance. If you don't project it, whatever your gender, you will not be well-received in Germany.

⊚ BUSINESS PRACTICES

Punctuality, Appointments, and Local Time

- Nowhere in the world is punctuality more important than in Germany. Be on time for every appointment, whether for business or social engagements.
- Arriving just four or five minutes late can be insulting to a German executive, especially if you are in a subordinate position.
- When writing the date, Germans write the day first, then the month, then the year (e.g., December 3, 2010, is written 3.12.10 or 3/12/10).
- Appointments should be made well in advance. Give at least one week's notice for an appointment made by telephone. If you don't have that much lead time, a short preliminary meeting may sometimes be arranged on a few days notice.
- E-mail has substantially changed the process for setting up appointments in Germany. Both the historical mode of communicating (sending a written letter to the firm in general rather than to an individual executive) and the lag time required for correspondence via the mail have been streamlined.
- Still, be aware that if your e-mail (or your posted letter) is addressed to an executive who is on vacation, the response may

be a long time in coming. Most Germans take at least six weeks of (paid) vacation per year.

- If two Germans sign a business letter, or if more than one German is consistently copied on e-mail, this indicates that both of them must be in agreement before a decision is made.
- Do not schedule appointments on Friday afternoons; some offices close by 2:00 or 3:00 P.M. on Fridays. Many people take long vacations during July, August, and December, so check first to see if your counterpart will be available. Also, be aware that little work gets done during regional festivals, such as the Oktoberfest or the three-day Carnival before Lent.
- In the former East Germany, businesses did not usually schedule appointments on Wednesdays. This has been changing since reunification.
- For Germany's official holidays, visit *www.kissboworshakehands.com*.
- Germany is one hour ahead of Greenwich Mean Time (G.M.T. + 1). This makes it six hours ahead of U.S. Eastern Standard Time (E.S.T. + 6).
- Germans use a twenty-four-hour clock. In German, midnight is *null Uhr* (zero hour).
- When identifying a half-hour, the usage in German is unlike the usage in English. Where an Englishman might refer to 9:30 A.M. as "half-nine," a German may call the same time "half-ten." If you are in doubt, ask for clarification.

Cultural Note

German negotiators can be very tough customers. Many of them view being forced to compromise as a personal failure. As some observers have noted, "Germans come in expecting 110 percent. They might settle for just 100 percent."

Negotiating

- The pace of German corporate decision-making is methodical—much slower than in Great Britain or the U.S.A.
- The decision-making process in German firms can be a mystery to outsiders. In addition to the official chain of command, German

companies often have a parallel "hidden" series of advisers and decision-makers. The approval of this informal "kitchen cabinet" is mandatory.

- Directness is appreciated. Germans may bluntly criticize your product or your company; don't take it personally.

- Germans abhor hype and exaggeration. Be sure you can back up your claims with lots of data. Case studies and examples are highly regarded.

- Be prepared to supply reams of information at short notice. Some of the requests may seem trivial; be assured that they are important to the Germans.

- The German reputation for quality is based (in part) on slow, methodical planning. Every aspect of the deal you propose will be pored over by various executives. Do not anticipate being able to speed up this process. This slowness extends through all business affairs. Germans believe that it takes time to do a job properly.

- German punctuality does not extend to delivery dates. Products may be delivered late without either explanation or apology.

- Germans also take a lot of time to establish a close business relationship. Their apparent coldness at the beginning will vanish over time. Once they get to know you, Germans are quite gregarious.

- German bookkeeping practices historically allowed a high degree of secrecy. It was exceedingly difficult (if not impossible) to get a German company to reveal a true and accurate financial record. Due to new EU requirements, this is changing.

- Even if the German executives speak your language, all promotional materials and instruction manuals should be translated into German.

- Bring plenty of business cards; quite a few Germans may wish to exchange them with you.

- If your company has been around for many years, the date of its founding should be on your business card. If you have a large number of employees, that number should be included too.

- Since education is highly respected in Germany, consider including any title above the bachelor's level on your card.

- Germans may or may not socialize before getting down to work. It is quite possible that you will walk into an office and start talking business immediately after introducing yourself.
- If your German associates decide to chat at the beginning of a meeting, expect to be asked about your flight, your accommodations, where you are from, and so forth.
- Germans smile to indicate affection. They generally do not smile in the course of business, either at customers or at coworkers.
- Business is serious; Germans do not appreciate humor in a business context.
- Compliments tend to embarrass Germans; they expect to neither give nor receive them. They assume that everything is satisfactory unless they hear otherwise.
- When a problem arises, be prepared to explain it clearly, in detail, and unemotionally. You may have to do this in writing. Germans are not accustomed to informally "passing the word."
- Never follow the U.S. business habit of saying something positive before saying something negative. This compliment/complaint juxtaposition will sound contradictory to Germans, and they may reject your entire statement.
- Privacy is very important to Germans. Doors are kept closed, both at work and at home. Always knock on a closed door and wait to be admitted.
- Avoid asking personal questions of a German executive. If a businessperson wants you to know if he or she is married or has children, he or she will find a way to communicate this to you. Family life is kept separate from work in Germany.
- Obviously, embarrassing political questions should be avoided. Do not ask about the Second World War or anti-Semitism.
- Germans tend to be well informed about politics and to have firm political opinions. They are also honest, and may tell you their opinions about your country (or its actions), even if these opinions are negative.
- Sports are a good topic for conversation. Many Germans are passionate soccer fans; skiing, hiking, cycling, and tennis are also

popular. Less well-known sports enjoyed by Germans include ice skating, curling, and gliding.

Business Entertaining

- Breakfast meetings are still somewhat uncommon in Germany. However, business lunches are customary.
- At lunch, be aware that business may be discussed before and (sometimes) after a meal, but never during the meal itself. If you are invited out to a luncheon, you may offer to pay, but expect your host to decline your offer. Insist on paying only when you have made the invitation.
- Be on time to social events. Drinks are served before the meal, but usually with few appetizers. The meal itself will start soon after.
- Germans do not often entertain business associates in their homes. If you are invited to a home, consider it an honor.
- When eating, always use utensils; very few items are eaten with the hands. Place your utensils vertically side by side on the plate when you are finished eating.
- If you smoke, always offer your cigarettes to everyone else before lighting up. Of course, ascertain if smoking is banned at your location.

⊚ PROTOCOL

Greetings

- In business situations, most Germans shake hands at both the beginning and the end of a meeting.
- The German handshake may be accompanied by a nod of the head. Although this gesture is subtle, it is important.
- While Germans are open and generous with close friends, they tend to be formal and reserved in public. You will not see many smiles or displays of affection on German streets.
- The avoidance of public spectacle is reflected in the way Germans will get quite close to each other before offering a greeting. Only the young and the impolite wave or shout at each other from a distance.

- To get someone's attention, raise your hand, palm facing out, with only the index finger extended. Don't wave or beckon.
- When sitting, cross one knee over the other, rather than resting your ankle over one knee. Do not prop your feet on anything other than a footstool.
- The eldest or highest-ranking person generally enters a room first.
- Many traditional practices of etiquette have changed in the last few decades; however, if you are with senior executives, behave in the most formal, reserved manner possible.
- Never talk to someone while chewing gum.
- Expect to be hushed if you so much as cough while attending an opera, play, or concert. German audiences remain extraordinarily silent, rarely even shifting in their seats.
- Carry a good supply of business cards.
- Extended, direct eye contact is expected when conversing. Failure to meet a German's gaze will give the impression that you are untrustworthy.
- Never put your hands in your pockets for longer than it takes to retrieve an object. Germans find it insulting when people speak to them with their hands in their pockets.

Cultural Note

Germans keep a slightly larger personal space around them than do most British or North Americans, and a much larger personal space than most Latins. Stand about six inches beyond handshaking distance.

Germans are also protective about the positioning of their office furniture. When invited into a German office, do not move your chair closer; a German executive could find that very insulting.

This expanded personal space extends to their automobiles. Expect an outburst from a German driver if you so much as touch his or her car. Never put a package down on any car except your own.

Titles/Forms of Address
- The order of names in Germany is the same as in most of Europe: the first name followed by the surname.

- Traditionally, only family members and close friends addressed each other by their first names. You may never establish a close enough relationship with your older German colleague to get to a first-name basis; however, younger Germans will move more quickly to a first-name basis.

- When speaking to persons who do not have professional titles, use "Mr.," "Mrs.," or "Miss," plus the surname. In German, these titles are

  Mr. = Herr
  Mrs. (or Ms.) = Frau
  Miss = Fräulein

- Fräulein is now used only for young women (under age eighteen). Any businesswoman you meet should be addressed as "Frau," plus her surname, whether or not she is married.

- It is very important to use professional titles. Attorneys, engineers, pastors, and other professionals will expect you to address them as "Herr" or "Frau" plus their title. This goes for anyone with a Ph.D. as well (e.g., Herr (or Frau) Doctor/Professor). However, make sure you know the correct professional title.

- When entering or leaving a shop, it is considered polite to say "hello" and "goodbye" to the sales clerk.

- There are significant regional variations in behavior throughout Germany. For example, Bavarians have a reputation for being warm, hospitable, and casual: they tend to progress quickly from formal to informal speech and from surnames to first names. Do not expect northern Germans to behave this way.

Gifts

- German businesspeople do not give or expect to receive expensive gifts. A gift should be of good quality but not of exorbitant cost. Gifts that are small in size are preferred.

- German civil servants are prohibited from accepting any form of gift whatsoever.

- Appropriate gifts include good-quality pens, reasonably priced electronics (MP3 players loaded with music that your associate will like, etc.), or imported liquor. Gifts from your home region or country are good choices, such as an illustrated book of your home city.

- The only article of clothing considered an appropriate gift is a scarf. Other clothing, perfume, and soap are considered too personal.
- An invitation to dinner at a German home is considered an honor, and you should send a bouquet of flowers ahead of time for your host. The bouquet should not be ostentatiously large and should have an uneven number of flowers (but not thirteen). Do not choose red roses; they are reserved for courting. Also avoid such funeral flowers as white carnations, white chrysanthemums, and calla lilies. In Northern Germany, do not include heather in a bouquet. (Because of its hardy nature, heather is often planted on graves, and deemed bad luck to bring into a house.)
- While an imported liquor is appropriate, a gift of a locally available wine might be interpreted as saying that your host's wine cellar is inadequate. However, a good wine brought from your home country (one not sold in Germany) or a top-quality imported red wine will be appreciated.
- Germans make some of the finest beers in the world, so it is unlikely that you could bring a foreign beer that would truly impress them.
- Business gifts are usually given at Christmastime, although many German companies restrict themselves to sending Christmas cards and/or a calendar.

Dress
- Business dress in Germany is very conservative. Virtually all businessmen wear dark suits, sedate ties, and white shirts. However, blue blazers and gray flannel pants are also considered formal. Khaki or seersucker suits are not acceptable! Women dress equally conservatively, in dark suits, pantsuits, and blouses of a neutral color.
- Follow the lead of your German colleague with regard to removing your jacket or tie in hot weather. Do not be surprised if he or she remains fully dressed in sweltering heat.

- Business wear is also appropriate for most formal social events: parties, dinners, and the theater. Remember that you are obliged to check your coat in German theaters; if you tend to be cold, bring a sweater. On the opening night of an opera, concert, or play, men are expected to wear their best dark suit or tuxedo, and women a long evening gown.
- Casualwear consists of comfortable shirts and jeans, although these clothes should be clean and in good repair. Most German men wear sandals during the summer.

Cultural Note

Keep your thinking linear in Germany. Thorough, methodical planning is how Germans have achieved their reputation for quality. Every aspect of every project will be examined in detail. This process can be very time intensive.

It is said that the British and American businesspeople first envision their goal, then plan backward on how to achieve it. The German process is different: everything is planned from the beginning. From this starting point, each step is meticulously envisioned, until the best possible result is divined. This may be an oversimplification, but it helps to explain why everything seems to take longer in Germany: the planning process is much more extensive.

Greece

Hellenic Republic
Local short form: Ellas or Ellada
Local long form: Elliniki Dhimokratia
Former: Kingdom of Greece

Cultural Note

Backgammon is the national pastime of Greece. Men can be found playing backgammon in every taverna. If you don't know how to play, learn before you go to Greece.

▶ WHAT'S YOUR CULTURAL IQ?

1. Even people who have never studied ancient Greek literature and philosophy have heard of Homer (the blind poet credited with writing the Iliad and the Odyssey), and the great Greek philosophers Plato and Aristotle. TRUE or FALSE? All three of these men were contemporaries.
   ANSWER: FALSE. Plato and Aristotle were contemporaries; Plato was Aristotle's teacher. But Homer lived several centuries before them.

2. The Greek language is written in the Greek alphabet, which is over 2,000 years old. Which of the following alphabets did *not* evolve from the Greek alphabet?
   a. The Coptic alphabet
   b. The Cyrillic alphabet
   c. The Phoenician alphabet
   ANSWER: c. The Phoenician alphabet came before the Greek alphabet. In fact, it is believed that the Phoenician alphabet inspired the Greek alphabet. Other alphabets, including the Coptic (used by Christian Egyptians) and the Cyrillic alphabet (used by Russians, among others) evolved out of the Greek alphabet.

3. Although many Greeks have immigrated to the United States, there has been a substantial amount of anti-Americanism in post-war Greece. What is the source of this?
   a. During the Greek civil war of 1945–1949, the United States (and the United Kingdom) intervened against the Communists, who had considerable popular support.
   b. The United States supported the right-wing military junta of 1967–1974; the junta drove many Greeks into exile.
   c. During the Cypriot crisis of 1974, the Greeks felt that the United States sided with Turkey over Greece.
   d. All of the above.
   ANSWER: d. However, this animosity is not usually directed toward individual citizens of the United States.

⊚ TIPS ON DOING BUSINESS IN GREECE

- Greeks tend to be physically demonstrative. They kiss, hug, and walk arm-in-arm with both relatives and friends. Even Greek soldiers often walk arm-in-arm. This is not private behavior; it can be seen every day in the streets, to a degree that surprises visitors from northern Europe and North America.
- The Greek Orthodox Church forms an integral part of the Greek identity. Unlike Western branches of Christianity, Greek Orthodoxy stresses individual choice and does not emphasize guilt or shame. Some view this as important to the Greek character.
- Greek (also called "Hellenic") is written in the Greek alphabet, rather than the Roman alphabet used by most western European nations. (Even Turkey uses the Roman alphabet.) The Cyrillic alphabet used by the Russians and Bulgarians is derived from this Greek alphabet.

⊚ COUNTRY BACKGROUND

History
The ancient Greeks are credited with the invention of democracy. However, the democratic era of Athens was relatively short-lived

and was followed by various forms of dictatorship. Occupation and domination by outsiders—Romans, Turks, and (in this century) Nazi Germany—has made the Greek people ferociously nationalistic.

During the Second World War, resistance to the German and Italian occupying armies was carried out by guerrilla bands, which fought each other almost as frequently as they fought the Nazis. With the end of World War II, Greece tried to form a democratic government, despite the presence of these competing guerrilla organizations.

The Communist guerrillas, seeing their brethren in neighboring Eastern European states come to power, decided to revolt. The Communist rebellion in Greece lasted from 1946 to 1949, and was ended only when neighboring Yugoslavia left the Soviet orbit. The Yugoslavs closed their borders to the Soviet-backed Greek Communists. The United States took over the responsibility for Greek reconstruction from an impoverished Great Britain, and U.S. intelligence agencies worked frantically to deprive the Communists of any power in the new Greek government. In 1952, Greece joined NATO and allowed the United States to create military bases on Greek soil in 1953.

At the time, Greece was a constitutional monarchy. Distressed by the inability of the Parliament to maintain stability, in 1966, King Constantine II authorized the formation of an extra-parliamentary government to rule until new elections could be held the following year. This resulted in a military coup d'état in 1967, first ruling "in the king's name" and then, when the king tried to stage his own coup, without the king.

The junta, ruled by Colonel George Papadopoulos, gave Greece stability and a degree of economic prosperity at the cost of some human rights. By 1973, opposition to the authoritarian regime had grown strong enough that Papadopoulos decided to institute reforms. The monarchy was formally abolished, civil liberties were promised, and free elections were scheduled. But the head of the Greek military police, General Ioannides, staged a coup in late 1973 before the planned elections could be held.

Within a year this new coup had yielded to the demand for elections. The new Greek Republic was declared on December 9, 1974. A new constitution was adopted in 1975, and Greece has had peaceful transitions from one government to the next ever since.

Greece became a full member of the European Economic Community (now the EU) in 1981.

Despite fears that the facilities would not be completed in time, the 2004 Summer Olympic Games in Greece took place in a secure, efficient, and successful manner.

Type of Government

Today, Greece is a presidential parliamentary republic. Its constitution dates from 1975. There is a president elected by the Parliament and served by an advisory body, the Council of the Republic. The president is the chief of state. The real power is held by the prime minister, who is the official head of the government. The prime minister is the leader of the majority party of the unicameral Parliament. The Parliament is called the Greek Chamber of Deputies.

For current government data, check with the Embassy of Greece at *www.greekembassy.org.*

Language

Greek is the official language. It is written in the Greek alphabet, which was developed around 1000 b.c. The second most commonly spoken tongue is Romanian.

Today, the Greek people speak a form of the Greek language known as Demotic Greek. This is a modern form of the Ancient Greek spoken 2,000 years ago. Classical studies programs usually teach Ancient Greek, not modern Demotic Greek.

In addition to Greek, linguists have identified fifteen languages, two of which are now extinct. (One of the languages classified as extinct is Ancient Greek, which is still used as a liturgical language by the Greek Orthodox Church.)

The Greek View

The Greek Orthodox Church is the official religion, and 98 percent of Greeks are members. Greek Orthodox principles are learned in school, and the state supports the church. However, freedom of religion is guaranteed. There is a small minority of Muslims, Roman Catholics, Protestants, and Jews.

Much of Greece's rural population has lived in privation for generations. While the quality of life has improved since the end of the Greek civil war in 1949, the memory of poverty is strong. Some attribute the Greek tradition of hard bargaining to this adversity.

Rainfall is sparse in Greece, making fresh water a valuable commodity. Wildfires are common in the parched woods and fields. Greece is also subject to periodic seismic activity, such as the devastating earthquakes in 1999. This contributes to a sense that humans are not in control of their fate.

The environment is a serious issue in Greece. In addition to the severe air pollution in cities like Athens, Greece suffers from severe deforestation. Ancient Greece was a country of forests and wooded hills. Since classical times, the trees have been stripped for lumber, for charcoal, and for fuel. What man did not destroy, wildfires and goats did. Reforestation efforts are still in their infancy in Greece and are hampered by the country's sparse rainfall.

Some foreigners doubted the ability of the Greeks to host the 2004 Summer Olympic Games. The fact that the games were peaceful and successful was uplifting to the Greeks, although they now have to deal with the exorbitant cost of the event.

Many older Greeks opine that the younger generation is becoming too Europeanized and losing its respect for Greek tradition.

☑ Know Before You Go

The greatest hazard to vacationers in Greece is probably sunburn in the strong Mediterranean sunlight. For business travelers in Greece, the risk is split between vehicular accidents and petty street crime (such as pickpocketing).

Greeks are heavy smokers; it is estimated that 45 percent of adults smoke. Smoking in many public places was outlawed in September 2002, but people often ignore the rules. (Greece is also a large tobacco producer.)

▶ CULTURAL ORIENTATION

Cognitive Styles: How Greeks Organize and Process Information

Greeks are open to discussion of most topics but may find it difficult to change their position on issues. They process information more from a subjective, associative perspective than an objective, abstractive one. Interpersonal relationships are of major importance in the overall scheme of things. This leads them to consider the specifics of a situation rather than making decisions on the basis of universal rules or laws.

Negotiation Strategies: What Greeks Accept as Evidence

Subjective feelings are the basis for the truth, although faith in various ideologies (religion, ethnocentrism) may strongly influence the outcome. Objective facts will not be accepted if they contradict either of these.

Value Systems: The Basis for Behavior

Greece is the historical home of democracy. Although it has toyed with other forms of government, it has always returned to a democratic form of government. The following three sections identify the Value Systems in the predominant culture—their methods of dividing right from wrong, good from evil, and so forth.

Locus of Decision-Making

The individual is responsible for all decisions, but he or she takes into consideration those who depend on him or her (family, group, and so forth). A person's private life is influenced by family, friends, and organizations. Through this process an individual develops opinions. Friendships are deep and carry obligations. One must establish a relationship with his or her counterpart before negotiations can be successful. Education is the primary vehicle for moving up the social ladder.

Sources of Anxiety Reduction

Greeks have a high index of uncertainty avoidance. As a result, Greeks use laws and morality to give structure to their worldview.

It is one's role in the social structure, the extended family, and deep friendships that give structure and security to the individual. There is a strong work ethic, but a laid-back approach to life contributes to an image of much activity but slow progress. There is a strong need for consensus in groups. Failures are often attributed to external circumstances.

Issues of Equality/Inequality

There is a definite social hierarchy, with some bias against classes, ethnic groups, and religions. Greeks have an inherent trust in people because of the social interrelationships between extended families and friends. There are extreme contrasts between rich and poor, but Greeks are people oriented, with quality of life and the environment being important considerations. Machismo is very strong.

▶ BUSINESS PRACTICES

Punctuality, Appointments, and Local Time

- Always be punctual, although you will note that punctuality is not generally stressed by your Greek counterparts.
- Scheduling an appointment is not always necessary, but it is courteous.
- It is not considered necessary to set a limited time for a business appointment.
- Greeks, like most Europeans, write the day first, then the month, then the year. For example, December 3, 2010, would be written 3.12.10 or 3/12/10.
- The work week may change. From May to October (Monday through Friday), it is generally 8:00 A.M. to 1:30 P.M. and from 4:00 P.M. to 7:30 P.M. From October to May, hours are usually from 8:00 A.M. to 1:00 P.M. and from 4:30 to 7:30 P.M.

- Greeks observe Orthodox Easter, (which is different from the Gregorian Calendar), however, they celebrate Christmas on the 25th of December. For a list of the official holidays of Greece, visit *www.kissboworshakehands.com.*

Negotiating

- The senior members of a group are always shown great respect. Authority usually rests with them.
- To do business in Greece, one must be patient, yet ready to use quick judgment. Greeks are excellent bargainers.
- It is advisable to have one side of your business card printed in English and the other in Greek. Present it with the Greek side up.
- Avoid making judgments about the Greek style of describing things. Many Greeks may use hyperbole in discussions; this is not unusual.
- Greece is two hours ahead of Greenwich Mean Time (G.M.T. + 2), making it seven hours ahead of U.S. Eastern Standard Time (E.S.T. + 7).

Business Entertaining

- Business is usually done over a cup of coffee—often in a coffeehouse or taverna.
- Lunch is the main meal of the day, between noon and 2:00 P.M.
- The elderly are always served first.
- Dinner is a small meal and is eaten at around 8:00 or 9:00 P.M.
- Often, many dishes are ordered and shared by all at the table.
- When dining in a Greek home, you will probably be offered seconds and thirds in an insistent way. Accepting more food is a compliment to your host.
- Bad topics to bring up include Greek conflicts with Turkey, Macedonia, or other nations. In general, just avoid political discussions.

⊚ PROTOCOL

Greetings
* Remember that Greek people tend to be physically demonstrative. Expect your Greek associates to stay in relatively close proximity to you.
* In first business encounters, a handshake is typical.
* The greeting can take many forms in Greece; a handshake, an embrace, or a kiss can all be encountered at first meetings or among friends and acquaintances.

Titles/Forms of Address
* Older people are greatly respected in Greece, and therefore are always addressed formally (using titles, etc.).
* The order of Greek names is the same as in North America: given name first, followed by surname.

Gestures
* The Greeks are an active and energetic people, and their mannerisms reflect this. Gestures tend to be strong and used frequently.
* Greeks gesture not only with their hands and heads, but with their eyes and lips as well.
* Greeks may exhibit nervous energy through foot tapping or fidgeting. This may be a reason why Greeks sometimes play with worry beads (called *kombologion*). This fidgeting does not necessarily indicate boredom or impatience.
* Traditionally, Greeks indicated "no" with an upward nod of the head. (This movement is also used to signify negation in Greek sign language.) This is not as common with the younger generation. Recently Greeks have begun to use North American gestures for "yes" and "no," which can be confusing.
* Anger is sometimes expressed by a smile.
* After giving or receiving a compliment, Greeks sometimes make a puff of breath through the lips to ward off the "evil eye."

- Sometimes Greeks express thanks by placing their right hands over their hearts. The gesture is usually accompanied by a verbal expression of thanks.

Gifts
- Greeks are very generous; if you compliment an object too enthusiastically, it may be given to you.
- For business associates, you do not need to give a gift during the first encounter.
- Avoid gifts that are too lavish or too skimpy, as well as gifts that are only a means of showing your company logo.
- If you are invited to a home, compliment the children of the household and give them a small gift; flowers or a dessert is also appropriate for the hostess.

Dress
- Conservative business clothing is best.
- Women should wear dresses or suits in subtle colors.

Hungary

Republic of Hungary
Local short form: Magyarorszag
Local long form: Magyar Koztarsasag

Cultural Note

For a relatively small country, Hungary has produced an astonishing number of top scientists. Many of the scientists who worked on the U.S. Manhattan Project (which produced the first nuclear bombs) were Hungarian expatriates. Some were Hungarian Jews who were fleeing fascism, some were Hungarian Christians, and others were born in the United States but had Hungarian ancestry.

▶ WHAT'S YOUR CULTURAL IQ?

1. No one can prove whether today's Hungarians are descended from the fifth-century warriors of Attila the Hun. TRUE or FALSE? Despite this uncertainty, "Attila" remains a fairly common name in Hungary.
   ANSWER: TRUE. It has been used both as a first name and a surname. Interestingly, whatever the legendary "Scourge of God" called himself, it wasn't Attila. The name "Attila" is a Gothic name derived from the Gothic word *atta*, meaning "father." Attila was probably a term given him by the Gothic peoples he conquered. The main alternative theory is that the ancestors of today's Hungarians arrived in Europe from Asia much later, sometime in the ninth century. This theory—that the Hungarians arrived after the empire of the Huns fell apart—was promoted by the Austrians and the Soviets. Both groups had a vested interest in blurring the Hungarian national identity. Neither wanted the Hungarians to think of themselves as descended from the most feared invaders Europe has ever known.

2. Hungary also has a number of well-known composers. Which of the following musicians is better known today for his efforts in music education?
   a. Béla Bartók
   b. Franz Lehár
   c. Zoltán Kodály
   ANSWER: c. There is a Zoltán Kodály Pedagogical Institute of Music in Hungary, as well as other institutes using his techniques all over the world. Lehár was a composer of operettas; he is best remembered for the operetta *The Merry Widow*.

3. TRUE OR FALSE: As in most Islamic countries, Jews were persecuted and expelled from both the Ottoman Empire and modern Turkey.
   ANSWER: FALSE. While there have been incidents of oppression, Jews have generally been welcomed in both the Ottoman Empire and Turkey. When the Jews were exiled from Spain in 1492, the Ottoman Sultan not only offered them refuge, but dispatched ships to bring them to Turkey.

▶ TIPS ON DOING BUSINESS IN HUNGARY

- Remember that Hungary is a landlocked nation, although a limited amount of shipping is done via the Danube River, which passes through the capital, Budapest. Hungary's infrastructure of highways and railroads has been improved, however, many roads are still in need of upgrades.
- The Hungarian language is called Magyar, and is difficult for outsiders to learn. Unlike most European languages, Magyar is not a member of the Indo-European linguistic family. It is a Finno-Ugric tongue, distantly related to Finnish and Estonian. Fortunately, Hungarians have a tradition of learning other languages. You can present written materials in English or German; many Hungarians read these languages.
- When holding important business discussions through an interpreter, stop and reiterate points on a regular basis. This avoids misunderstandings. Magyar has suffixes that convey degrees of ambiguity and subtleties, which can easily be lost in translation.

▶ COUNTRY BACKGROUND

History

King Stephen (later canonized), is credited with uniting the Hungarian people and adopting Roman Catholicism as the national religion. The dates of his rule are usually given as A.D. 1000 to 1038. The Arpád dynasty he established ruled Hungary for some 300 years.

After the fall of Constantinople in 1453, the Hungarians became Europe's front line of defense against the Ottoman Turks. The two groups fought off and on for some 300 years. Finally, the Turks managed to conquer the Hungarians

At the Battle of Mohács in 1526, the Ottomans dealt the Magyars a crushing defeat and slew the Hungarian king. The Ottomans occupied the then-capital of Buda. All of southern Hungary became a vassal state of the Ottoman Empire. The Habsburg kings of Austria took control of the northernmost remnant of Hungary, and they slowly pushed back the Ottomans. By 1683, they had expelled the Turks from central Hungary, and they incorporated most of Hungary into their empire.

Unhappy under Habsburg rule, the Hungarians revolted in 1848. The Austrians were unable to put down the revolt by themselves, and accepted an offer of Russian aid. The Hungarian revolt was crushed in 1849.

Realizing that they could not permanently stifle Hungarian nationalism, the Habsburgs created the dual monarchy: Hungary became a separate state under the Habsburg Crown. The name of the empire was changed to the Austro-Hungarian Empire.

The Austro-Hungarian Empire entered the First World War in 1914. When the war ended in 1918, Hungary was dismembered along with the rest of the Austro-Hungarian Empire.

Hard hit by the Great Depression, Hungary developed its own fascist movement, the Arrow Cross. When the Second World War began, both Hungary and Romania allied themselves with Nazi Germany. Hungary suffered great destruction, and emerged from the war both reduced in size and under the control of the USSR.

As in its neighboring countries, Hungary was forced to accept a Communist government. In 1956, the Hungarian government tried to withdraw from the Warsaw Pact. This resulted in a Soviet military crackdown, during which many Hungarians died, others fled to the West, and Prime Minister Imre Nagy was executed.

The liberalism that swept Eastern Europe in the late 1980s fostered changes in Hungary. Long-time Communist leader János Kádár was forced to resign in 1988. The Communists became just another political party, and were roundly defeated in the elections of 1990.

Hungary joined NATO in 1991 and the European Union in 2004.

Cultural Note
An amazingly fertile country, Hungary was intentionally kept agricultural while it was part of the Austro-Hungarian Empire. After the Second World War, the Communists instituted massive industrialization projects. Industry now provides almost half of the Hungarian GNP. Besides the soil's fertility, Hungarian resources include coal, natural gas, and bauxite.

Type of Government
The Republic of Hungary is now a multiparty republic. There is a single legislative body, the National Assembly.

The prime minister is the head of the government. The state president of Hungary is commander in chief of the armed forces, in addition to being head of state; this gives the position more importance than in most European countries.

Formerly one of the most prosperous members of the Warsaw Pact, Hungary underwent a relatively smooth transition from a one-party Communist state to a democracy.

For current government data, check with the Embassy of Hungary at *www.huembwas.org*.

Language
The official language of Hungary is Hungarian, which the Hungarians call "Magyar."

Although Hungary has a significant minority population (primarily German, Slovak, Romanian, and Gypsy), over 95 percent of the people speak Magyar.

The Hungarian View

The majority of Hungarians are Roman Catholic; approximately 28 percent belong to Protestant denominations. Other religions are also present. By and large, Hungary marks the end of Catholic and Protestant Europe. Romania and Bulgaria are Orthodox countries. Some believe that Hungary's economic success is due in part to the "Protestant Work Ethic"—something which is relatively absent in Romania and Bulgaria.

Hungarians have a reputation for melancholy. Rates of depression in Hungary are difficult to measure, but the suicide rate is relatively high.

On the bright side, Hungarians also rank among the top in number of Olympic medals per capita.

☑ Know Before You Go

As in many former members of the Warsaw Pact, street crime is present. There are also various scams, from bars that charge foreigners outrageous prices for drinks, to elaborately plotted scams using criminals disguised as police officers.

Under the Communist regime, Hungary suffered massive environmental pollution. This is slowly being ameliorated. Hungary has substantial deposits of coal, but new regulations require many coal-fired plants to be shut. They are usually replaced with power plants using natural gas, which Hungary must import. Hungary also uses aging, Soviet-built nuclear power plants, the safety of which is cause for concern.

Although most Hungarians were anxious to join NATO, they still want to balance military and environmental concerns. In 2004, protesters halted the construction of a NATO radar station near Pecs in southern Hungary.

Hungary's overriding international concern is the treatment of ethnic Hungarians living in Romania, Serbia, and the Slovak Republic. In addition to this, Hungary and the Slovak Republic have long-standing disagreements over a dam on the Danube River.

▷ CULTURAL ORIENTATION

Cognitive Styles: How Hungarians Organize and Process Information

Hungary engaged in a degree of free-market enterprises before the collapse of Communism. Consequently, there is now an entire generation of businesspeople with experience in capitalism.

Under Communism, the educational system taught most Hungarians to process information associatively. Today, between a more diverse educational system and training abroad, there are a substantial number of Hungarians who think more abstractively. Hungarians have a tendency to see laws as something written by those in power for the benefit of those in power, not as something to protect the powerless. Personal relationships tend to be valued more than stringent adherence to regulations.

Negotiation Strategies: What Hungarians Accept as Evidence

The cataclysmic demise of the Communist Party as the ideological focus for all arguments has opened the door to other forms of reasoning. The more exposed to outside influences the participants are, the more they may use objective facts in their reasoning rather than subjective feelings or faith in the ideology of party or group. Intentions, feelings, and opinions are now openly expressed. Because it is considered better to be direct than devious, spontaneity of action is favored.

Surrounded by peoples (especially Slavs) who speak languages radically different from their own, Hungarians tend to feel isolated. Their typical worldview is that Hungarians are a misunderstood, put-upon people, oppressed by their neighbors. Information is often filtered through this worldview.

Value Systems: The Basis for Behavior

With the fall of Communism, Hungary is now open to explore the values of other systems and is subject to all the internal turmoil this brings. The following three sections identify the Value Systems in the predominant culture—their methods of dividing right from wrong, good from evil, and so forth.

Locus of Decision-Making

As the movement toward freedom and privatization advances, it is putting the responsibility for decision-making on the shoulders of the individual. In many instances the individual may transfer this responsibility to the group as a whole or to a consensus of privileged individuals. It is not clear yet whether the model to be followed will be that of capitalist or socialist democracy.

Sources of Anxiety Reduction

Formerly, the party structure, power, and full employment were the primary stabilizing forces in the lives of the people. Now there is a great deal of day-to-day anxiety over job and family security. The family unit is still recognized as a stabilizing force in society. Hungarian churches, which have always been influential in family life, are taking a more active role.

Except for a minority of successful entrepreneurs, Hungarians tend to have low expectations out of life. For example, when Hungary joined the European Union, most Hungarians surveyed said that they thought EU membership might bring a degree of prosperity to future generations, but not to their own.

Issues of Equality/Inequality

The removal of Communist Party control has allowed perceived feelings of inequality to surface. Ethnic disputes have become visible, along with humanitarian needs for equality and the establishment of strong, hierarchically structured systems in government, business, and society.

While Hungarian women hold important positions in academia and various professions, business is still dominated by men. Although Hungarian tradition demands that men treat visiting women with great courtesy, this does not apply to the women they see on a daily basis. In mixed company, men tend to dominate the conversation.

▶ BUSINESS PRACTICES

Punctuality, Appointments, and Local Time

- Punctuality is expected in all matters related to business: appointments, deliveries, payments, and so forth.
- Establish a relationship with a Hungarian representative prior to your visit. This individual can initiate contacts for you and accompany you to your appointments. Select this contact person carefully, because your new Hungarian clients will expect you to keep that representative ad infinitum.
- Request your appointment via e-mail or by regular letter as far in advance as possible. Always reconfirm the day before the meeting.
- Business letters may be written in English. While all businesses can translate letters from English, not all of them have staff members who can speak it. Consider hiring an interpreter.
- Avoid making business trips to Hungary during July and August, and from mid-December to mid-January. These are holiday and vacation periods.
- For further information on official holidays in Hungary, see *www. kissboworshakehands.com.*
- Hungary is one hour ahead of Greenwich Mean Time (G.M.T. + 1) and six hours ahead of U.S. Eastern Standard Time, (E.S.T. + 6). There is a daylight-saving system in the summer; the clocks are turned one hour ahead from April to September.

Negotiating

- It is difficult to predict how long it will take to negotiate a deal. Under the Communists, any type of contract would take months. However, some of Hungary's entrepreneurs will be anxious to move quickly.
- Whether fast or slow, deals in Hungary cannot be finalized without a lot of eating, drinking, and entertainment.
- Except for businesspeople trained abroad, Hungarians do not tend to stick to a linear agenda. Foreigners may perceive a Hungarian

business meeting as loud and disorganized. Despite this perception, Hungarians are effective at accomplishing their goals.

- Have someone in your party take notes during meetings.
- Bring plenty of business cards, and give them out to everyone you meet.
- If you speak English, it is not necessary to have your business card translated into Hungarian. Indeed, Hungarian has many foreign loanwords, so your title in English may be similar to what it would be in Hungarian.
- Hungary's relations with its neighbors (especially those it ruled during the days of the Austro-Hungarian Empire) have not always been cordial. Do not bring up your background if you are of Romanian, Slovak, Polish, or Gypsy descent.

Business Entertaining
- Hungarian hospitality is legendary. You will have to fight with your Hungarian counterparts to pay a bill.
- Meals are primarily social occasions. Very little can be accomplished during a lunch, and nothing related to business should be brought up at dinner.
- Expect dinners to last a long time; restaurants usually have musicians or entertainers in the evening.

Cultural Note

Hungary produces a variety of fruit brandies, and an excellent selection of wines. The best-known Hungarian wine-producing region is Tokaj, which produces wines by that name (known as "Tokay" outside Hungary).

When offering a toast, Hungarians will toast to your success—not to their own. In response, you should toast to their success—even if you are all in business together. Hungarians believe that toasting one's own success is pompous and arrogant.

- If your schedule will not permit a full night's entertainment, suggest a business lunch instead.
- Once you have signed or completed a contract, throw a cocktail party at a prestigious hotel.

- Hungarian food, wine, horses, and sightseeing are good topics to discuss. So are sports: football (soccer) is the most popular sport, and chess is a national preoccupation. Hungarians consider themselves a "nation of horsemen." If you get outside the city, invitations to go horseback riding are not uncommon.

▶ PROTOCOL

Greetings
- A handshake is customary not only when being introduced, but also when departing. Men sometimes wait for women to extend their hands before shaking.
- Only close friends will greet each other with an embrace. For men, the sequence goes as follows: shake hands, embrace, and make cheek-to-cheek contact on the left cheek, then on the right cheek. Close female friends do the same but omit the handshake.
- Hungarians typically "talk with their hands," using a lot of gestures.
- Personal space is small in Hungary; people talk at a closer distance than is common in northern Europe or North America.
- Extended eye contact is expected. Failure to meet a Hungarian's gaze will convey that you are untrustworthy.

Titles/Forms of Address
- Relatives and close adult friends address each other on a first-name basis; they will also call children by their first names. Young people typically use each other's first names. However, it is prudent to address adults by their titles and surnames until you are invited to do otherwise.
- In Hungary, the surname is listed before the given (first) name. Thus, the Hungarian musicians Béla Bartók and Franz Liszt are known in their homeland as Bartók Béla and Liszt Franz (or, more precisely, Liszt Ferenc, since Ferenc is the Hungarian equivalent of Franz). Foreign names, however, are listed in the order that is customary in their country of origin.

- Always use professional titles (Doctor, Director, Minister, and so forth) when addressing someone. Either use a title and surname (Professor Szabo) or add "Mr.," "Mrs.," or "Miss" to the title (Mrs. Architect).

Gifts

- When visiting a company, it is not always necessary to bring gifts. However, if you do, bring many small gifts and give them out freely.
- Because of a housing shortage, you may not be invited into a Hungarian home. This is especially true in Budapest, where some 20 percent of the total Hungarian population resides. If you are asked to visit, Western liquor (not wine, as Hungarians are proud of the wines they produce) and wrapped flowers (but not red roses or chrysanthemums) are appropriate.

Dress

- Dress tends to be conservative, especially among businesspeople.
- Appropriate business dress for men is a dark suit, a white shirt, and a tie. Women should wear suits or dresses.
- Jeans are standard casualwear. Shorts are somewhat uncommon in the city, and are best reserved for the beach or the countryside.
- Standard business wear is appropriate for formal social occasions, restaurants, and the theater.
- Hungarians enjoy dressing up for their many formal events. Dark suits, tuxedos, and formal gowns are popular.

Cultural Note

Chess is one of the most popular past-times among Hungarians. Hungary has produced world-class chess players, including two grandmasters: Judit and Zsuzsa (Susan) Polgár, and their sister, Zsófia (Sofia), an International Master. Judit is regarded as the strongest female player of all time, and has defeated almost every top player in the world, including Garry Kasparov. Susan was the top-ranked female chess player in the world by the age of fifteen.

Inviting your Hungarian prospects to play a game of chess might be an excellent opening move.

Ireland

The Republic of Ireland
Local short form: Éire

Cultural Note

The Republic of Ireland joined the European Community in 1973, and trade with the European Union moved Ireland out from under the United Kingdom's shadow. Originally one of the poorest members of the EU, Ireland became eligible for EU loans and assistance, and many multinational corporations placed their headquarters there. EU influence also helped women to achieve more equality in Ireland. Historically a male-dominated society, Ireland now has many women in politics—including its recent presidents.

▶ WHAT'S YOUR CULTURAL IQ?

1. What service did the Irish render after the fall of the Roman Empire?
   a. They protected England from invasion by fierce Icelandic Vikings.
   b. They preserved Roman and Greek literature and disseminated it throughout Europe after the continent had been overrun by illiterate Germanic tribes.
   c. They became the primary provider of alcoholic beverages to the world.

   ANSWER: b. Greco-Roman heritage was lost to much of Europe after the fall of Rome. Irish priests and monks kept literary treasures safe within their monasteries while the western Roman Empire collapsed. Then, Irish missionaries spread out over Europe to convert the barbarians. In the process, they introduced them to Greek and Roman literature.

2. TRUE or FALSE? English is the sole official language of the Republic of Ireland.

ANSWER: FALSE. They have two official languages: Irish (a.k.a., Irish Gaelic, or Erse) and English.

3. Which of the following Irish-born authors did *not* win the Nobel Prize for literature?
   a. Samuel Beckett
   b. Seamus Heaney
   c. James Joyce
   d. George Bernard Shaw
   e. William Butler Yeats

ANSWER: c. Joyce might be the most famous novelist of the twentieth century, but he never won the Nobel.

▶ TIPS ON DOING BUSINESS IN IRELAND

- The Irish have an ambivalent attitude toward wealth. The founding father of the Irish Republic, Eamon De Valera, envisioned Ireland as a pastoral land of simple virtues. Moneymaking was not included as a virtue. People who have achieved financial success are not automatically respected. Ostentation is frowned upon, except in giving to charity.

- Irish hospitality and friendliness are well known. Most Irish look forward to chatting with friends and strangers alike over a cup of tea or a pint of Guinness (naturally, in a country with such a changeable climate, the weather is a constant topic). It would be considered impolite not to talk to anyone in whose company you found yourself, whether in a waiting room or a pub.

- In the 1990s, Ireland experienced unprecedented economic growth. Ireland's rates of employment and growth outstripped that of most other European Union nations. After decades of seeking work in other countries, Irish emigrants began returning home. This has brought the Irish a degree of satisfaction, but not the exuberance one might expect. The Irish continue to have a deep strain of pessimism. Many feel that success today is no guarantee of success tomorrow.

▶ COUNTRY BACKGROUND

History

Although Ireland's economy and image have changed incredibly since 1990, its history reaches back to around 350 B.C., when Ireland was occupied by Celtic tribes from Europe. They overwhelmed the original inhabitants and became Ireland's dominant culture. Written Irish history began circa A.D. 400, and in A.D. 432, Saint Patrick brought Christianity to Ireland.

Anglo-Norman troops conquered most of Ireland in 1170, and the overlords loosely ruled a portion of Ireland known as the Pale for the next 400 years. In 1541, the Irish Parliament granted Henry VIII the title of King of Ireland, and the king's establishment of the Church of England eventually resulted in the persecution of Irish Catholics. The harp (which became Ireland's national symbol) was first used on Irish coinage under Henry VIII.

In 1801, the Act of Union made Ireland part of the United Kingdom and dissolved the Irish Parliament. Then in 1916, a rebellion in Dublin called the Easter Rising became a rallying point for Irish nationalism. The Anglo-Irish War, between the Irish Republican Army and the Royal Irish Constabulary, followed from 1919 to 1921. Years of negotiations resulted in independence from the United Kingdom for twenty-six southern Irish counties in 1921. The other six counties in the North (known as Ulster) remained part of the United Kingdom.

The Republic of Ireland formally withdrew from the British Commonwealth and became fully independent in 1948. In 1973, it joined the EC (now the EU).

"The Troubles" began in 1970, when the Irish Republican Army began fighting the Protestant government in Northern Ireland. Relatively little violence occurred in the Republic of Ireland. A peace settlement for Northern Ireland, called the Good Friday Agreement, was approved in 1998, but has not been implemented.

Type of Government

Ireland is a parliamentary democracy. Its president, or chief of state, is a somewhat ceremonial figure elected by popular vote to a seven-year term. According to the Irish Constitution, the president needs advance cabinet approval of speeches and travel.

The prime minister is the head of government and is nominated by the House of Representatives and appointed by the president.

The Bicameral Parliament, or Oireachtas, is comprised of the Seanad or Senate and the Dail Eireann or House of Representatives. The Dail representatives are elected by universal suffrage for a maximum of a five-year term. Members of the Senate also hold office for a five-year term; however, eleven Senate members are nominated by the prime minister and the remaining are elected by local universities and from panels of candidates in the following five areas: cultural and educational, agricultural, labor, industrial and commercial, and administrative. The Dail is the more powerful body. The electoral system features proportional representation in multicandidate constituencies. Current government data can be found at the Embassy of Ireland at *www.irelandemb.org*.

Cultural Note

In 1957, corporate taxes on foreign multinationals that invested in Ireland were almost eradicated. Low corporate taxes, free trade with the United Kingdom, relatively low wages, and English as an official language made Ireland extremely attractive to many corporations. After the setbacks of the 1970s, the Republic of Ireland experienced tremendous growth in the 1990s and was nicknamed the Celtic Tiger.

Language

Ireland has two official languages, English and Irish (also called Irish Gaelic, Erse or Gaeilge).

Irish is from the Gaelic (aka, Goidelic) group of Celtic languages, which includes Scottish Gaelic and the now-extinct Manx; Welsh is a more distant relation. It was suppressed by the English overlords of Ireland and was close to dying out by the end of the nineteenth century. It survived in the most rural areas of Ireland (such regions were known as *Gaeltacht*). Organizations such as the Gaelic League helped revive its use. When Ireland achieved independence, the new government encouraged the use of Irish. Politicians gave speeches in Irish (often to audiences with little knowledge of the language). Today, some programs are broadcast in Gaelic, and Irish is a mandatory subject in schools. Proficiency in Irish is a qualification for a successful career in academia and the civil service. For those who master it, Irish is a second language. English is the everyday language of Ireland.

Ireland is not unique in the European Union for having two official languages. However, Ireland is alone among EU members in that one of those tongues is a revived language—Irish was near extinction until the Gaelic League revived it in the early twentieth century.

The Embassy of Ireland has a deeper explanation of Gaeilge at *www.irelandemb.org/gaeilge.html.*

Cultural Note

The Irish character can seem complex and contradictory at times. (Sigmund Freud is alleged to have said that the Irish are the only people who cannot be helped by psychoanalysis.) Ireland is still a Catholic country, yet the Irish people are inevitably described as rebellious by nature and sarcastic about authority. Ireland has the lowest rate of marriage per capita in the European Union, yet the highest fertility rate (2.1 children per woman). And even when Ireland was a poor country with high unemployment, the Irish often gave more per capita to charities than far wealthier nations.

The Irish View

It is not possible to define the Irish identity without reference to two seminal influences: the British Empire and the Catholic Church.

Ireland was invaded by the British many times. Subjugation began in earnest after Henry VIII changed England's official religion from Catholicism to Protestantism, which had the side effect of making wealthy Catholic monasteries into legitimate military targets. The Irish were dispossessed and the Protestant gentry set up farms known as "plantations." In the North of Ireland, even the plantations' tenant farmers were Protestant Englishmen. Southern Ireland was brutally subjugated by Cromwell the Protector in the 1650s. Catholic Irish lands were confiscated. By the eighteenth century, Catholics owned less than 15 percent of Irish lands.

The height of British misrule of Ireland occurred during the Potato Famine of the 1840s. The potato crop failed in 1842, and then failed again in 1846. While 1 million Irish starved and another million fled Ireland, British-owned plantations in Ireland continued to export grain. By the time the famine eased, the population of Ireland had dropped from over 8 million to some 6 million. Emigration had become a way of life, and continued until the economic turnaround of the 1990s. As in other occupied countries, the Church became a guardian of the national identity during the hard years.

While Ireland has no official religion, about 92 percent of the citizens of Éire claim to be Catholic. The Church's influence has waned in recent history, and there is a more liberal view on sexuality. A referendum was narrowly passed in 1995 to allow divorce, and contraceptives are now widely available. (Condoms were illegal until 1980; after that, they could only be sold to married couples—by prescription.) Abortion is still illegal, but there are no sanctions against women traveling to England for abortions.

The Irish are exceedingly proud of their history and of their tremendous successes in the last few decades.

☑ Know Before You Go

Ireland does not have any natural hazards, unless one includes winter weather. But business travelers may even enjoy the look of the Isle in the misty rain and cold—it certainly makes pubs look warm and inviting.

There is some water pollution from agricultural runoff, and Ireland has been listed as a transshipment point for illicit drug trade.

▶ CULTURAL ORIENTATION

Cognitive Styles: How the Irish Organize and Process Information

Historically, Ireland has been seen as a traditional, conservative country—however they have always been interested in outside information and different opinions. Over many decades, the Irish have shown they are comfortable with risk. Their strong cultural identity has allowed them to accept the rapid changes that foreign investment and economic success have brought.

Negotiation Strategies: What the Irish Accept as Evidence

Historically, the Irish primarily used a combination of feelings and facts to discern the truth in a situation. With the recent changes in Ireland, younger Irish are more prone to consider the validity of facts as the primary basis for evidence. However, ones feelings for an individual still weigh heavily on business decisions. Again, they are comfortable with a short-term risk and may perceive a work decision almost like a bet.

Value Systems: The Basis for Behavior

The Irish are generally ambivalent about authority, and despite recent economic growth, do not feel as though immense success and wealth is an attractive goal. There is a belief that the poor should receive the same respect as the powerful. Besides the structure of the family and the Catholic Church, the Irish do not require additional rules to make them feel secure.

Locus of Decision-Making

Decisions are often made individually, usually by a senior executive, after some discussion with associates. The Irish will be polite, but are more straightforward with good or bad news about business situations than in the past. An individual's right to make his or her own decisions is vital.

Sources of Anxiety Reduction

The immediate and extended family are the primary units of social organization, and they give the Irish a strong sense of identity and stability. This is followed by the precepts of Catholicism. The Irish are relatively open with their emotions, but may have an aversion to saying a definitive "yes" or "no." Pressurized deadlines generate large amounts of stress.

Despite the economic gains that Ireland has made, there is often a sense of melancholy and cynicism that is expressed in songs and literature.

Issues of Equality/Inequality

There is a high level of masculinity in the culture, and sex roles were historically differentiated in a clear manner. The Irish are becoming more open to equality for women, as evidenced by recent elections and more women in executive positions. The Irish are very competitive and will grasp at opportunities as they arise.

▶ BUSINESS PRACTICES

Punctuality, Appointments, and Local Time

- As in most countries, the Irish write the day first, then the month, and then the year (e.g., December 3, 2010, is written 3.12.10 or 3/12/10).

- Punctuality is expected for business appointments. The rules for social engagements, especially between friends, are more flexible.

- Perhaps because of the Irish tendency to do things differently from the British whenever possible, the Irish have traditionally taken a more relaxed view toward time.

- Because promptness has not historically been valued in Ireland, some Irish companies instituted unusual measure to encourage people to pay their bills on time. For example, the Irish telephone and electric utilities automatically enter paid-on-time bills into a raffle!

- Irish attitudes toward time may extend to deadlines and delivery dates. Do not automatically expect something to be executed at the time or date promised, unless you have been careful to explain why that deadline must be met.

- Avoid scheduling many appointments around July and August, because many Irish executives will be on vacation. Most businesses also close from December 24 through January 2 during the Christmas period.

- Ireland's national holiday is Saint Patrick's Day, on March 17. For a list of the holidays of Ireland, visit *www.kissboworshakehands .com.*

- Ireland, like England, is on Greenwich Mean Time. This is five hours ahead of U.S. Eastern Standard Time (E.S.T. + 5).

Negotiating

- Historically, the Irish did business with people they knew and liked. They still feel far more comfortable working with people they know, but have extended their personal contacts into the global market.
- Money was minimally discussed, and seemed to be an almost embarrassing topic.
- A handshake and a verbal promise were good enough for many Irish, as was the fact that a delivery date was an approximation.
- It can still be considered poor manners to directly tell someone "No, we haven't any of those products" or "No, we cannot do that work for you." A softer answer (which may stretch the truth a bit), is more civilized.
- With the economic changes over the last two decades, negotiations have taken on a more assertive tone. Do not expect the Irish to accept initial offers—they will expect to bargain for the best possible margin that they can.
- A fast cash profit is generally viewed as better than a long-term market share.
- However, the Irish will still want to do business on a personal level, and even brief meetings for coffee can be the key to building a valuable relationship.
- Never cancel an appointment without a serious reason—it is insulting to not only that potential contact, but all his or her close contacts as well.
- Many Irish businesses are family owned, and nepotism is considered as a good thing. This is one reason it can be difficult to enter a network without an appropriate contact or introduction. The Irish like to work with their own, and they do not offer referrals or introductions without trusting you first.
- Never praise England or use any British symbolism during your negotiations with the Irish.
- Balance your presentations with both good and bad data. Present your information in a factual, concise manner.
- Never make inflated claims about your product or yourself. The Irish do not like hype.

- Since sports are generally a good topic, you might want to use a sports analogy in your presentation—that is, if you are up-to-date with popular Irish teams.

Business Entertaining
- Offer to take your Irish associates to a popular restaurant or pub. Make sure you confirm that you are picking up the tab, and do not try to initiate a serious work discussion until after the meal is over.
- Do not expect table service at a pub. Go to the bar to order your pint of Guinness.
- After-hours Guinnesses or ciders are primarily for establishing social relationships; you may never get to the topic of business in a pub.
- Going to the pub is traditionally a daily routine for many Irish. Be aware of your limitations.
- Avoid bringing up topics of discussion like abortion, religion, and politics with older Irish citizens—they will generally have conservative views. If these topics do arise, refrain from commenting unless you fundamentally agree with your Irish hosts.
- Younger Irish citizens are far more liberal and open to change; however, do not expect them to appreciate your views. Many foreign executives feel too comfortable too soon chatting with the Irish, and air their opinions far too readily.

⊙ PROTOCOL

Greetings
- A handshake is the most common form of greeting. The grip is generally firm. Both men and women shake hands.
- Foreigners should not initiate a hug.
- Give your Irish associates enough room to stand a few feet apart from you after the handshake is over.
- Generally, the further you are from an urban setting, the further the acceptable personal distance.

- Whether it is a formal introduction in a business setting, or a chance meeting with a stranger in rural Ireland, you will find yourself spending time chatting about yourself, where you come from, your trip, etc. Always allocate enough time to visit a bit; the Irish will want to know something about you. Do not rush them.
- Whether you are leaving a serious meeting at headquarters or a little shop on a corner street, always say "goodbye."

Titles/Forms of Address

- During introductions, the Irish may use "Mr." or "Ms." and a last name with each other for the first meeting. However, many people go to first names right away (particularly younger members of the work force).
- Most Irish have two Christian, or given names which are conferred upon them at baptism. Usually, people use just one of their first names, along with their family name (another name is bestowed upon Catholics during the Sacrament of Confirmation). This means that many Irish Catholics have rather long names (e.g., Patrick Joseph Sían Conaway).
- Many women do not take their husbands' last names. Alternatively, they may combine their own names with their husbands'.
- You may hear some of your Irish associates called by either Gaelic or English versions of their names. For example, Liam is William, and Máirín is Maureen. Some Gaelic names have no English equivalent.
- The prefixes "Mac" and "O" originally meant "son of." For example, Brendan MacCarthy meant Brendan, "son of" Carthy ("Mac" was changed to "Mc" by the English).
- Some names originally indicated an occupation; for example, Ms. Rose MacGowan would have been the daughter of a blacksmith—in Gaelic, she would be Ms. MacGabhann. (*Gabha* is Gaelic for "blacksmith.")

Gestures

- The Irish are comfortable with prolonged eye contact. Do not shift your gaze around when speaking with someone.

- Men do not usually touch or hug each other, unless they are participating at a sporting event.
- Winking is usually inappropriate.
- At work, the Irish are rather restrained in their gestures. Do not gesticulate emphatically during a presentation.

Gifts
- Gift giving is not common at work; however, a small, thoughtful present will be appreciated.
- Extravagant gifts can make the Irish uncomfortable. Dinners, visits to a pub, tickets to sporting events, etc., are more advisable.
- Bring wine, chocolates, and gifts for the children when you visit someone's home.

Dress
- Although business dress is usually casual among the Irish, they will expect you to wear more formal attire because you are a foreign executive.
- Fashions are changing in Ireland, so be adaptable.
- Visiting female executives will not want to wear any low-cut attire at work.
- While it may sound conservative, your garments will be scrutinized, so you should be more formal in order to maintain your credibility.

Cultural Note
Remember that Éire, Ireland, the Free State, the Republic, and the South all mean the Republic of Ireland. If you confuse it with Northern Ireland, the North, or Ulster, you have definitely started out on the wrong foot with your Irish Republican associates. Northern Ireland is part of the United Kingdom. The Republic of Ireland is not.

Italy

Italian Republic
Local short form: Italia
Local long form: Repubblica Italiana
Former: Kingdom of Italy

Cultural Note

The Italians—and their ancestors, the Romans—invented many of the business practices we use today. Their innovations included banking, insurance, and even double-entry bookkeeping. Do not let Italian friendliness and chatter lull you into forgetting that they are very astute businesspeople.

▶ WHAT'S YOUR CULTURAL IQ?

1. Leonardo is the name of an Italian police database that tracks what?
   a. Illegal drugs
   b. Stolen art
   c. Suspected terrorists
   ANSWER: b. According to the United Nations, more than half of the world's cultural treasures are in Italy. At least for now. Thousands of precious and historic artifacts are being smuggled out every year, and the Italian police have the formidable job of investigating and prosecuting the Italian art crime wave—with the help of "Leonardo."

2. The Italian language has many dialects, some of which are not mutually intelligible. From which region did modern Italian evolve?
   a. Rome
   b. Sardinia
   c. Tuscany

ANSWER: c. Since the 1500s, Tuscan has been the preferred dialect, in large part because it was favored by some of Italy's greatest writers of the Middle Ages (such as Dante, Petrarch, and Boccaccio).

3. The former Italian prime minister, Silvio Berlusconi, drew a lot of attention in January of 2004 because:
   a. After four years of legal battles, he was cleared of charges of corruption.
   b. He revealed his new, cosmetically enhanced face.
   c. His right-wing party, Forza Italia, eradicated the budget deficit.

ANSWER: b. The sixty-seven-year-old thanked his wife, Veronica, for convincing him to undergo plastic surgery.

▶ TIPS ON DOING BUSINESS IN ITALY

- Italians generally behave in a formal, refined manner—or with a *bella figura*—what Western executives might call a "consultative image." It can mean anything from an attractive-looking appearance, to appropriate behaviors, to a good performance. Dignified, smooth mannerisms are important from the first meeting—through each dining experience—to your final departure.

Cultural Note:
July and August are poor months for scheduling appointments, since many firms close for vacation. The observance of many regional holidays may also close businesses, and if a holiday falls on a Tuesday or Thursday, Italians tend to extend their weekend to the holiday—giving themselves a four-day weekend. And of course, many businesses celebrate Christmas and New Year's for at least a week. Check with your local representatives to confirm whether offices may be closed during your visit.

- While you may be extremely well prepared with factual details for your meetings, you should also invest a great deal of effort in developing a strong, trusting relationship with your Italian associates. Initially they will care more about you, and whether you are worth knowing personally, than the specifics of your product.

- The Italian bureaucracy and legal system is notoriously slow. One reason for this is because Italy is burdened with over 2,000 years of laws. While new laws are added, old ones are rarely removed from the books—even laws dating back to the Roman Empire still exist!

▶ COUNTRY BACKGROUND

History
Italy has been the name of this region for over 3,000 years. Evidence of early Latin/Italic tribes dates from 2000 B.C. The Etruscans arrived around 1200 B.C., bringing their own culture and laws, and conquered vast central areas of the peninsula.

Greek civilization dominated southern Italy around 600 B.C., and much of Greek culture was subsequently adopted by the Romans. The Roman Empire had tremendous impact on Italian social, legal, political, artistic, and military culture.

With 3,000 miles of coastline, Italy proved a logical prey for invaders. After the fall of the Roman Empire, there were repeated invasions from many countries, including France, Austria, Spain, and Germany. Italy became a country of sharply diverse city-states.

By 1870, Italy had become a politically unified monarchy. The final monarch abdicated in 1946.

The most notorious political figure from Italy's recent past is Mussolini, the fascist dictator known as Il Duce. Mussolini controlled Italy's government from 1922 to 1943. He supported Hitler during World War II, until the Allies' Italian supporters assassinated him and overthrew the Fascists.

Italy did not become a politically unified constitutional republic until the 1946 national elections. Corruption scandals in the early 1990s tainted most major political parties, resulting in the 1994 election of reform candidates led by Prime Minister Silvio Berlusconi.

Type of Government
The Italian Republic is a multiparty parliamentary republic. There are two legislative bodies, a Senate and a Chamber of Deputies. The

president is the chief of state, while the prime minister is the head of the government.

For current government data, check with the Embassy of Italy at *www.italyemb.org.*

Language

Italian is the official language. There are many diverse dialects. Modern Italian originally evolved from spoken Latin. Although modern Italian is spoken in most of Italy, many Italians also speak one of the regional dialects as their first language. English is spoken by many businesspeople.

The Italian View

The vast majority of Italians are raised Roman Catholic, although the Republic of Italy has no official religion. While the Catholic Church remains very influential in Italy, it was unable to prevent the legalization of divorce and abortion in the 1970s.

Historically, Italy's geographic structure produced distinct regions, each with its own dialect, politics, and culture. These regions frequently warred with one another, which was one of the reasons why family life became a central focus. The motto "Family First" reflected Italians' need to preserve and protect not only their relatives but their regional cultures. However, while there is great respect in Italy for the family, for age, and for the power of the patriarch and matriarch—the institution of the family has changed.

Recently, both a falling birth rate and economics have changed the family. Currently, Italy's birth rate is not even sufficient to offset its death rate. Households now need two incomes, so more women work, and many Italians have actually moved away from their traditional homes in search of employment. Today the extended family, with several generations living under one roof (and most of the adults working together in the family business) is the exception, not the rule.

Italians do appreciate the more refined aspects of life. They have a cultivated awareness of art, science, history, literature, music, fine wines, beautiful clothes, excellent meals, the list goes on. . . . They will respect a well-educated, civilized businessperson with accomplishments beyond just the workplace.

☑ Know Before You Go

Although it is not a consistent issue, traveling by train in Italy can be problematic.

In January of 2005, railway workers went on strike to protest unsafe practices. The strike followed a head-on collision between two trains, which resulted in the death of seventeen people (five of whom were railway workers). Developments for increasing the safety standards, as well as the efficiency of the trains are ongoing.

Italy's natural hazards vary by region. Mudflows, landslides, volcanic eruptions, and avalanches can occur, but there are more gradual issues that are of great concern as well—like Venice's land subsidence.

Crimes like money laundering and smuggling are well publicized, but business travelers who are cautious will probably not even encounter a pickpocket. (Unless they ride the subway in Rome.)

Cultural Note

Italian firms tend to have a fairly rigid hierarchy, with little visible fraternization between the ranks. This doesn't necessarily indicate a lack of communication. Even though you may be dealing with senior executives, lower management will probably also be evaluating your proposal.

⊙ CULTURAL ORIENTATION

Cognitive Styles: How Italians Organize and Process Information

In Italy, information is readily accepted and great discussions occur, but little movement is seen in the opinions of the participants. Information tends to be processed subjectively and associatively. Italians will look at the particulars of each situation rather than appeal to a law or rule to solve a problem.

Negotiation Strategies: What Italians Accept as Evidence

Subjective feelings are more important than faith in an ideology or objective facts when deciding what is true. However, the ideologies of the Church do permeate many transactions. Italians who have a higher education tend to use facts to back their arguments.

Value Systems: The Basis for Behavior

The ideologies of the Roman Catholic Church exert the most influence. The following three sections identify the Value Systems in the predominant culture—their methods of dividing right from wrong, good from evil, and so forth.

Locus of Decision-Making

The individual is responsible for his or her decisions but is often expected to defer to the interests of the family or organizational unit. There is an admiration for urban life and an enduring loyalty to region and family.

Sources of Anxiety Reduction

The extended family is getting smaller but is still the major source of security, order, and stability. Anxiety, as well as security, is produced by seeking success in the eyes of the extended family and society. There are strong Catholic and Communist segments that can work in opposition, but they are not completely incompatible. The Church gives a sense of structure to the majority. Italians are remarkably diverse, but they also have a strong capacity for social and cultural resilience and continuity.

Cultural Note

Everyone tends to speak at once at Italian gatherings. This goes for business meetings as well as social events. Of course, it is possible for Italians to conduct a meeting in a more orderly fashion, if those parameters are established at the beginning—but do not take offense at being interrupted.

Issues of Equality/Inequality

There are extreme contrasts between rich and poor. The population is stratified by income. Patron-client relationships provide a strong social and political base. Even though there is a large German-speaking group in the north, and many mutually unintelligible dialects, there is one standard language that binds the country together. Women have made progress toward equality.

▶ BUSINESS PRACTICES

Punctuality, Appointments, and Local Time

- Be on time, especially in the industrial north, where business is often conducted with pressure and efficiency.
- Italian businesspeople prefer to deal with people they know, even if that acquaintance has been a perfunctory handshake at a trade fair. Before you invest in travel to Italy, be sure to engage a strong representative who can make appropriate introductions and appointments for you.
- Write first for an appointment, in Italian if you want an immediate reply.
- Follow up your letter by phone and by e-mail.
- Be very aware of summer vacation periods. Most firms are closed in August. If you write for an appointment in mid-July, you may not get a satisfactory reply until September.
- Italians like to get acquainted and engage in small talk before getting down to business. They are hospitably attentive. Expect to answer questions about your family.
- Plan appointments between 10:00 and 11:00 A.M., and after 3:00 P.M.
- Northern business hours are usually 8:30 A.M. to 12:45 P.M. and 3:00 to 6:30 P.M., Monday through Friday. Many businesses are open Saturday mornings.
- In central and southern Italy, business hours are generally from 8:30 A.M. to 12:45 P.M., then 4:00 or 5:00 to 7:30 or 8:00 P.M., Monday through Friday, and 8:30 A.M. to 12:45 P.M. Saturday. The southern business pace is more relaxed.
- There may be fewer public holidays in Italy than in many Latin countries, but businesspeople must be aware that practically every Italian city celebrates the feast of its patron saint as a legal holiday and much of the city literally shuts down.

- For a list of the official holidays of Italy, visit *www.kissboworshake hands.com*.
- Italy is one hour ahead of Greenwich Mean Time (G.M.T. + 1), or six hours ahead of U.S. Eastern Standard Time (E.S.T. + 6).

Cultural Note

Corporations often have a horizontal chain of authority. Italians call it a *cordata* (which actually means a team of mountain climbers on the same rope). This parallel channel is based on levels of personal, reciprocal concern—and should never be taken lightly.

Negotiating
- It is important to understand corporate hierarchy. Titles may not coincide with a foreigner's conception of responsibility. Authority often goes with the individual, not necessarily the title. Status is exceedingly important, and respect for authority pervades work and social environments.
- The cordata concept is very difficult to explain fully to outsiders. But it exists and, to facilitate business, one should have a reliable contact who has full knowledge of a company's internal structure.
- The pace of negotiations is usually relatively slow. The more important the contract, the more study is going on behind the scenes. Any obvious sense of urgency is thought to weaken one's bargaining position.
- A dramatic change in demands at the last minute is often a technique to unsettle the other side. Be patient and calm; just when it appears impossible, the contract may come together.
- One does not exchange business cards at social occasions, but it is normal at business functions—especially because an Italian would feel it impolite to ask a foreigner to spell out her or his name.
- Italian cards are often plain white with black print. Usually, the more important the person, the less information is on the card.
- Conversational subjects that are highly appreciated are Italian culture, art, food, wine, sports such as bicycling and especially soccer, family, Italian scenery, and films.

- Your host may be negative about something in his or her country or its politics, but don't agree too strongly and never offer criticisms of your own.
- Avoid talking about religion, politics, and World War II.
- Italians do not usually tell off-color jokes and are uncomfortable when acquaintances do.
- Never ask someone you have just met at a social gathering about his or her profession. To do so is considered gauche, even insulting.

Cultural Note

When dining, Italians keep both hands above the table, not one resting on the lap. There may be three plates to start: a small one for antipasto, a deep dish for pasta or soup, and a large plate on the bottom—which may be for the main course, or may be removed with the soup, and replaced with a fresh plate.

Business Entertaining

- Italian hospitality plays an important role in business life, and most often means dining in a restaurant. No matter how you feel, refusing an invitation will be offensive.
- Use your utensils (not your fingers) to pick up cheese, and don't eat any fruit except grapes or cherries with your hand.
- Italians consider wine as a food to be sipped, not as a means of relaxation. Therefore, to drink too much is considered rude.
- Business dinners involve only a small, important group. If you are the host, consult with your Italian contact before extending invitations. You cannot be aware of all the "inside" personalities and ranks, so ask for help.
- Ask your Italian client's secretary to suggest a favorite restaurant.
- Dining is a serious business, and prestige can be gained or lost at the table. At the propitious moment one may bring up business.
- Paying may equate to prestige, and Italians may even slip the waiter a generous tip before dinner to make sure you do not get the bill.

- The check will not be brought until you ask for it. And female executives may find it extremely difficult to pay.
- Keep the receipt for the restaurant bill. Sometimes "tax police" check restaurant bills outside for adherence to tax laws.
- In a restaurant you will have to ask for ice, because Italians usually do not serve drinks cold (they think ice-cold things are unhealthy—except for "gelato").

Cultural Note

Breakfast *(la prima colazione)* is usually around 8:00 A.M. and consists of rolls, bread, butter, perhaps some jam, and strong coffee or chocolate.

Lunch *(la colazione)* is the full-course, main meal of the day, and serving starts at 1:00 P.M.

Dinner *(la cena)* is again a light meal. Service starts around 7:00 P.M. and may be served until after 10:00 P.M.

▶ PROTOCOL

Greetings

- As a guest, you will probably be introduced first. The most senior or eldest person present should also always be given special deference.
- Shake hands with everyone present when arriving and leaving. At a large gathering, if no one is giving formal introductions, it is proper to shake hands and introduce yourself.
- Handshakes may include grasping the arm with the other hand.
- Women may "kiss" good friends on either cheek (it is rather more like pressing the sides of each face together).
- Close friends and male relatives often embrace and slap each other on the back.

Titles/Forms of Address

- Do not use first names unless you are invited to—formality is still appreciated.

- Traditionally, executives and subordinates in offices would not address one another by their first names; however, this is changing.
- Professors and doctors are highly esteemed; use the title *Dottore* for a man and *Dottoressa* for a woman. It is better to use a title (even if you are unsure); always err on the side of caution. It will be accepted as an understanding of "status earned" even if not academically achieved.
- Personal titles are used in all forms of address, spoken and written. Like "Dottore," they can be used with or without the surname. Attorney Green is "Avvocato Verdi," Signorina Avvocata is "Miss Attorney," and so forth. Find out these details before the meeting if possible.

Gestures
- Latins "talk with their hands," and most gestures are usually both expressive and innocuous.
- You may see a disgruntled man quickly stroke his fingertips under his chin and thrust them forward. This is a sign of defiance and/or derision, somewhat like thumbing your nose in the United States.
- Another gesture has two versions: Holding your hand palm down with the index and little fingers straight out, and the others curved inward, symbolizes the devil's horns, and the message is to ward off evil. If the same gesture is done with the fingers pointing upward, it is an obscene message.
- Further information on gestures is accessible at *www.kissbowor shakehands.com.*

Gifts
- Business gifts are sometimes given at a senior managerial level. They should be well designed and made by craftsmen of prestige.
- Consumables like liquors or delicacies, or crafts from the visitor's country, may be appropriate.
- Do not give gifts that are obviously a vehicle for your company's logo.

- Note that some Italian firms have privately published glossy, top-quality illustrated books suitable for display on a bookshelf or coffee table.
- A small gift may be given to any staff member who has been particularly helpful. Travel alarm clocks, pens, electronic gadgets, silver key chains, or local handicrafts from your home are good gifts. If it is not a handicraft, be certain that you purchase prestigious name brands.
- If you require a more substantial gift, consider loading an iPod with a gracious message from your CEO to the recipient, or music from a prestigious orchestra in your country.
- Flowers or chocolates are acceptable for a secretary.
- If you are invited to someone's home, bring gift-wrapped chocolates, pastries, or flowers. Never give an even number of flowers. Do not give chrysanthemums; they are used for funerals. Do not give a brooch, handkerchiefs, or knives, all of which connote sadness.
- If you give wine, be certain it is of excellent vintage—many Italians are oenophiles.

Dress
- In the business world, good clothes are a badge of success. Women dress in quiet, expensive elegance; men's ties and suits should also be fashionable and well cut.
- Keep in mind Italy is a major center of European fashion. Even casual clothes are smart and chic.
- Women wear pants in cities, but shorts are a rarity. You may be stopped if you try to go into a church while wearing shorts, a shorter than knee-length skirt, or a sleeveless top.
- Italians appreciate refined clothes, and they will take note of your garments. But again, your clothes are just part of your image. Italians value a *bella figura* and will consider all aspects of the individual simultaneously—from their attire and the scent they wear, to their technical knowledge and reputation in the field. Investing some time in your personal appearance, as well as your technical research, before you arrive in Italy, will help you to be successful.

Holy See (Vatican City)

The Holy See (State of the Vatican City)
Local short form: Santa Sede (Città a del Vaticano)
Local long form: Santa Sede (Stato della Città del Vaticano)

Cultural Note
On April 2, 2005, Pope John Paul II passed away at the age of eighty-four. He served as the bishop of Rome for twenty-six years, and he was succeeded by Pope Benedict XVI, who was formally inaugurated on April 24, 2005.

▶ COUNTRY BACKGROUND

History
Although the Holy See's history reaches back to the fourth century, the pope's court has only been permanently established at the Vatican since 1311, when it returned from Avignon, France. It was recognized as an independent state in 1929. The Lateran Pacts between Pope Pius IX and the government of Italy acknowledged its 109 acres as the sovereign State of the Vatican City.

Vatican City contains the Basilica of St. Peter, the Apostolic Palaces, the Museums, the Gardens, and many offices. There are also thirteen buildings in Rome, and Castle Gandolfo (the pope's summer residence), which have extraterritorial rights.

During John Paul II's term as pope, 996 Catholics were beatified and 447 canonized. Some critics cited these numbers as "inflated" because more occurred under Pope John Paul II than in the previous three centuries. However, representatives of the Church affirmed that the increase in the numbers of saints is a positive development.

According to canon law, five years must pass before a cause for sainthood can be opened. However, there have been exceptions to the protocol. For example, Pope John Paul II initiated the process for Mother Teresa only two and a half years after her death. And in May of 2005, Pope Benedict XVI (formerly Cardinal Joseph Ratzinger) announced that he was starting the process for Pope John Paul II's beatification six weeks after the Pontiff's death.

There is an immense history associated with the Holy See. Further information is available at the Vatican's Web site, *www.vatican.va.*

Cultural Note

Vatican City, the smallest sovereign state in the world, generally operates on a budget of less than U.S.$300 million annually and may be the oldest continuously operating institution in existence.

Type of Government

A papacy, the Vatican is the ecclesiastical governmental and administrative capital of the Roman Catholic Church. The pope has supreme legislative, executive, and judicial power over not only the Holy See, but indirectly, over the Roman Catholic Church and its approximately 1 billion members worldwide.

The Holy See has diplomatic relations with 174 nations, is present on every continent, and is heavily involved in many international organizations. Only the United States has a larger diplomatic representation worldwide.

Vatican City has a Pontifical Commission, which handles internal administrative duties, such as the post office, publishing house, and Radio Vatican. The Roman Curia administers high-level Church affairs.

The College of Cardinals is divided into ranks: cardinal-bishops, cardinal-priests, and cardinal-deacons. There are various curial institutions, which oversee everything from missionary activities to the appointment of bishops. Tribunals in the judicial branch are responsible both for civil and criminal matters within Vatican City, as well as rulings pertaining to the Holy See. There is a Prefecture for Economic Affairs, which has final oversight authority for all of the Holy See's financial matters, including the Vatican bank.

Suffrage is limited to cardinals less than eighty years old.

While the Swiss Guard provides security for the Vatican and is directly responsible for the safety of the pope, Italy also assumes some accountability for defense of the Vatican.

Cultural Note

Requests for papal audiences are made through the Prefecture of the Papal Household.

Phone numbers and e-mail addresses are available on the Vatican's Web site under "Hospitality" and "Ticket Services." There is also a Vatican Tourism office in the Piazza di San Pietro, which distributes tickets.

Language

Latin is the official language; Italian, French, and others are commonly used.

There are various sign languages used in Monastic communities; these are not languages for the deaf, but are second-languages used to communicate while observing vows of silence.

Cultural Note

Estimates vary, but Vatican City is reported to have approximately 900 citizens living inside its walls. Some 3,000 more work in various positions. The labor force includes priests, nuns, dignitaries, the Swiss Guard, and lay workers. Many prestigious families are honored to have a son or daughter serve in the Vatican.

⊚ BUSINESS PRACTICES

Punctuality, Appointments, and Local Time

While Vatican City is an independent country, it is integrated into the Italian postal code and telecommunication systems. If you want to use the postal system (which has improved over the last decade—but is still problematic), be sure to include the correct code. For example, the mailing address for tickets for a papal audience is through the Vatican's "Tourist Office" at:

Prefecture of the Papal Household
Piazza Pio XII
4-00120 Città del Vaticano

Titles

- The pope has many titles, which reflect his many roles:
  Bishop of Rome and Vicar of Jesus Christ
  Successor of St. Peter, Prince of the Apostles
  Supreme Pontiff of the Universal Church
  Patriarch of the West
  Primate of Italy
  Archbishop and Metropolitan of the Roman Province
  Sovereign of the Vatican City State
  Servant of the Servants of God

Dress

- Refined, well-cut clothing is a vital aspect of doing business in the Vatican. Always wear elegant, subtle fashions.
- Modest, appropriate attire is required to enter the Basilica of Saint Peter and the Sistine Chapel. Shorts, bare shoulders, revealing garments, and so on, will prevent the wearer from gaining access. If necessary, visitors can purchase suitable clothing from the Vatican.

Cultural Note

There are many rules for behavior in the Vatican besides modest attire. Strict silence is required in many areas (cell phones must be turned off), and many items are banned from specific areas for security purposes. There are various levels of protocol for access to virtually anyone or anything in the Holy See—from the Vatican Library to the Museum to His Holiness the Pope.

Do not take pictures of anyone—particularly the Swiss Guard—without their permission. (Surprisingly, many mourners took pictures of the deceased Pope John Paul II lying in state—which, while morbid and ill-mannered, was permitted by the Vatican.) Guidelines for appropriate behavior within the Vatican are available on their Web site at *www .vatican.va*.

The Netherlands

Kingdom of the Netherlands
Local short form: Nederland
Local long form: Koninkrijk der Nederlanden

Cultural Note

The Kingdom of the Netherlands is often incorrectly called Holland. Holland refers only to a specific area in the Netherlands, encompassing the major cities of Amsterdam, Rotterdam, and the Hague. It is no more correct to call all of the Netherlands "Holland" than it would be to call all of Germany "Bavaria" or all of Spain "Andalusia."

▶ WHAT'S YOUR CULTURAL IQ?

1. Match the following notable Dutchmen with their fields of achievement:

a. Christiaan Huygens	1. Biology/Microscope
b. Rembrandt van Rijn	2. Philosophy
c. Baruch (Benedict) de Spinoza	3. Painting
d. Anton van Leeuwenhoek	4. Mathematics and Physics

   ANSWERS: a. 4; b. 3; c. 2; d. 1

2. TRUE or FALSE: It is acceptable to discuss prostitution, soft drugs, and euthanasia with your open-minded Dutch coworkers.
   ANSWER: FALSE. Although all are legal in the Netherlands, none are an appropriate topic of conversation in a work environment.

3. TRUE or FALSE? During the 1600s, the Netherlands became a world power, with a globe-spanning fleet and a far-flung network of colonies.

ANSWER: TRUE. The Dutch fleet even outclassed the British fleet in the early 1600s. Dutch supremacy started to unravel when both Britain and France attacked the Netherlands in 1672.

▶ TIPS ON DOING BUSINESS IN THE NETHERLANDS

- The Netherlands continues to rank among the top dozen trading nations in the world. Expect Dutch businesspeople to be experienced and sophisticated.
- The Dutch are a low-context, straight-speaking people. They can be blunt spoken and critical without meaning to offend.
- Do not make any promises you cannot keep. The Dutch expect honesty; any backpedaling on what they perceive as a promise will cause you to lose credibility. Even an offhand promise—such as "We'll take care of it"—is likely to be taken at face value.

▶ COUNTRY BACKGROUND

History
Julius Caesar's troops fought Germanic tribes in what is now the Netherlands. The strongest of these tribes were not subdued until 13 B.C. The Romans were neither the first nor the last to invade the Netherlands.

Following the collapse of the Roman Empire, Charlemagne incorporated the Netherlands into his Kingdom of the Franks.

The Low Countries, as the Netherlands and Belgium were then known, were subsequently claimed by one ruler after another, from the French duke of Burgundy to the Austrian House of Habsburg. All of these rulers were absentee landlords; they controlled blocks of land in scattered locations throughout Europe. Lacking any political power, the Dutch put their energies into trade and industry.

When Charles I of Spain came of age in A.D. 1516, he inherited title to the Netherlands. But a nation as distant as Spain was bound to have difficulty ruling the increasingly self-sufficient Dutch. The

Protestant Reformation increased Dutch opposition; many Dutch became Calvinists and resisted Catholic Spain on religious grounds.

The Dutch revolution spanned eighty years, from 1568 to 1648. Although Spain was then the most powerful nation in Europe, it was unable to subdue the Dutch rebels.

The northern districts of the Low Countries formally united in 1579 under the Union of Utrecht; this is often used as the date of origin of the Netherlands. An equally valid date is 1781, when those northern districts formally declared their independence from Spain. The Spanish agreed to a twelve-year truce with the Dutch in 1609, but did not recognize the Dutch Republic as an independent nation until the Peace of Munster in 1648. The southern Low Countries (Belgium) remained under Spanish control.

The Netherlands survived and prospered. They experimented with several forms of government, with and without kings. The current Kingdom of the Netherlands dates to the ascension of Prince William I as king in 1813.

Beginning in the seventeenth century, the Netherlands enjoyed a "golden era" of economic supremacy as its trade spanned the world. Dutch colonies were founded in Asia and the Caribbean. However, the tiny size and small population of the Netherlands made it inevitable that Dutch economic supremacy would be eclipsed by Britain, France, and Germany.

The Netherlands remained neutral in World War I. However, in World War II, they were invaded and occupied by the Nazis. The Netherlands' last major colony, Indonesia, was occupied by the Japanese during WWII as well. The Dutch never truly regained control of Indonesia after the war, and Indonesia became independent in 1949. The Dutch still rule the Netherlands Antilles and Aruba in the Caribbean.

In 1995, Dutch confidence in their military was shaken when their peacekeeping troops stationed in Bosnia failed to prevent the Srebrenica massacre. Subsequently, the Dutch were shocked again when the controversial Dutch politician Pym Fortuyn was assassinated in May of 2002.

Type of Government

The Kingdom of the Netherlands is a constitutional monarchy. There is a bicameral Parliament, with a First Chamber and a Second Chamber. The monarch is the chief of state; the prime minister is the head of the government.

The Netherlands is a member of both NATO and the European Community.

Although the Dutch are known for frugality in their personal lives, they have a very generous social welfare system. The government is seeking ways to reduce this system, which is seen as a burden on the economy.

For current government data, check with the Embassy of the Netherlands at *www.netherlands-embassy.org*.

Language

The official language of the Netherlands is Dutch. A minor percentage of the population speaks Frisian, Turkish, and Arabic.

The Dutch are among the most accomplished linguists in Europe. A majority of Dutch people speak at least one additional language. English is widely understood.

The Dutch View

There is no official religion in the Netherlands. Although the Netherlands is thought of as a Protestant nation, Roman Catholics have a slight majority. The Dutch Reformed Church and Calvinists are the significant Protestant denominations. The largest group consists of persons professing no religion at all: nearly 40 percent.

The Dutch live with the knowledge that their tiny country was once, in the seventeenth century, the world's pre-eminent mercantile power. This is a source of great pride and gives business a great importance even today.

For better or worse, the Dutch also have to live with their legacy as a former colonial power, which involves them in the affairs of places such as Indonesia.

Much of their land is below sea level. Only their elaborate system of dikes protects them from the North Sea.

Equality and tolerance are important aspects of Dutch society. A
wide range of behavior is tolerated, as long as it is kept private.

Cultural Note

The Dutch have a very egalitarian society, which respects the rights of every citizen. They do
not respond well to persons who project superiority or elitism. In a Dutch company, every
individual—from president to secretary to janitor—is considered worthy of respect.

☑ Know Before You Go

The Netherlands is a very safe country, although there is the ever-present worry about
the system of dikes that hold back the North Sea. Failure in the dike system would
devastate the country and take thousands of lives. This occurred in 1953, when nearly
2,000 people died when storm waters breached the dikes. Then in 1995, serious flooding
occurred again, and 250,000 people were evacuated.

Street crime and vehicular accidents are probably the greatest hazards to visitors.
The term "vehicular accidents" includes bicycle accidents; the Dutch are avid cyclists. By
some reckonings, one-fourth of daily trips made by the Dutch are via bicycle. Bike theft
is a problem.

▶ CULTURAL ORIENTATION

Cognitive Styles: How the Dutch Organize and Process Information

The Dutch are circumspect toward outside information. They
are abstractive and process information objectively and analytically.
There is an obligation to the universal rules of behavior, rather than
to the individual. Friendships develop slowly and are very selective.

Negotiation Strategies: What the Dutch Accept as Evidence

Truth lies in the accumulation of objective facts, influenced by
a strong faith in a social democratic ideology. Minimal credence is
given to subjective feelings. The Dutch tend to offer as little information as possible, and moderation is the rule. Subjective, emotional
arguments are not accepted.

Value Systems: The Basis for Behavior

Planning is a way of life in the Netherlands. Planning, regulating, and organizing are of major importance to the Dutch. The following three sections identify the Value Systems in the predominant culture—their methods of dividing right from wrong, good from evil, and so forth.

Locus of Decision-Making

The Dutch are strongly individualistic, but cultural history must be considered in the decision-making process. Individual privacy is considered a necessity in all walks of life.

Decision-making is slow and involved, as all peripheral concerns must be taken care of in the process. Once the decision is made it is unchangeable.

Even though universal values are adhered to, it is important to develop the respect and friendship of the participants.

Sources of Anxiety Reduction

Universal rules and regulations combined with strong internal discipline give stability to life and reduce uncertainty.

There is a high need for social and personal order and a low tolerance for deviant behavior. Everything is organized, including leisure time. The Dutch rarely show emotions, because of strong internal structure and control. But the Dutch have great faith in the ability of scientific method to solve human problems.

Some sociologists believe that the Dutch have a high index of uncertainty avoidance. As a result, they generally use laws and morality to give structure to their worldview.

Issues of Equality/Inequality

The Netherlands is a distinctly hierarchical society, with classes established to fill organizational roles and give structure and order. Protest in the Netherlands is a crucial part of the democratic process, because the densely populated and overly structured country breeds dissent.

Equal rights for all are guaranteed by law, but may not be prac-
ticed in the marketplace. There is some racism (although its presence
is often denied).

Although there is still a strong paternal nuclear family orientation
(including well-defined roles for males and females), this structure is
beginning to erode as more females enter the work force.

Cultural Note
The Dutch do not usually give compliments to individuals. Everything is considered a team
effort, and accolades are awarded to the group, not to individuals. Conversely, individuals are
not usually singled out for blame. When something goes wrong, it is considered the fault of
a system that failed to exercise proper oversight. The Dutch find self-aggrandizement to be
abhorrent.

▶ BUSINESS PRACTICES

Punctuality, Appointments, and Local Time

- The residents of the Netherlands, like most Europeans, write the
  day first, then the month, then the year (e.g., December 3, 2010, is
  written 3.12.10 or 3/12/10).
- Punctuality is very important in the Netherlands. Be certain to be
  on time for both business and social engagements.
- The Dutch place great importance on planning and efficient use
  of time. Arriving even a few minutes late to a business meeting
  may cause the Dutch to doubt your ability to utilize time well. In
  the Netherlands, a person who is late is suspected of being either
  incompetent or untrustworthy—or both!
- Another important aspect of punctuality in the Netherlands
  involves response time. Note that any company that cannot
  promptly deliver price quotes upon request will fail to win Dutch
  customers. It is also important to deliver products and services
  quickly.
- A very high percentage of Dutch businesspeople are fluent in
  English. In almost every situation, someone who can translate
  from English to Dutch will be close at hand.

- Appointments will be carefully scheduled; do not assume that they can be changed on short notice. Spontaneity is not considered a virtue in the Netherlands.
- Give as much notice as possible for an appointment made by telephone or e-mail.
- Always acknowledge the receipt of important communications immediately (contracts, price quotes, letters of intent, and so forth).
- Business letters may be written in English. Keep your letters formal, businesslike, and grammatically correct. When addressing individuals in writing, be sure to use their full and correct title, even if you are on a first-name basis.
- Many Dutch executives take long vacations during June, July, August, and late December, so confirm that your counterpart will be available.
- For the official holidays of the Netherlands, visit *www.kissbowor shakehands.com*.
- The Netherlands is one hour ahead of Greenwich Mean Time (G.M.T. + 1), or six hours ahead of U.S. Eastern Standard Time (E.S.T. + 6).

Cultural Note

Avoid conveying information that you want kept confidential. The Dutch prefer to keep their operations open to suggestions from all employees in a company, so all personnel are given access to information. Furthermore, the Dutch are generally uncomfortable with secrets.

Negotiating
- Do not be surprised if meetings begin with little or no preliminary socializing. The Dutch value the effective use of time and do not like to waste it on small talk.
- Dutch executives are often straightforward and efficient. However, the pace of corporate decision-making may be slower in the Netherlands than in North America.
- Decisions in Dutch firms are based upon consensus. Every employee who may be affected will be consulted. All opinions will

be listened to, regardless of the status or seniority of the person. The process can take a good deal of time.

- Dutch society values diversity of opinion. Everyone has his or her say, and they do not have to agree. An effort will be made to accommodate all divergent positions. This will include an attempt to make dissenters change their minds.

- Once a positive decision has been reached, Dutch firms will move swiftly. Everyone will be committed to the project and will be prepared to act quickly.

- A negative decision may be slower in coming. The one area in which many Dutch are not blunt is in saying "no." They may prevaricate or predict insurmountable complications instead of giving a direct "no."

- The Dutch admire modesty and abhor exaggeration or ostentation. Be sure you can back up your claims with lots of data. Keep your presentation clear and straightforward.

- Keep every promise you make, no matter how minor. A person who cannot be trusted to be punctual or to deliver a proposal on time will not be considered responsible enough to fulfill a contract.

- Most executives in the Netherlands understand English, so it is not necessary to have your business cards translated. However, all promotional materials and instruction manuals should be translated into Dutch.

- History is very important in the Netherlands. If your company has been around for many years, the date of its founding should be on your business card.

- Education is well respected in the Netherlands; include any degree above the bachelor's level on your card.

- It is quite possible that you will walk into an office and start talking business immediately after introducing yourself. In a country with centuries of experience in commerce, Dutch executives believe that they can judge whether they wish to work with someone quickly.

- In addition, it is also possible that a Dutch executive will have had background research done on prospective clients. This gives the executives hard data to back up their impressions, while maintaining a reputation for being "canny judges of human character."
- When the Dutch decide to chat before getting down to business, expect to be asked about your flight, your accommodations, where you are from, and so forth. Contacts are vital to doing business in the Netherlands, so know the name of every possible person who could give you or your company a good reference. Be aware of recent political events, both in your own country and in the Netherlands; the Dutch frequently discuss politics.
- The Dutch respect honesty and forthrightness. It is better to be blunt than to appear devious or evasive.
- When an individual must be either complimented or chastised, the Dutch always do so in private.
- Always avoid giving an impression of superiority. Egalitarianism is a central tenet of Dutch society. Everyone in a Dutch company, from the boss to every laborer, is considered valuable and worthy of respect.
- Privacy is very important in the Netherlands. Doors are kept closed, both at work and at home. Always knock on a closed door and wait to be admitted.
- Keep personal questions superficial; if your counterpart wants you to know any detail about his or her family, he or she will tell you. Avoid talking about sex, including the fact that prostitution is legal in the Netherlands.
- The Dutch tend to stand somewhat further apart than North Americans when talking. The positioning of furniture reflects this, and you may find yourself giving a sales pitch from a chair that seems uncomfortably far away. Do not move your chair closer; it is not your place to rearrange the furniture.
- Dutch family life is kept separate from business dealings. However, executives do take work home with them and may be phoned at home about business matters.

Cultural Note
Although business is considered a serious matter, the Dutch occasionally enjoy humor in
formal business presentations and official speeches. The Dutch sense of humor tends to be
good-natured and earthy; wit, sarcasm, and verbal legerdemain are not prized.

Business Entertaining

- Although the Netherlands is not known for its cuisine, food constitutes an important part of Dutch entertainment.
- In addition to three meals a day, the Dutch often break for a snack at 10:00 A.M. and 4:00 P.M. Coffee is available at the morning break; the afternoon drink is usually tea.
- The Dutch enjoy hosting foreign businesspeople at lunches and dinners. These are usually held in restaurants rather than in Dutch homes.
- All social events will be carefully scheduled and planned. The Dutch do not appreciate spontaneity, and they do not "do lunch" on a moment's notice.
- Remember to be on time to social events.
- Fine coffee is prized in the Netherlands; expect to drink a lot of it.
- When eating, always use utensils; very few items are eaten with the hands. Many Dutch even eat bread with a knife and fork!
- At the dinner table, do not rest your hands in your lap. Keep both hands above the table, with your wrists resting on the tabletop.

Cultural Note
As an alternative to a formal dinner, the Dutch often invite guests to come to their home after
dinner. The guests are offered numerous hors d'oeuvres, plus alcohol and coffee. The amount
of food and drink at these events can rival a full meal, but the setting is more relaxed and
informal.

▶ PROTOCOL

Greetings

- Virtually everyone shakes hands in the Netherlands, both upon greeting and upon departure. Men shake hands, firmly but briefly, with other men, with most women, and even when being introduced to a child.
- Upon introduction, repeat your last name while you are shaking hands. It is not traditional to utter any greeting phrase (such as "How do you do?"), although many Dutch businesspeople will do so to make a foreigner feel at ease.
- When you have not been formally introduced to everyone at a business or social gathering, it is your job to introduce yourself. Failure to do so may leave a bad first impression.
- Avoid standing with your hands in your pockets, and never leave your left hand in your pocket while shaking hands with your right.
- Aside from handshakes, there is very little public contact in the Netherlands. Close friends or relatives may hug briefly.

Titles/Forms of Address

- The order of names among the Dutch is first name followed by surname.
- As a foreigner, it may take you a long time to establish a close enough relationship with a Dutch colleague to get to a first-name basis. However, Dutch associates will usually use their first names amongst themselves at work.
- On the other hand, many Dutch executives are experts at dealing with foreign businesspeople. Your Dutch counterpart may quickly suggest going to a first-name basis. Understand that he or she is trying to make you feel comfortable.
- Dutch surnames can be confusing to foreigners, especially when they are preceded by a prefix. Common Dutch prefixes include: *de, der, den,* and *het* (which all mean "the"); *op* means "on," and *van, van't, van den,* and *van der* all mean "from."

- There is usually a space between prefixes and the surname in the north of the Netherlands. In the south, the prefixes may be combined and attached to the surname. For example, the form "van der Heyde" is common in the north, while "vanderHeyde"—all one word—is common in the south.
- Professional titles are not always used when speaking. Usually, an attorney, engineer, or doctor who wishes you to use a title will introduce himself or herself to you that way.
- Written communication in the Netherlands is very formal. Know the recipient's correct professional title and be sure to use it in the letter or e-mail.
- When entering a shop, it is considered polite to say "good day" to everyone present, customers and employees alike. However, do not interrupt—Dutch clerks will wait on only one person at a time.

Gifts
- Any gift to a Dutch executive should be of good quality but not of exorbitant cost.
- Appropriate gifts to businesspeople include imported liquor, good-quality pens, pocket calculators, or any new gadget. Wine collecting is common, so do not give a gift of wine unless you can make an appropriate selection for that person.
- If you are invited to dinner at a Dutch home, bring a bouquet of unwrapped flowers for your host; or, you may send a bouquet or a plant the following day.
- Avoid bringing wine as a gift to dinner; you don't want to imply that your host's wine cellar is inadequate.
- Chocolate or candy is also a good gift when you are invited to a Dutch home, especially if there are children in the house.

Cultural Note
The Netherlands is not the place to "dress for success." The wealthier and more successful a Dutch executive has become, the harder he or she must work at appearing ordinary. Wealthy Dutch citizens often may not wear fancy clothes, drive exotic cars, or live in expensive mansions. In a crowd, a Dutch CEO might not be distinguishable from a low-ranking executive.

Dress

- Business dress in the Netherlands is fairly conservative, but it varies with the industry. In the financial industries, most businessmen wear dark suits, sedate ties, and white shirts; women dress in dark suits and white blouses. Expect to wear the same clothes when invited to dinner.
- However, some industries allow very informal dress. Quite a few executives save their ties and jackets for outside the office.
- Surprisingly, the higher a person's rank, the more informally he or she can dress (in some industries). You may find the sales clerks in suits and the boss in jeans and a sweater.
- When the occasion calls for it, the Dutch enjoy dressing up. A tuxedo for men and an evening gown for women may be required for formal social events. These include formal parties, dinners, and opening night at the theater.
- Casualwear is essentially the same as in North America. However, shorts are worn only when jogging or hiking.

Norway

Kingdom of Norway
Local short form: Norge
Local long form: Kongeriket Norge

Cultural Note

Norway has been ranked as the best place to live in the world by the United Nations—for four consecutive years! The criteria include average income (U.S.$36,600 in 2004), life expectancy (seventy-nine years), and education levels (enrollment levels of 98 percent). Norway's vast oil and gas reserves help generate a high level of wealth, and their relatively small population uses that wealth to develop and sustain an economically and politically equal society with a high quality of life.

▶ WHAT'S YOUR CULTURAL IQ?

1. Norwegian names like Olsen, Hansen, and Nilsen originated as patronymics—that is, they originally meant "son of Ole," "son of Hans," and "son of Nils." TRUE or FALSE: All Norwegians use their patronymic as their surname.
ANSWER: FALSE. In 1923, all Norwegians were ordered by law to adopt a hereditary last name. Many simply took their patronymic and used that. However, other surnames were adopted as well. Many took the name of the farm they worked on as a surname.

2. Which of the following cultural figures is *not* Norwegian?
   a. Composer Edvard Grieg
   b. Playwright Henrik Ibsen
   c. Painter Edvard Munch
   d. Composer Jean Sibelius
   ANSWER: d. Sibelius is from Finland, and his work comes from a different cultural tradition.

3. Norway was occupied by Nazi Germany during the Second World War. TRUE or FALSE? Norwegians wore a paper clip on their clothing as a sign of opposition to the Nazi occupation.
ANSWER: TRUE. The invention of the modern paper clip is credited to Norwegian Johan Vaaler. (Although Norway had no patent law when he created the device in 1899.) During the occupation, wearing this Norwegian invention on one's clothing became a sign of Norwegian patriotism. It irritated the Germans so much that wearing a paper clip made one subject to arrest.

▶ TIPS ON DOING BUSINESS IN NORWAY

- Norwegians tend to be more informal than other Scandinavians (especially the Swedes, whom they generally consider stuffy).
- Many observers consider the Norwegians to be the least punctual people in northern Europe. A fifteen-minute delay is not uncommon. However, as a foreigner, you are expected to be prompt.
- Norwegian businesspeople are sometimes uncomfortable communicating in writing, especially in a foreign language. Many prefer to do business by telephone rather than by letter. When writing is necessary, it will often be as short as possible: a brief e-mail message or fax suffices.

▶ COUNTRY BACKGROUND

History

The Vikings (also called "Norsemen") were feared for their raids throughout northern Europe from the eighth to eleventh centuries. These Vikings eventually became the Norwegians, the Swedes, and the Danes.

Political power became concentrated in Denmark, which came to rule much of Scandinavia, including Norway. Eventually, Sweden became a rival power. Denmark sided with Napoleon during the Napoleonic Wars. To punish Denmark, the postwar Congress of Vienna took Norway from Denmark and gave it to Sweden in 1815.

The fishermen, sailors, and merchants of Norway had little in common with the aristocrats of Sweden. Friction developed.

Fortunately for the Norwegians, their rugged, rocky nation could not be divided up into the vast farming estates preferred by the Swedes. After a century of Swedish occupation, Norway peacefully gained its independence in 1905.

The Norwegian parliament invited a Danish prince to become their constitutional monarch, so King Haakon VII became the first king of Norway.

Norway remained neutral in World War I. However, despite its neutrality, Norway was occupied by Nazi Germany during World War II. For this reason, the Norwegians shifted from a belief in neutrality to one in collective security.

Norway signed the North Atlantic Treaty of 1949 and participated in the foundation of the United Nations.

Oil was discovered off Norway's coast in the late 1960s, and production of North Sea oil began in the 1970s. Today, Norway is the world's third largest producer of crude oil, behind Saudi Arabia and Russia. Norway also provides over 10 percent of the natural gas used in Europe. Oil revenues have made Norway one of the wealthiest nations in the world.

Norway declined to join the European Union in 1994. In 2001, Norway agreed to fight terrorism by sending troops to Afghanistan. However, Norway opposed the invasion of Iraq because it was not supported by the United Nations.

Type of Government

Norway is a multiparty (hereditary) constitutional monarchy. There are three branches of government. The executive branch is made up of the king, who is chief of state, the prime minister, who is the head of government, and a cabinet, also termed the Council of Ministers.

Executive power actually resides in the Council of Ministers in the name of the king, or King's Council. The prime minister sits on this council. The prime minister is chosen by the leading political parties. The legislative branch is a modified unicameral parliament, known as the Storting. Members of the Storting are elected according to a system of proportional representation. They serve for four years.

Women comprise a strong percentage of the representatives in the Storting.

Norway became a major oil and gas producer in the 1970s. The income from this sector allowed it to further advance its social welfare system. Currently, it hopes to make the non-oil sector of its economy more efficient and less dependent on subsidies.

For current government data, check with the Embassy of Norway at *www.norway.org.*

Cultural Note

In accordance with the wishes of Swedish industrialist Alfred Nobel, five of the six Nobel Prizes are awarded by Sweden. The sixth prize—the Peace Prize—is awarded by Norway. No one knows for sure why Nobel wanted the Norwegians to award the Peace Prize, but it may have been because Norway lacked Sweden's militaristic history.

Language

The official language of Norway is Norwegian, which is a Germanic language related to Icelandic, Danish, and Swedish. It has two forms, a "book language," known as *Bokmål*, used in schools and broadcasting, and a commonly spoken language, known as *Nynorsk*. According to law, Nynorsk must sometimes be used in instruction and in the media.

Most Norwegians have studied English; it is widely spoken in business meetings and in major cities.

Cultural Note

As in Danish and Swedish, the Norwegian alphabet has twenty-nine letters. The additional three letters are listed at the end of the alphabet. The Æ is the twenty-seventh character, the Ø is the twenty-eighth, and the Å is the final, twenty-ninth letter of the Norwegian alphabet.

The Norwegian View

Norway has complete religious freedom, but it does have an official state church, the Evangelical Lutheran Church, or Church of Norway. About 94 percent of the people belong to this church.

The traditional occupations of Norwegians—farming the rocky soil or fishing—were very hard lifestyles. Norwegians attribute many of their national characteristics to this: toughness, stubbornness, and self-sufficiency.

Older Norwegians complain that, due to the country's growing wealth, young Norwegians are losing some of their self-sufficiency. Some affluent young Norwegians hire people to do gardening and home repairs—to the horror of their elders. Egalitarian Norwegians like to boast that there are no private housemaids in Norway, but that may not be true for long.

Protection of the environment is a major concern for Norwegians. In March of 2000, a dispute over whether or not to build power plants fired by natural gas (which cause air pollution) resulted in a change of government.

☑ Know Before You Go

Norway is an extremely safe country. The primary hazard to visitors comes from Norway's weather, particularly in winter.

Oddly, there have been recent terrorist threats against Norway by groups presumably related to Al Qaeda.

Norway has two territorial disputes. The most serious one concerns fishing rights in the Barents Sea, which are also claimed by Russia.

The second dispute is about Antarctica. Norwegian explorers were among the first to explore the continent, and their territorial claims overlap those of other nations.

⊙ CULTURAL ORIENTATION

Cognitive Styles: How Norwegians Organize and Process Information

Norwegians are generally cautious toward outside information. New products and new ways of doing things are viewed with circumspection.

Their education system has become more abstractive, and people are beginning to process information conceptually and analytically. Although they are deeply concerned with social welfare, their individualism dictates that everyone be subject to the same rules and regulations.

Negotiation Strategies: What Norwegians Accept as Evidence

Proud of the country they have built, Norwegians put their faith in the ideologies of their culture and their social welfare state. Truth tends to be viewed through this filter. Within that context, objective facts are preferred to subjective feelings.

Norwegians tend to be blunt and direct; subtlety is not a typical trait. This makes them more likely to accept evidence at face value. However, their acceptance of facts as evidence does not result in quick decisions.

Value Systems: The Basis for Behavior

Norway has a highly nationalistic culture with a liberal philosophy of tolerance for dissent and deviation. Independence is highly valued.

Debts of all sorts are avoided, since such obligations are seen to impinge upon an individual's freedom.

The following three sections identify the Value Systems in the predominant culture—their methods of dividing right from wrong, good from evil, and so forth.

Locus of Decision-Making

There is a strong belief in individual decisions within the social welfare system. Self-sufficiency is prized. There is an emphasis on individual initiative and achievement, with a person's ability being more important than his or her station in life.

Although the dignity and worth of the individual is emphasized, there is a strong feeling of obligation to help those who are not able to help themselves.

Sources of Anxiety Reduction

Life's uncertainties are accepted and anxiety is reduced through a strong social welfare system. Life is given stability and structure by a strong nuclear family. Young people are encouraged to mature early and take risks to develop a strong self-image.

Issues of Equality/Inequality

Nationalism transcends social differences, and ethnic differences are minimized within a largely homogeneous population. Norway has a fiercely democratic and egalitarian society.

Norwegians have been charted as having a very low masculinity index. This is indicative of a society free of gender roles, in which women have no limitations on their behavior. Child care duties are shared by Norwegian husbands and wives.

High taxes have helped to produce a middle-class society that strives to minimize social differences. There are no privileges granted to wealthy or high-status Norwegians—not even to government officials or the royal family.

▶ BUSINESS PRACTICES

Punctuality, Appointments, and Local Time

- Norwegians are not quite as insistent on punctuality as many Scandinavians. However, as a foreigner, you should always be punctual, both for business and social events.
- Norwegians generally get to work exactly at the start of the business day. They also like to leave exactly at the end of the day. They have even been known to hang up in the middle of a phone call at the end of the workday!
- Norwegians, like most Europeans, write the day first, then the month, then the year (e.g., December 3, 2010, is written 3.12.10 or 3/12/10).
- The work week is generally Monday through Friday, 8:00 A.M. to 4:00 P.M. Businesspeople leave their offices promptly and go home for dinner, which is typically held at about 5:00 P.M.
- It is best to avoid business trips to Norway around Easter and in July and early August—when most people take vacations.
- Norway's Constitution Day is May 17. For more official holidays, visit *www.kissboworshakehands.com*.

- Norway is one hour ahead of Greenwich Mean Time (G.M.T. + 1), or six hours ahead of U.S. Eastern Standard Time (E.S.T. + 6).

Negotiating

- Norwegians are relatively informal (far more so than the neighboring Swedes).
- It is wise to set a time limit on the meeting. However, Norwegians will abide by the schedule, so be ready to end the meeting at the designated time, whether or not there are matters left to discuss.
- Norwegians may adopt a "take it or leave it" attitude, and will not appear dismayed if you reject their proposal and the deal falls through.
- Norwegians are wary of the American concern with legal matters. Written confirmation of business deals is sufficient; if you must mention bringing in a lawyer, be discreet.

Business Entertaining

- If you have a late morning meeting, invite your Norwegian colleague to lunch.
- In most Norwegian restaurants, alcohol is served only after 3:00 P.M. and only from Monday through Saturday.
- You may discuss business at any time during the meal.
- Good topics of conversation include family, Norwegian history, sports, and nature.
- Many affluent Norwegians have a second home in the country, where they can hike and ski.
- Norwegians will appreciate your knowledge about the differences among the Scandinavian countries.
- Avoid personal topics (employment of your host or family members, health issues, etc.)
- Avoid criticism of other peoples or political systems. The Norwegians stress tolerance. Chastising Norwegians for permitting the hunting of whales will not win you any friends.
- Don't complain about the cost of living in Norway. Norwegians know how expensive their country is.
- Norwegians usually eat dinner early, starting at 5:00 or 6:00 P.M.

- When you go to a Norwegian home, wait to be asked in; wait again until you are asked to sit down. At the table, wait until the host invites everyone to begin eating.
- Some Norwegians have a cocktail before dinner; others do not. It is possible that you will be directed to the dinner table as soon as you arrive. Arrive on time.
- The fork is held in the left hand; the knife remains in the right hand.
- Hands should not be kept in the lap at the table.
- A dinner in a Norwegian home may have numerous courses and last several hours. Pace yourself.
- At the end of the meal, people thank the hostess by saying *takk for maten*, or "thank you for the food"; you will please your hosts by saying this in Norwegian.
- You should initiate your own departure, as your hosts will not. Expect the evening to end around 10:00 P.M. in the winter. However, in the summer, the sun does not set until around midnight. Your hosts may suggest a walk after dinner, followed by a final drink. In the summer, expect to leave around 11 P.M.

Cultural Note

There was a turn-of-the-century fashion in Norwegian interior design for disguising interior doors. You may have to search for a door in older homes; do not be surprised if the door is covered by wallpaper. Doors are traditionally kept shut.

▶ PROTOCOL

Greetings

- The handshake is the standard greeting for men and women.
- People greet each other by saying "Morn" (which means "morning") at any time of day.
- Norwegians are quiet people; avoid speaking loudly.

Titles/Forms of Address

- The order of names is the same as in most of Europe: first name followed by surname.
- Follow the lead of your hosts as to whether or not to go to a first-name basis. Many Norwegians prefer to be addressed solely by their surnames, without even a "Mr." in front.
- Among older people, titles are used; among younger people, usage varies. In general, professional titles (Doctor, Engineer, Professor, and so forth) are used, followed by a surname; business titles (Director, President, and so forth) are not typically used. With government officials, it is appropriate to use titles. Oddly, lawyers and clergymen do not use titles.

Gestures

- A toss of the head means, "come here."
- Norwegians do not always rise when another person enters the room. Don't be offended by this.
- However, do rise when you are being introduced to someone.
- Talking with your hands in your pockets is considered too casual.
- The North American "okay" gesture (thumb and forefinger forming a circle) is considered insulting.

Gifts

- Gift giving is not part of doing business in Norway. Anti-bribery legislation makes giving any gift in a business setting problematical.
- Flowers, liqueurs, wine, liquor, or chocolates are appropriate gifts for your hostess when invited to a Norwegian home.
- When giving flowers, avoid the following, since they are all used only for funerals: lilies, carnations, and all white flowers, as well as wreaths.
- Alcohol taxes are high, so fine alcohol is an appropriate gift.
- If you do decide to give a business gift, be sure it is wrapped in good-quality paper. Make the gift neither too extravagant nor too skimpy.

Dress

- In general, Norwegians dress more informally than North American businesspeople; however, visitors should dress as they would in a business context at home.
- Men should always wear a tie for business appointments, but a sports jacket rather than a suit is usually acceptable.
- Women may wear suits, dresses, or pants.
- Clean blue jeans and T-shirts are standard casualwear, but torn clothes are unacceptable. Shorts are worn for hiking; they are not common in urban areas.

Poland

Republic of Poland
Local short form: Polska
Local long form: Rzeczpospolita Polska

Cultural Note

The Communist regime was overthrown in 1989, so an entire generation of Poles has grown up in a free society. While they are not nostalgic for that era, there is an ironic appreciation among some young people for the "socialist-realist style." Propaganda posters from the Stalinist era have recently become collectibles.

▶ WHAT'S YOUR CULTURAL IQ?

1. The name "Poland" describes the country's geography. What does "Poland" mean in Slavic?
   a. The hill country
   b. The flatlands
   c. The borderlands
   d. That unpronounceable place straddling the Vistula River
   ANSWER: b. Poland is mostly flat.

2. TRUE or FALSE? Although the Poles have been in their current location for some 2,000 years, the country of Poland has sometimes disappeared off the map of Europe.
   ANSWER: TRUE. Most notably, Poland was partitioned three times, with Polish land divided up by Germany, Russia, and Austria. Poland vanished entirely in 1795, and did not reappear as an independent entity until 1918.

3. Several Polish writers have won the Nobel Prize. Match the following Nobel Laureates with their works or genre:

a. Czeslaw Milosz (1911–2004)

b. Wladyslaw Stanislaw Reymont (1867–1925)

c. Henryk Sienkiewicz (1846–1916)

d. Isaac Bashevis Singer (1904–1991)

1. *Quo Vadis?* and historical novels

2. Poetry, essays, and translations

3. Stories on Jewish life

4. The peasants and epic novels

ANSWERS: a. 2; b. 4; c. 1; d. 3. Singer, although he was born in Poland and worked in Warsaw as a journalist before moving to the USA in 1935, wrote in Yiddish, not Polish.

▶ TIPS ON DOING BUSINESS IN POLAND

- Polish is one of the more difficult European languages for native speakers of English. It is complex, subtle, and formal. Certain sounds in Polish—notably the soft s, sh, cz, and szcz—are particularly hard for English speakers to master. However, learning even a few phrases in Polish will endear a foreigner to the Polish people. Polish businesspeople often speak German or English.

- In common with other Slavic groups, Poles give the appearance of being rather dour. Smiles are reserved for friends; they are rarely used in public.

- Despite theoretical equality under the law, Poland is still a male-dominated society. International businesswomen report that Poland is one of the more difficult places in Europe to be taken seriously. Businesswomen must also consider how they want to socialize with Polish executives—a process which invariably includes large quantities of alcohol.

▶ COUNTRY BACKGROUND

History

The very existence of Poland is a testament to the tenacity of the Polish people, considering that it has disappeared from the face of Europe several times.

The Slavic tribes that would later become the Polish people settled in this northern corner of Eastern Europe more than 2,000 years ago. The nation took its name from one of these tribes, the Polane (the people of the plain). The Polish nation dates its existence to the tenth century, with the ascension of King Mieszko I in A.D. 963. Mieszko adopted the Roman Catholic faith in 966, and the country remains staunchly Catholic to this day.

Poland flourished culturally and economically, but not politically. The country's flat, fertile plains and lack of defensible frontiers have made it a constant target for its aggressive neighbors. In 1386, the Polish state opted for unification with neighboring Lithuania, and for a time Polish fortunes were strengthened. But again political decline set in, and the country was partitioned three times between the German, Russian, and Austrian empires. By 1795, the time of the third partition, Poland had vanished.

The 1815 Congress of Vienna decreed that a Kingdom of Poland still existed, but only within the confines of the Russian Empire, where it was legally ruled by the Russian czar.

For the next hundred years the Poles continually worked for independence, with Catholicism serving as a rallying point against their Russian Orthodox overlords.

It was World War I that returned Poland to the map. When Russia sued the Central Powers for peace, the Treaty of Brest-Litovsk in 1918 dismembered the Russian Empire. Poland re-emerged as an independent state. But this independence proved to be short-lived. World War II began when Nazi Germany invaded Poland. Over 6 million Poles, including virtually the entire population of Polish Jews, died during the occupation. The Germans were pushed out by the Soviet Army in 1945, and the Polish borders were redrawn in their current configuration.

But Poland was not yet free. Instead, Poland became a Communist state under Soviet domination. Again, the Poles protested against their Russian overlords.

The first glimmering of success came in 1981 with the organization of the Solidarity labor union. Martial law was unable to stifle the will of the people, and (after the Polish regime ascertained that the Soviets would not intervene) Solidarity was legalized in 1989.

Political liberalization and a transition to a market economy were followed by the election of Solidarity leader Lech Walesa as the leader of the Polish Republic in late 1990.

Despite the opposition of Russia, Poland joined the North Atlantic Treaty Organization (NATO) in 1999. Poland joined the European Union in May of 2004.

Type of Government

The Republic of Poland is a multiparty democracy. The president is the chief of state; the prime minister is the head of government. There are two legislative houses: the upper house (the Senate) and the lower house (the Sejm). Within the legislative branch of the government, the Sejm has most of the power; the Senate may only suggest amendments to legislation passed by the Sejm or delay it. Both bodies are democratically elected.

Poland contributed troops to the U.S.-led Coalition in the occupation of Iraq in 2003.

For current government data, check with the Embassy of Poland at *www.polandembassy.org*.

Cultural Note
Pope John Paul II, the first Polish pope of the Roman Catholic Church, remains a hero to Poles. They also believe that he had a major role in preventing the USSR from crushing the Solidarity Movement in the 1980s, which eventually led to Poland becoming free of Soviet domination.

Language
Polish is the official language. Closely related to Czech, Polish is placed in the Slavic branch of the Indo-European linguistic family

(English is also part of this family). Polish is written in a modified Latin alphabet, not the Cyrillic alphabet of Russian.

The Polish View

Catholicism is essentially the only religion in Poland today. Only 1.5 percent of the population is identified as belonging to another religion (Orthodox), although almost 10 percent of Poles are nonreligious (an atheist legacy of Soviet-dominated Poland).

During centuries of foreign domination, the national aspirations of the Polish people were sublimated into the Catholic Church. The Church was the single most important influence in preventing Poland's cultural absorption by Lutheran Prussia and Orthodox Russia. The Polish people are in debt to their Church for preserving their cultural identity.

With Poland free and independent at last, it is not surprising that the Catholic Church should want to collect on that debt by having a say in how Poland is run. Poland is now challenging Ireland for the honor of being "the most Catholic country in the world." As in Ireland, the major friction arises over the Church's prohibition of contraception and abortion. But unlike Ireland, Poland had abortion on demand during the decades of Soviet domination. New restrictions on abortion have been passed, but they are opposed by many Polish citizens. Businesses (including medical insurers) whose products or services touch on birth control issues should be prepared for further changes in Poland.

While capitalism has been more successful in Poland than in any other former Warsaw Pact nation, it has also created a society of haves and have-nots. While most Poles are better off than they were under Communism, some (including farmers, miners, pensioners, and teachers) are not.

Despite the fact that virtually all of Poland's Jews were exterminated by the Nazis in World War II, anti-Semitism is still extant in Poland. Anti-Semitism can be found in many sectors of Polish society.

The overriding concern for Poles is national security. After centuries of domination by Russians and Germans, the Poles are determined to maintain their freedom. The Polish government does not believe that their fellow Europeans will guarantee their security, so they place their faith in the United States. Poland is the greatest ally the United States has in Europe; Poland even sent 2,600 troops to support the occupation of Iraq, and led a multinational force (most from Eastern Europe) of 8,000.

Poland and Russia are locked into a complex historical relationship that colors all cross-border interactions. Many Poles see Russia as the architect of Poland's misfortunes. Some interactions that involve Poles and Russians will involve these beliefs.

In the short-term, Poles seem to be open to change, and welcome the introduction of new business products or ideas.

☑ Know Before You Go

As with other Eastern European countries, the greatest hazard to travelers is property crime. Pickpocketing, theft from hotel rooms, and auto theft are common. Violent crime is rare but is an increasing problem.

The weather can be a hazard. Poland is subject to a highly variable climate. Winters can be very cold and snowy, or mild and wet. Summers are sometimes very hot and dry, especially in the eastern portion of the country. Poland is very flat, and flooding is common.

Much of Poland's infrastructure is in need of repair. Be cautious of road conditions when driving. Rural roads can be dangerous at night.

Poland has had some problems with bribery, and several Polish politicians have been removed for corruption.

Most business travelers come away from Poland with no more damage than a hangover (from trying to keep pace with Poles drinking vodka).

▶ CULTURAL ORIENTATION

Cognitive Styles: How Poles Organize and Process Information

The Polish culture has always been open to information from the West. With the demise of Communism, many aspects of education in Poland are in a state of flux. Poles tend to be abstractive, processing information conceptually and analytically. However, Poles also value personal relationships as much as the law.

Cultural Note

Interpersonal relationships are all-important to Poles, even in business. This makes business use of the Internet problematical. Although Internet access is substantial, few small to medium-sized businesses currently make purchases online.

Poles are not technophobes, though. Cell phones and electronic gadgets are popular, and text messaging is widespread.

Negotiation Strategies: What Poles Accept as Evidence

In Poland, truth rests on both objective facts and the subjective feelings of the moment. Faith in ideologies that may change an individual's perspective on the truth has changed, shifting from the ideologies of the Communist Party to those of nationalism, democracy, and the Catholic Church.

Value Systems: The Basis for Behavior

Since the fall of Communism and the rise of democracy, the value systems of Poland are being influenced more and more by those of the West. This includes both the United States and Poland's fellow members in the European Union.

Poles are discovering a newfound respect for the law. In the past, Poles often felt that rules were made to benefit the rulers (who were often not Polish). Today, Poles make their own rules. How well Poles will adhere to the multitudinous regulations of the European Union remains to be seen.

The following three sections identify the Value Systems in the predominant culture—their methods of dividing right from wrong, good from evil, and so forth.

Locus of Decision-Making

In the new, democratic Poland, more decision-making responsibility has been placed on individuals. Poles have a strong sense of individualism and democracy, plus a belief that all citizens should influence the way the society is governed. In many instances, the individual may transfer decision-making responsibility to the group as a whole or to a consensus of privileged individuals. There is a tendency to expect decisions to be made at a higher level.

Sources of Anxiety Reduction

Studies have shown that Poles have a high index of uncertainty avoidance. As a result, Poles use laws and morality to give structure to their worldview.

Post-Communist freedom is perceived as threatening most of the structures the Poles have depended upon for stability and security. However, since most Poles are Catholics, the Church is a significant factor in filling this need. Polish Catholicism has been described as emotional and traditional, and the Poles are considered the most devout of all European Catholics. A strong extended family also helps to give structure and security. Many Poles are unsure about whether Poland's membership in the European Union will be a benefit or a detriment.

Issues of Equality/Inequality

Traditionally, Poles have lived in a hierarchical society. The structure of the organization is dictated from above.

Although Poland has a largely homogeneous population, there are substantial inequalities between its citizens. There is some disjunction between private and public morality.

Poland is a male-dominated society. Only recently have a substantial number of women advanced beyond clerical status in Polish businesses.

▶ BUSINESS PRACTICES

Punctuality, Appointments, and Local Time

- As a foreigner, you are expected to be on time for any and all appointments.
- Poles have become more punctual since the end of the Communist regime. Today, most Poles will be prompt for business appointments.
- The Polish workday starts early, generally at 8:00 A.M. Do not be surprised if someone offers you an 8:00 A.M. appointment.

- Many Polish workers do not take a lunch break, but work straight through the end of the day. Factory workers tend to be finished by 3:00 P.M.; office workers by 4:00 P.M. Even executives are usually done by 5:00 P.M. Many people also work on Saturday.
- Business "lunches" are often held quite late, around 4:00 or 5:00 P.M., after the end of the business day. No one goes back to work after lunch, so only the time of day differentiates the business lunch from a business dinner. Dinner in Poland starts around 8:00 or 8:30 P.M.
- Requests for appointments should be made in writing (via e-mail) when possible. Translating the request into Polish will make a good impression.
- Poles count six distinct seasons. In addition to spring, summer, winter, and fall, they recognize early spring (przedwiosnie) and early winter (przedzimie).
- Sunday is the traditional day for visiting family and friends in Poland.
- Poland's Independence Day is celebrated on 11 November. For further official holidays in Poland, visit *www.kissboworshake hands.com.*
- Poland is one hour ahead of Greenwich Mean Time (G.M.T. + 1), and thus six hours ahead of U.S. Eastern Standard Time (E.S.T. + 6).

Negotiating
- It is difficult to predict how long it will take to negotiate a deal. Poles used to be very cautious, and contracts could take months to complete. However, Poland's new entrepreneurs are more amenable—almost anxious to move quickly. This is more common with small enterprises.
- Poles can be very tough customers, insisting on their own terms. They sometimes take pride in being difficult—as the rest of the European Union found out once Poland became a member.
- The single most commonly heard objection in Poland is "the price is too high." Foreign companies must be flexible to penetrate the

Polish market. For example, some foreign companies ship their products unassembled to reduce Polish import duties.

- Office doors are usually kept closed in Poland. Knock and wait before you enter. Either you will be told to enter or the occupant will open the door.

- A local Polish representative will be vital to successful operations. Polish business runs on relationships, and, as an outsider, you will need a Polish native for his connections. He will also be able to get you things in short supply, from prestigious office space to scarce restaurant reservations.

- Bring plenty of business cards and give one to everyone you meet. Poles tend to bring more than one person to a meeting, so you should bring a good supply of cards.

- One side of the card should be in your native language, the other in Polish. However, because English is the most popular second language, opinions differ on whether or not it is necessary to translate an English business card into Polish.

- Proposals, reports, and promotional materials should be translated into Polish. If graphics are included in this material, make sure they are well done and neatly printed. Standards are high, because Poland has graphic artists that are the equal of any in Europe.

- While your presentation materials are important, Poles tend to operate on their gut feelings. If no bond has been established between you and your Polish counterparts, no presentation will be good enough.

- In order to counter objections from your Polish prospects (who may be somewhat more risk-averse), cite examples of similar deals that were successful.

Business Entertaining

- Business lunches and dinners are popular, but breakfast meetings are virtually unknown.

- Poland is still recovering from a housing shortage. Because apartments can be very cramped, do not be surprised if a Polish businessperson does not invite you home. Most entertaining is done in clubs and restaurants.

- The person who issues the invitation to a restaurant is usually the one who pays the bill. However, it is customary for a foreigner to offer to pay. Foreign businesswomen should intercept the waiter before dinner starts in order to arrange to pay. This will avoid any controversy over the tab, since Polish men may not want to let a woman pay.

- As a foreigner, you may get more attention and better service in restaurants and clubs than Poles—but only if people realize that you are a foreigner.

- Despite having to go to work early, Poles love to stay up late, talking and drinking. Leaving early may insult them, so be prepared for a long night.

- Although there is an effort to promote beer as an acceptable drink (most Poles consider beer a chaser), vodka is still the drink of choice. (Poland makes an excellent potato vodka.) Don't get trapped in a vodka-drinking contest with Poles; you'll lose. Expect your glass to be refilled every time it is empty until the vodka runs out.

- Learn to give a Polish toast: "Na zdrovya" and the optional answer "Dai bozhe"—God grant it.

- Do not bring up your background if you are of German, Hungarian, or Russian descent. Poland's relations with those neighbors have not always been cordial.

- Anti-Semitism is also a subject to avoid. Remember that the Nazis located most of the death camps on Polish soil, not in Germany itself.

⊙ PROTOCOL

Greetings
- Shake hands when you meet, and when you leave.
- You may want to wait for a Polish woman to extend her hand before offering to shake hands. If you feel an additional expression of respect is called for, simply make a short bow.
- Close Polish friends or relatives may greet each other effusively, with much hugging and kissing of cheeks. These are most common between women or between women and men, but Polish

men occasionally kiss each other on the cheek. Three kisses, each one on an alternate cheek, are traditional.

- Food and sports are good topics to bring up, but expect conversations to be wide-ranging.
- Most of the businesspeople you meet will be male. Admonishing Poles for sexist attitudes, real or perceived, will not help your relationship.

Titles/Forms of Address

- As in some other Slavic cultures, the final letter in a woman's surname may be different from that of a man's. Where this is the case, a woman's surname will end in the letter a—thus, it is Mr. Solski and Mrs. Solska.
- The simplest way to address a Polish professional is by using "Mr.," "Mrs.," or "Miss" and their job title.
  Mr. = Pan ("Pahn")
  Mrs. = Pani ("Pah-nee")
  Miss = Panna ("Pah-nah")
  Mr. Executive = Pan Dyrektor
  Mr. Reporter = Pan Redaktor
- If a Pole lacks a title, be sure to address him as Mr., plus his surname. Only close adult friends will address each other by their first names.

Gestures

- In social situations, when a Pole flicks his finger against his neck, he is inviting you to join him for a drink (probably vodka).
- Do not chew gum while speaking to someone.
- Do not litter; Poles are shocked at the sight of anyone throwing trash anywhere but in a trash receptacle.
- Avoid loud behavior in public; Poles tend to be a quiet people. You will notice that Poles speak more softly than North Americans do.
- Polish men tend to have traditional views of acceptable female behavior. Women who speak forthrightly may encounter resistance from Polish men.

- When asking directions from strangers, a woman should approach either a police officer or another woman. Approaching a man will probably be interpreted as flirting.

Gifts
- A foreign gift is appropriate the first time you meet a Polish businessperson. Liquor (anything except vodka) is a good choice.
- Always bring a gift when visiting a Polish home, even for a brief visit. Flowers are the most common gift. Give the flowers, unwrapped, to your hostess. Always bring an odd number of flowers, and avoid red roses (used for courting) and chrysanthemums (used at funerals).
- For further information on culturally correct gifts for your Polish clients, see *www.kissboworshakehands.com*.

Dress
- Business dress is formal and conservative: suits and ties for men, dresses for women. Colors tend to be muted.
- For casualwear, jeans are ubiquitous for both men and women. Jeans with a dressy shirt or blouse will get one through most non-business situations. Exceptions are:
  - Expensive restaurants, the theater, and the opera (these require suits and ties or dresses)
  - Dinner invitations in a Polish home (these require jackets and ties or dressy pants or skirts)
  - Formal invitations, as on New Year's Eve (these require tuxedos or gowns)

Cultural Note
Living in a hostile environment, often ruled by enemies, the Poles have developed two separate codes of behavior. In public, Poles can be demanding, distant, and abrupt. But in private, among friends or relatives, Poles tend to be warm, generous, and talkative. Long conversations lasting late into the night are a Polish tradition.

To see private behavior in a public setting, go to a train station or an airport. There, Poles engage in intimate farewells that last until the transport pulls away. There is a Polish saying that goes, "The English leave without saying goodbye. The Poles say goodbye but do not leave."

Portugal

Portuguese Republic
Local long form: Republica Portuguesa

Cultural Note

Although Portuguese is related to Spanish, and many Portuguese understand Spanish, foreigners should never presume that knowledge of Spanish is sufficient to do business in Portugal. The Portuguese consider it insulting when foreigners constantly try to communicate in Spanish.

▶ WHAT'S YOUR CULTURAL IQ?

1. Like Rome, Lisbon—the capital of Portugal—was built on seven hills near a river. Tradition holds that Rome was founded by Romulus. Which mythological character is credited with founding Lisbon?
    a. Aeneas
    b. Apollo
    c. Bacchus
    d. Ulysses
    ANSWER: d. According to local legend, Ulysses founded Lisbon (which the Romans called Olisipo) during his wanderings after the fall of Troy.

2. TRUE or FALSE? Geographically speaking, Portugal is not a Mediterranean country.
    ANSWER: TRUE. Portugal's only coastline is on the Atlantic Ocean. It is not on the Mediterranean Sea at all. However, its culture has much in common with other Mediterranean nations.

3. The fado is the most important indigenous style of music in Portugal. TRUE or FALSE? The fado is a happy, celebratory harvest song associated with the Portuguese countryside.
ANSWER: FALSE. The fado is associated with urban life, and is invariably melancholy and wistful.

▶ TIPS ON DOING BUSINESS IN PORTUGAL

- Portugal was a highly stratified society for hundreds of years, and hierarchy remains important in the business climate. If an owner of a firm basically runs the company for his own benefit, that is accepted as natural. The owner can use it as an employment vehicle for members of his family or friends, or dispose of the firm as he wishes.
- This emphasis on social and business positions helps explain why it is vital to develop contacts and relationships with Portuguese executives. When the network is open, business is done.
- Women should be aware that machismo is a cultural norm in Portugal. Be certain to present a professional, capable image at all times, and do not be surprised if your Portuguese contacts consistently look to the men on your team for answers—even if you are the senior executive at meetings. Resolve this problem before the first meeting by briefing your male employees; in order to confirm your position, they should defer to you during discussions, and reinforce your opinions.

▶ COUNTRY BACKGROUND

History

Over the course of history, Portugal's coastline has been populated by a succession of cultures. Ancient Phoenicians, Carthaginians, and Greeks preceded the Romans, who conquered the region in 27 B.C. Subsequently, the Visigoths and the Moors governed until the twelfth century. In 1140, Portugal became an independent nation under King Alfonso Henriques. During the fourteenth and fifteenth centuries, Portuguese explorers immensely expanded their empire.

Both Spain and France temporarily ruled Portugal before the Republic of Portugal was established in 1910.

Type of Government

From 1974 to 1976, Portugal underwent a nearly bloodless transition from an authoritarian government to a constitutional democracy. Today, Portugal is a multiparty parliamentary democracy.

The parliament is known as the Assembly of the Republic. It is unicameral, and its members are elected by direct universal suffrage. Deputies serve for four years. The president is the chief of state, while the prime minister is the head of the government.

The 1976 constitution was revised in 1982 and 1989. It placed the military under civilian control and eliminated the Marxist rhetoric and socialist goals of the first document. This led to the privatization of many sectors of the economy, such as the financial and telecommunications industries. It also called for increasing decentralization of the administration. Portugal joined the European Community (now the European Union) in January of 1986. Membership stimulated liberalization of economic policy, which resulted in one of the best economic performances and one of the lowest unemployment rates in the 1990s. Performance diminished in recent years, partly based upon a poor educational system.

For current government data, check with the Embassy of Portugal at *www.portugal.org*.

Language

Portuguese, a Romance language, is spoken throughout Portugal. Outside Portugal, (i.e., in Brazil) the language has altered somewhat due to the influence of other language and speech patterns.

The Portuguese View

As a colonial power, Portugal retained its colonies far longer than most other European powers. Italy, Germany, and Belgium held their colonies for less than a century; England, the Netherlands, and France held most of theirs for less than 200 years. Spain lost Latin

America after about 250 years, and the Philippines after about 330. But Portugal's final African colonies were lost only after some 400 years of contact! This may help explain the Portuguese melancholy for past glories.

> **Cultural Note**
>
> Many people who have written about Portuguese characteristics mention several terms: a sense of *saudade* (the sad knowledge that one is living in diminished times); *siso* (which is similar to a sense of prudence), and *loucura* (which would almost be the opposite of prudence—more like "excess"). While these terms are often quoted and may apply to many Portuguese, viewpoints are changing as the economy improves, and a younger generation looks to the future more than to the memories of the country's glory days.

Portugal, like Spain, emerged from decades of repression under a dictator in the 1900s. This suddenly gave social and political freedom to a tightly controlled society. A rising standard of living (in large part due to Portugal's joining the EU) has generated more economic choices and opportunities, and the Portuguese finally have personal and political freedoms.

This change has lightened the *saudade* attitude that has been referred to in literature about Portugal. Portuguese culture is slowly changing with developments in their economy and technology.

There is a Portuguese tradition of delegating hard or distasteful labor to others. They do not consider work to be the purpose of living, and will not generally dwell long on conversations about their jobs.

☑ Know Before You Go

Portugal's Azores are subject to severe earthquakes. Water pollution is a serious problem in the coastal areas, and has affected the fish populations.

Smoking is still common.

Portugal does have a drug problem since it is a gateway country for Latin American cocaine and Southwest Asian heroin entering the European market (especially from Brazil); it is reported to be a transshipment point for hashish from North Africa to Europe.

▶ CULTURAL ORIENTATION

Cognitive Styles: How the Portuguese Organize and Process Information

In Portugal, information is readily accepted for the purpose of discussion, but negotiations may be extensive with little movement from the initial perspective. Teaching is formal and innovation is discouraged, which fosters a subjective, associative mode of information processing. Because interpersonal relationships are of major importance, Portuguese are more inclined to maintain a relationship than to abide by rules and laws.

Negotiation Strategies: What the Portuguese Accept as Evidence

Truth is found in the personal feelings of those involved in a situation. While faith in the ideologies of humanitarianism and religion may influence their perspective, the Portuguese will not often let objective facts unduly sway their opinions.

Value Systems: The Basis for Behavior

The Portuguese's value systems are still in transition from the old authoritarian political and economic systems to the present democratic and capitalistic systems. The following three sections identify the Value Systems in the predominant culture—their methods of dividing right from wrong, good from evil, and so forth.

Locus of Decision-Making

Individuals are responsible for their decisions, but they are usually subject to the pressures of the family or the working group. The elite control all seats of power, intermarry for stability, and rely on extended kinship ties for control. One's self-identity comes from the history of one's extended family and one's position in society. A person's connections are much more important than his or her expertise when finding a job.

Sources of Anxiety Reduction

Most Portuguese are members of the Catholic Church, and its teachings and social structure provide stability and security to the individual. Friendship and patronage networks are the cement of Portuguese society and the primary means of communication within and between social classes. The family is the primary unit of social interaction, and it is an individual's role in the social structure and the presence of the extended family that give a sense of stability and security to life.

Issues of Equality/Inequality

There is ethnic and linguistic homogeneity in Portugal and this brings a sense of equality to the people. Although there are extreme contrasts between rich and poor, with a small upper class, a larger middle class, and a massive lower class, in general people feel that they are all equal because they are all unique. Failures are often attributed to external circumstances rather than personal inadequacies. It is a strongly macho society.

▶ BUSINESS PRACTICES

Punctuality, Appointments, and Local Time

- Punctuality is not a high priority in Portugal. Although foreigners are always expected to be on time, your Portuguese counterpart could easily be thirty minutes late. This indigenous casual attitude toward punctuality is affected by rank. A person of high social standing has the option to show up late to a meeting with a person of lower rank.
- Prior appointments are necessary.
- Remember that many Europeans and South Americans write the day first, then the month, then the year (e.g., December 3, 2010, is written 3.12.10 or 3/12/10). This is the case in Portugal.
- Lunch has traditionally been from noon to 2:00 P.M.; however, businesspeople may take shorter lunches. Try to avoid appointments between noon and 3:00 P.M.

- For a list of the official holidays of Portugal, visit *www.kissbowor shakehands.com.*
- Portugal is one hour ahead of Greenwich Mean Time (G.M.T. + 1), or six hours ahead of U.S. Eastern Standard Time (E.S.T. + 6).

Negotiating

- Establishing a strong rapport through constant personal contact is essential.
- Emphasize your commitment to your clients; frequent visits are highly recommended. Do not expect negotiations to proceed at a rapid pace.
- Persistence and patience are vital. Nothing is accomplished quickly in Portugal. The Portuguese do not consider themselves slaves to the clock. Appreciate their viewpoint, and you will have little difficulty conducting business there.
- After-sale service of your product is necessary. You must prove to your clients that this support will be provided.
- Good topics of discussion are the family, the excellent food, positive aspects of Portuguese culture, and personal interests.
- Avoid discussing politics and government.
- Avoid sounding too curious about your associates' personal matters.
- Many Portuguese study British English, so avoid idioms from the United States.
- Business cards are used. It is best to have yours translated, so that English is on one side and Portuguese on the other.
- Present your business card to your colleague with the Portuguese side facing him or her.

Business Entertaining

- Lunch is the main meal of the day and is eaten at approximately 1:00 P.M. Business lunches are common.
- Wine is generally the typical beverage consumed with meals.
- If you are invited out to lunch or dinner, be certain to reciprocate; however, do not mention that you "owe" the other person the favor.

- Women eating alone in a restaurant may be approached unless they obviously take work with them.
- The fork is held in the left hand and the knife remains in the right hand.
- Hands should not be kept in the lap at the table.
- It is impolite to eat while walking down the street.
- People often meet at tea houses (casas de chá).

▶ PROTOCOL

Greetings
- A warm, firm handshake is the standard greeting.
- For social occasions, men greet each other with an embrace.
- Women kiss on both cheeks when greeting each other.
- The Portuguese tend to be less physically demonstrative in public than Spaniards.

Titles/Forms of Address
- The order of names is first name followed by the surname.
- Use of first names has traditionally been reserved for friends, but this is changing.
- Some professionals are introduced as "Doctor" or "Doctora" even if they are not officially doctors.

Gestures
- "Come here" is indicated by waving the fingers or hand, with the palm facing down.
- It is considered very impolite to point.
- To call a waiter to your table in a restaurant, simply raise your hand.

Gifts
- It is not appropriate to give a business gift at the first meeting.
- When you give a business gift, do not include your business card; instead, include a handwritten card.
- Do not make your gift too extravagant or too cheap.

- The gift should not be a vehicle for your company logo.
- It is not necessary to bring a gift when you are invited to a home. Instead, you may invite your hosts out at a later date.
- If you do wish to give something to your Portuguese hosts, fine chocolates or other candy is the preferred gift.
- If you send flowers to your Portuguese hosts, have them sent ahead, and do not send thirteen of them, as that number is considered bad luck. Do not send chrysanthemums or roses. Do make sure that the bouquet is impressive; a gift of cheap flowers will have a negative effect.

Dress

- Conservative, formal dress is essential. Portuguese men may wear jackets and ties even when going to the movies!
- Despite the hot Portuguese weather, men should not remove their jackets unless their Portuguese colleagues do so first.
- Portuguese businesswomen usually wear subdued colors, so avoid the red power suit.

Romania

Romania

Cultural Note

Romanians consider themselves a Mediterranean people who just happen to live in Eastern Europe. Despite their central European location, the Romanians identify more closely with Italy and France. Between WWI and WWII, the Romanian capital, Bucharest, was known as "the Paris of the East."

▶ WHAT'S YOUR CULTURAL IQ?

1. TRUE or FALSE? Modern Romania is situated in the province known in the Roman Empire as Dacia.
   ANSWER: TRUE. The Romans conquered the Dacians in the second century A.D. The territory of Dacia was approximately the same as present-day Romania.

2. Nazi Germany considered it vital that they controlled Romania during the Second World War. TRUE or FALSE: This was because of Romania's coastline on the Black Sea.
   ANSWER: FALSE. It was because the Nazi war machine needed oil, and Romania had the largest petroleum reserves then known in continental Europe.

3. Match the following
   a. Constantin Brâncuşi   1. Symbolist poet; founder of Dadaism
   b. Eugène Ionesco   2. Nobel prize winner for medicine
   c. George Palade   3. Sculptor
   d. Tristan Tzara   4. Absurdist playwright
   ANSWERS: a. 3; b. 4; c. 2; d. 1

◉ TIPS ON DOING BUSINESS IN ROMANIA

- Romanians have reputations as hard bargainers. One useful technique is to delineate the limits of what your negotiators can and cannot do. This should be done at the beginning of a meeting.
- Romanians also have reputations as risk takers. Unpredictability, spontaneity, and boldness are considered part of the Romanian character. So is their sense of humor, which includes a fine appreciation of the absurd.
- Filing paperwork at Romanian government offices can try the patience of a saint. It may involve waiting in line at a half-dozen offices.

◉ COUNTRY BACKGROUND

History

Modern Romania can be dated to 1861, when the principalities of Moldavia and Wallachia were freed from the control of the Ottoman Empire and united as the Romanian nation.

Despite having a Prussian king, Romania did not join the Central Powers at the outbreak of the First World War. When the Allies offered Transylvania to Romania, the Romanians joined their side. But without Allied armies on the ground, the Romanians were no match for German and Austrian armies. The Central Powers occupied Romania, while the Romanian government retreated to Moldavia, where the Russians protected them.

Russian protection ended with the Bolshevik Revolution of 1917. Romania surrendered to the Central Powers in May 1918. But the Central Powers soon collapsed. Romania retracted its surrender and occupied both Bessarabia and Transylvania. Romanian troops even briefly occupied the Hungarian capital of Budapest.

The Romania that emerged from the First World War was the largest it had ever been, but it had earned the enmity of all its neighbors. The victorious Allies allowed Romania to keep its winnings, provided that they sign a treaty with Hungary. The Trianon Treaty was signed in 1920.

As the Second World War swept over the Balkans, the Romanian army became involved. They assisted the Austrians and the Italians in the invasion of Yugoslavia. Then, once Hitler invaded the USSR, Romanian troops marched into Ukraine. The Romanians also exterminated the Jews in the Soviet land they occupied.

When the war turned and the Red Army marched into Romania in August of 1944, the Romanians switched sides. The Romanian army fought the Germans with the same fervor they displayed in Ukraine. The Red Army occupied Romania until a Communist government was established.

Gheorghe Gheorghiu-Dej took power in 1953. He deviated from Moscow's orders by encouraging anti-Hungarian and anti-Russian nationalism. These policies were continued by his successor, Nicolae Ceauşescu, who came to power in 1965. Ceauşescu ultimately held dictatorial power over Romania for twenty-four years.

As Moscow's control over the Warsaw Pact nations began to slip, desperate Romanians began to protest against their government. An underground movement, the National Salvation Front, rose up to oppose the regime. A populist uprising in late 1989 overthrew the government. Ceauşescu and his wife were captured, tried, and executed—which was videotaped and subsequently broadcast on television—on Christmas Day, 1989.

After the overthrow of the Ceauşescu regime, an interim government led by the National Salvation Front took control. The National Salvation Front leader, Ion Iliescu, was elected president in May of 1990, despite his Communist background and close ties to the Ceauşescu government. Because former Communist officials remained in charge, some refer to the events of 1989 as "the stolen revolution."

Iliescu remained in power until 1996, when the National Salvation Front lost the elections to an opposition group, the Democratic Convention of Romania. Their leader, Emil Constantinescu, became president for just four years. In the 2000 elections, Ion Iliescu's party gained a majority and he returned to the presidency.

Romania joined NATO on March 29, 2004, and is scheduled to be admitted to the European Union in 2007.

Type of Government

Romania is now a multiparty republic with two legislative bodies: the Romanian Senate and the Assembly of Deputies. The president is the chief of state. The prime minister is the head of the government.

Previously one of the poorer countries in Europe, Romania's efforts toward improving their economy is generating positive results.

For current government data, check with the Embassy of Romania at *www.roembus.org*.

Language

The official language of Romania is Romanian. Romanian is mutually intelligible with Moldavian; many consider the two to be dialects of the same language.

Romanian is derived from Latin, and it is in the same linguistic family as Italian, French, Spanish, and Portuguese.

While French had been the most popular foreign language in Romania for decades, English has recently supplanted it. Many young Romanians study English and attend English-speaking universities.

The Romanian View

Some 87 percent of the population belongs to the Romanian Orthodox Church. The remainder of the population is Protestant, Roman Catholic, Greek Orthodox, Jewish, Islamic, or atheist.

Romanians consider themselves to be descended from the native Dacians and the Roman legions who conquered them in A.D. 101. Of course, this original population has been influenced by some 1,650 years of subsequent conquest and migration by many other peoples.

Foreigners have often commented on the fierce intensity of Romanians. They are fearless soldiers.

In Orthodox churches and at funerals, Romanians sometimes display a religious fervor that sedate—or repressed—foreigners find frightening. And in business, Romanians attack obstacles with a will—particularly when their path is clear.

Romania is subject to occasional serious earthquakes, which may contribute to the Romanian mindset that they are not in control of their destiny.

☑ Know Before You Go

The greatest hazard for visitors to Romania is probably nonviolent crime, such as pick-pocketing. Visitors also complain about being gouged by taxi drivers, who often drive without meters or with nonoperational meters. Violent crime seems to be on the rise, ranging from simple muggings to sophisticated confidence schemes in which a criminal impersonates a law officer.

Romania is the second largest nation in Eastern Europe (after Poland). Consequently, it has a wide variety of terrain and climate. These include mountains and coastlines, each of which present different hazards. Romania is subject to occasional earthquakes, floods, and mudslides. Romania's prevailing weather patterns flow through Ukraine and Russia, yielding hot summers and cold winters.

While public transportation in Romania is in good repair, the roads are not—especially in rural areas. Travelers on rural roads at night should be especially careful of pedestrians, bicyclists, and horse-drawn carts—none of which will probably be carrying lights. Also, be aware that Romanian traffic laws are very strict. Romanian police may confiscate your driver's license for infractions, even if it was issued in your home country.

As in other former Warsaw Pact nations, little thought was given to the environment in the past fifty years. There is severe industrial and chemical pollution in parts of Romania. And Romania's first nuclear power plant was built on the country's most active earthquake zone.

There is a high degree of computer competence in Romania. Cybercrime is a growing problem, especially for foreign companies (which are the most frequent targets). Typical cybercrimes include: Internet fraud, credit card fraud, auction site fraud, and hacking or extortion schemes.

▶ CULTURAL ORIENTATION

Cognitive Styles: How Romanians Organize and Process Information

The people in Romania have always been independent (even under Communist rule) and open to outside information. Their basic education fosters associative thinking, but most of them are now processing information conceptually and analytically. They are also returning to personal involvement in situations rather than following the rules of a party line.

Negotiation Strategies: What Romanians Accept as Evidence

The more educated the participants are, the more they will use objective facts to define the truth. Subjective feelings are still strong, but faith in an ideology, other than freedom, does not cloud the issue of truth.

Value Systems: The Basis for Behavior

The following three sections identify the Value Systems in the predominant culture—their methods of dividing right from wrong, good from evil, and so forth.

Locus of Decision-Making

As the movement toward freedom and privatization advances, it puts the responsibility for decision-making on the shoulders of the individual. The individual may, in turn, transfer this power to the group as a whole or to selected experts within the group. It is not clear yet who will be the beneficiary of the individuals' decision-making skills: the decision-maker or the people as a whole. It seems that the Romanian tendency is to work for the betterment of the people.

Sources of Anxiety Reduction

Family cohesion is the basic social unit that gives identity and security to the individual. However, this has changed somewhat as more women work outside the home. Romanians are very nationalistic, which has been augmented by the departure of Communist rule. Religion fills some of the need for structure and security.

Issues of Equality/Inequality

A discernible hierarchy of classes has evolved, from the peasant to the bureaucratic elite. Although egalitarianism is favored, some resentment is found among the various ethnic and social groups. Hungarian and German minorities are very distinct, with their own languages, and present potential social and political problems. The ethnic Romanians do not hide their emotions; they tend to express their intentions, feelings, and opinions freely. In marriage both spouses have equal rights, and their roles are not clearly delineated.

▶ BUSINESS PRACTICES

Punctuality, Appointments, and Local Time

- Romanians tend to be very punctual; be on time.
- Appointments should be made well in advance.
- Appointments may be requested by e-mail or mail. Business letters can be sent in English. Not only do Romanians expect to translate foreign correspondence, but such a letter may be accorded more attention than one written in Romanian.
- An interpreter will be necessary for the meeting unless you are positive that you and your Romanian counterpart are fluent in a common language.
- Because more Romanian students now study at English universities than French, English is the most widely spoken foreign language. French is still widely studied as well, and many other languages are heard in various parts of Romania. For example, Hungarian is spoken in Transylvania, and Russian is common near the Romanian-Russian border. Older Romanian business-people tend to speak some German. Major hotels and resorts have English-speaking staff members.
- Official holidays include January 1 and 2, Easter Sunday and Monday, May 1 (Romanian Labor Day), December 1 (National Day) and December 25 and 26. For further holidays of Romania, visit *www.kissboworshakehands.com.*
- Romania is on Central European Time, two hours ahead of Greenwich Mean Time (G.M.T. + 2), or seven hours ahead of U.S. Eastern Standard Time (E.S.T. + 7).

Negotiating

- Patience is necessary for establishing business contacts in Romania; the process can seem glacially slow. However, once the connection is established, one can expect to continue the relationship for a very long time.
- Stay at one of the more prestigious international hotels. Staying elsewhere will diminish your importance in the eyes of Romanians.

- Like many Eastern Europeans who lived under totalitarian regimes, older Romanians learned to communicate obliquely. Even today, they are not accustomed to answering questions directly. Instead, they prefer to respond to questions with long stories that suggest an answer.
- Be prepared to hand out a large number of business cards. Your cards need not be translated into Romanian; a card in English or French is satisfactory. Your title and any advanced degrees should be listed on the card.

Business Entertaining

- Remember that Romania remains one of the poorer countries in Europe. As a foreigner, your hard currency gives you priority access to available goods. You should also bring some gift items with you from home.
- Your Romanian colleagues will do the majority of the entertaining. However, if you wish to reciprocate, begin with an invitation to lunch or dinner at your hotel.
- Romanian business lunches typical last at least two hours and involve the consumption of alcohol. Romania produces excellent wine and plum brandy; these are commonly served drinks.
- Romanians are avid fans of soccer (fútbol). Not only does soccer make an excellent topic of conversation, be aware that everything stops during the World Cup when a Romanian team is in contention.
- Basketball and volleyball run a distant second and third in popularity to soccer. Other sports of interest include any Olympic sports in which Romanians have recently won medals.
- Other good topics include famous Romanians, scenic sights in Romania, and the Romanian language.
- Bad topics of conversation include all the ethnic groups with whom Romanians have fought over the last hundred years—which covers many of their neighbors.

▶ PROTOCOL

Greetings

- Romanians shake hands constantly: when they are introduced, when they leave someone, and every time they meet. No matter how many times they run into each other during the day, they will shake hands each time. Men should wait for a woman to extend her hand first.
- Men may still rise when being introduced to someone; women may remain seated.
- Good friends will greet each other expansively. Romanians may kiss each other on both cheeks. Men may kiss each other.
- At social gatherings, wait for your host to introduce you to everyone there.

Titles/Forms of Address

- The order of names in Romania is the same as in most of Europe: first name followed by surname.
- Historically, only close adult friends and relatives addressed each other by their first names. This may change when working with younger Romanians. Adults address the young by their first names.
- Surnames commonly end in escu or eanu. The escu ending means "son of"—Ionescu means "son of Ion" (Ion is the Romanian version of John). The eanu ending indicates a location—Constantinescu means "from Constantin."
- Always address Romanian professionals by their title (Doctor, Engineer, Professor, and so forth) and surname.

Gestures

- Romanian gestures tend to be expansive, reflecting both Italian and Slavic influences.
- The "fig" gesture—the thumb between the index and middle fingers of a clenched fist—is an insult.

Gifts

- Gift giving is very much a part of business in Romania. Sometimes it can be hard to decide where gift giving becomes bribery.
- While substantial gifts are expected on holidays (such as Christmas) and contract signings, it is also useful to stock up on items such as pens, calculators, or lighters discreetly imprinted with your company name for incidental meetings.
- Items that are produced in your home state or region are of interest. Local artifacts (Native American handicrafts, etc.) or gourmet items may be appropriate. A more significant gift would be an iPod, or whatever advanced portable electronic tool is currently hot.
- If you are invited to dinner at a private home, bring wine, liquor, or have flowers sent ahead. Roses (but not red) are a good choice.
- Romanians have a tradition of hospitality. Indeed, some have called it aggressive hospitality. Romanians typically refuse to allow a guest to leave for hours, and attempt to give all manner of items to the guest.
- If you are staying at a Romanian home, you can try to repay their hospitality by offering to help with some household chores, although your offer will probably be refused. You may be allowed to purchase groceries.

Cultural Note

Despite anticorruption regulations, bribery is still common in Romania. The country has been described as "a nation of brown envelopes," referring to the typical enclosure for a bribe.

Dress

- Casual Western-style dress is common; jeans are everywhere. However, businesspeople are still expected to dress in conservative business apparel. Men wear dark suits except during the summer, when short-sleeved shirts with ties are acceptable; women wear suits and heels. Make sure your shoes are well polished.
- Business wear will generally suffice for formal occasions.

- Shorts are appropriate only for the country or the shore, not the cities.
- Unless specified otherwise, assume that invitations to a Romanian house or restaurant call for the same clothes you wear for business.
- Women should wear a skirt that covers their knees, and have their shoulders covered when entering an Orthodox church. Covering up one's hair is generally not required, but it is wise to carry a scarf just in case.

Russia

Russian Federation
Local short form: Rossiya
Local long form: Rossiyskaya Federatsiya
Former: Russian Empire, Russian Soviet Federative Socialist
Republic

Cultural Note

Russia is developing at an intense pace, absorbing new viewpoints and business styles. In some aspects they have changed their negotiating styles substantially (they rarely lose their tempers and walk out of meetings anymore). However, one crucial characteristic remains the same: they have tremendous patience. Russians prize endurance, which often puts impatient North Americans at a disadvantage.

▶ WHAT'S YOUR CULTURAL IQ?

1. The USSR launched the first artificial satellite in 1957. TRUE or FALSE: The Soviet space program shut down with the breakup of the USSR and has not launched since.
   ANSWER: FALSE. The program is still operational. The Russians run it out of the old USSR launch site in Kazakhstan. Currently, it is supporting the manned international space station Freedom.

2. Which of the following Russian authors have won the Nobel Prize for Literature?
   a. Ivan Bunin
   b. Boris Pasternak
   c. Mikhail Sholokhov
   d. Alexander Solzhenitsyn
   e. All of the above

ANSWER: e. Pasternak, however, was persuaded by the Kremlin not to accept the prize.

3. The Russian Federation has many different ethnic, religious, and linguistic groups—some of whom, like the Chechens, want to be independent of Moscow. TRUE or FALSE? Ethnic Russians are actually a minority within the Russian Federation.
ANSWER: FALSE. Although the Russian Federation is the largest single nation on Earth, its population contains approximately 87 percent ethnic Russians.

▶ TIPS ON DOING BUSINESS IN RUSSIA

- When managing Russian employees, be clear and precise in your communications. Don't try to be subtle and make "suggestions," assuming that Russians will "take the hint." Give concise instructions. Russians accept authority figures; be one.
- If necessity is the mother of invention, Russians are very, very inventive. Historically faced with shortages of funds and equipment, they have learned how to improvise. Do not be surprised to find creative solutions to every type of problem everywhere you look.
- Very little is done in Russia without using *blat*—which is Russian for "connections" or "influence." Blat involves an exchange of favors; when you do something for someone, they now owe you a favor. Gifts—monetary or otherwise—are often part of this exchange.

▶ COUNTRY BACKGROUND

History
The former USSR, also known as the Soviet Union, lasted from 1917 through 1991. Before 1917, most of the territory in the USSR was part of the Russian Empire. The Russian Empire expanded outward from Moscow, the historic capital of the Russian Republic and of the Soviet Union itself. (Czar Peter the Great moved the capital in 1712 from Moscow to Saint Petersburg—Peter's "window on the

West"—but the Communists moved the capital back to Moscow in 1918.)

The authoritarian, one-party rule of the Communists collapsed with surprising speed. Theories for this collapse abound. The precipitating event was the August 1991 coup attempt, when hard-line Communist leaders briefly imprisoned President Mikhail Gorbachev. Faced with resistance on all sides (from Gorbachev, who refused to acknowledge their authority; from President Boris Yeltsin, who became a popular hero for facing down tanks in the streets; and from thousands of Russians who took to the streets in protest), the coup failed in less than a week. The coup attempt ended the careers of the coup leaders (the "gang of eight") and of Gorbachev as well; Gorbachev had appointed the very men who had plotted against him.

In disarray, Moscow was unable to prevent the non-Russian republics from leaving the Soviet Union. The USSR ceased to exist on December 25, 1991. The Russian Soviet Socialist Republic was renamed the Russian Federation, and remains the largest and most powerful of the former republics.

As the hero of the popular uprising against the coup attempt, Boris Yeltsin became the first president of the independent Russian Federation. Initially a strong head of state that encouraged decentralization of power, Yeltsin became increasingly isolated as his health deteriorated. Corruption and favoritism had grown to alarming proportions by the time of his resignation at the end of 1999.

Various regions of the Russian Federation (especially those populated by non-Slavs) agitated for autonomy. The republic of Chechnya, whose population is predominantly Muslim, went further and declared independence. Russian troops invaded Chechnya late in 1994, and virtually destroyed the capital city of Grozny. A pro-Moscow government was eventually installed, but much of the country was never pacified. Chechen terrorists began attacks both inside Chechnya and in other areas of Russia—even in Moscow itself.

Russia's second president, Vladimir Putin, was elected in 2000. He initiated reforms in the economy and the legislature, and cut back military expenditures. He also promised to combat corruption.

His term was marred by more combat in the breakaway region of Chechnya.

In 2004, Muslim terrorists held hostage and slew hundreds of schoolchildren. Following his re-election to the presidency, Putin used this as a justification to consolidate power in his hands, to "protect Russia from terrorism."

Type of Government

The Russian Republic is a federal multiparty republic with a bicameral legislature.

There is an upper house called the Federation Council, and a lower house, the State Duma.

The Russian president is the chief of state. The Russian prime minister is the head of the government.

Although there has been a considerable amount of legal reform (especially as it relates to business), Russian law remains in a state of flux. For years after the breakup of the USSR, multiple authorities tried to impose taxes—so many that taxes sometimes exceeded the gross income of businesses. As it was impossible to pay such a tax burden, most businesses in Russia declined to pay their taxes. In 2004, the administration of President Putin tried to enforce reformed tax legislation; it remains to be seen how successful this effort will be.

For current government data, visit the Embassy of Russia's Web site at *www.russianembassy.org.*

Language

Russian is the official language. The literacy rate is approximately 99 percent. The Web site *www.ethnologue.com* cites 105 languages for Russia, including both European and Asian regions. Of those, 101 are living languages and 4 are extinct.

The Russian View

The Russian Federation is so huge and contains so many ethnic, religious, and linguistic groups that it is impossible to generalize about its citizens. For example, the Russian Federation includes the autonomous republics of Chuvashia and Tatarstan, both of which are populated predominantly by Turkic peoples. However, the Chuvash adopted the Russian Orthodox faith centuries ago. The Tartars (or Tatars), like most Turkic peoples, remain Muslim.

That said, the following information should be considered to apply to the predominant culture of Russia, which is mostly ethnic Russian.

The USSR was officially an atheist nation; religion was suppressed, and some 50 percent of the population considered themselves nonreligious or atheist. Religious worship is now permitted. Many religions are represented in Russia, including Russian Orthodoxy, Protestantism, Islam, and Judaism. Religious participation is increasing.

Periodic hostility exists between officials of the Russian Orthodox Church and religions seen as not native to Russia. This hostility is often directed at the Roman Catholic Church, but can be aimed at missionaries of any religion operating in Russia.

To older Russians who remember the constant shortages and endless lines of the USSR, the plethora of modern consumer goods available today is a source of amazement. But there is also a new generation of Russians who grew up amid this consumer culture; to them, it is normal.

There is substantial dissatisfaction among young Russians today. They face high levels of unemployment, poverty, and drug addiction. Emigration is more common, and the birth rate is low. Russia's population is shrinking.

☑ Know Before You Go

Russia is so large that almost any type of natural disaster can (and does) occur within its borders, including earthquakes, blizzards, floods, and forest fires.

As in other former republics of the USSR, street crime is present.

Russian roads are not in good condition.

While there has been some improvement in the Russian health care system, the U.S. State Department recommends that foreigners who experience medical emergencies in Russia seek medical evacuation for treatment elsewhere.

Although the 1986 Chernobyl nuclear accident occurred in Ukraine, the prevailing winds blew some of the fallout into Russia. However, there are many sources of radioactive and chemical pollution within Russia. Recently, dozens of radioactive hot spots were found around Moscow itself, from badly stored nuclear waste and decades-old experiments.

The incidence of HIV and AIDS is growing rapidly in Russia.

▶ CULTURAL ORIENTATION

Cognitive Styles: How Russians Organize and Process Information

Historically, Russians have not been open to outside information. With the downfall of Communism, many Russians acknowledge that they must learn new ways. But it is a struggle, and they may once again close themselves off from outside information. Their tendency is to process information subjectively and associatively. Some Russians are able to transfer this predilection to the abstract rules of science and technology.

Negotiation Strategies: What Russians Accept as Evidence

Some executives—especially those trained in Western business traditions—will let objective facts dictate the truth. Others will still look to faith in some ideology or their own personal feelings to guide them to the truth.

Value Systems: The Basis for Behavior

Having rejected the values of Communism, Russians are still struggling to master those of a free-market economy and democracy. The following three sections identify the Value Systems in the predominant culture—their methods of dividing right from wrong, good from evil, and so forth.

Locus of Decision-Making

Although the Russians are by nature collectivistic, Communist Party rule put decision-making in the hands of the party. Soviet executives made their decisions in line with party policy; as long as the party rules were followed, the decision could not be wrong. Now these individuals have to make decisions on their own—and take responsibility for those decisions. In many instances, executives are delegating this authority to the group as a whole or to specialists within the group.

The presence of a strong, yet predictable, boss actually works to reduce anxiety in many Russians.

Sources of Anxiety Reduction

The demise of Communism has abolished many of the structures the people depended upon for stability. This stability is now being sought in religion, social groups, the family, or elsewhere. The transition to a free-market economy and democracy will not succeed unless the people can be shown that these changes provide increased security and stability.

Issues of Equality/Inequality

Today, the most obvious area of inequality is ethnicity. Terrorism is associated with Russians from the Caucasus area, so there is suspicion of anyone with darker skin. (People from the Caucasus resemble Mediterraneans more than pale-skinned Slavs.) In Moscow and other predominantly-Slavic areas, dark-complexioned people are frequently stopped on the street by security forces. They also find it difficult to get hired or to rent lodgings.

Despite the Communist premise of gender equality, there had always been a great deal of inequality between the sexes. Russian women are still struggling for equality with men, but more female business leaders are emerging. Despite new legal standards, sexual harassment is still extant in business and government.

Cultural Note

The avoidance of people in power has a long tradition in Russia. Even in modern businesses, employees tend to avoid talking to the boss. They do not even voice complaints to the boss (although they will to everyone else). Often, the first time a Russian boss knows that an employee is unhappy is when that employee resigns.

Western managers who have run businesses in Russia state that it is extraordinarily difficult and time consuming to get feedback from employees. Sometimes, the best solution is to ask the same question in several different ways at different times.

⊙ BUSINESS PRACTICES

Punctuality, Appointments, and Local Time

- Always be punctual, but do not be surprised if the Russians are not on time. It is not unusual for Russians to be fifteen to thirty minutes late.
- Historically, patience, not punctuality, was considered a virtue in Russia.
- Allow plenty of time for each appointment. Not only may they start late, but they may run a bit longer than originally planned.
- Remember that the date is written differently in many countries. In Russia and the CIS, the day is normally listed first, then the month, then the year. (For example, 3.12.10 or 03.12.10 means December 3, 2010, not March 12, 2010.)
- Obtaining an appointment can be laborious. Be patient and persistent. Once your appointment is scheduled, avoid a cancellation.
- Russia's Independence Day (from the Soviet Union) is August 24 (1991), and their National Holiday is Russia Day, June 12.
- Moscow and Saint Petersburg are both in the westernmost time zone, three hours ahead of Greenwich Mean Time (G.M.T + 3), or eight hours ahead of U.S. Eastern Standard Time (E.S.T. + 8).

Negotiating

- It is said that Russians are great "sitters" during negotiations. Traditionally, Russians regard compromise as a sign of weakness. Some even see compromise as morally incorrect. Russians would rather out-sit the other negotiator—and gain more concessions from the other side.
- Be certain that all members of your negotiating team know and agree on exactly what you want out of the deal. Write this down (perhaps adding a few "nice to haves" that can be given away later) and bring it with you. Do not show the Russians anything other than unity among your team.
- Be factual and include all levels of technical detail.

- "Final offers" are never final during initial negotiations. Be prepared to wait; the offer may be made more attractive if you can
  hold out.
- Until you have a signed, formal agreement, do not get overconfident about the deal at hand. And never expect that you can renegotiate later for a better deal. This contract is as advantageous as
  you will ever get.
- The Russians may request that some funds be paid to them directly
  in cash, or to an account in a foreign bank. This may be because of
  their historic concern over the oppressive Russian tax system and the
  rarity of being paid in cash. Be prepared to propose various options.
- One Russian tactic is to allow (after long negotiations) the foreign
  partner to own 51 percent of a joint venture. However, contracts
  usually require unanimity among the partners for major decisions
  anyway, so 51 percent is not a controlling interest.
- Include a clause requiring the joint venture partners to submit to
  arbitration in a neutral country if they can't come to an agreement.
  Sweden is the most popular choice for third-country arbitration.
- Russian regulations represent the biggest liability to a successful
  joint venture. These regulations are in constant flux (reforms are
  being made all the time), so don't count on your Russian partner
  to have a full grasp of the legal issues involved. Get your own
  expert in Russian law. Don't be surprised when something you
  did yesterday is disallowed tomorrow; some laws are nebulous,
  and their interpretation is subject to change.
- Appearances can be deceiving. Russian firms may look prosperous
  and full of potential. Select a partner based upon full knowledge
  of the assets it owns or controls.
- Since it is not customary for Russians to disclose their home
  phone, or other personal telephone numbers, no official residen-
  tial phone books are issued at all. However, various directories are
  produced, and many of them are accessible free on the Internet.
- Be sure to take enough business cards and expect to hand them
  out often. Russian businessmen usually now have business cards
  as well, and will exchange them freely.

- In many countries—such as Japan—people tend to respond to a question by saying "yes." In the USSR, the tendency used to be just the opposite; managers and bureaucrats said "no" at every opportunity. However, Russian executives now often say yes to proposals—even if they lack the authority to do so. They make promises in order to buy time, and expand the contacts they want with foreigners.

- Historically, there were many reasons why Russians said no to business proposals. One was that innovation was traditionally discouraged. Also, Russians were afraid that if they gave the go-ahead and a project failed, they would be held responsible. Another reason had to do with the position of an individual in a rigid, hierarchical bureaucracy. You rarely met a Russian bureaucrat who had the power to push a project forward without the agreement of others. But one individual could cancel a project, all by himself or herself. Often, the ability to say no was the only real power many bureaucrats possessed; not surprisingly, they used it frequently.

- Peace, international relations, the changes in Russia, and difficult economic situations are all common topics of conversation. People will ask what you think of Russia and what life is like in your home country.

Business Entertaining

- Always have a good supply of soft drinks, tea, coffee (not in plastic cups!), Danish, cookies, snacks, and so forth, on the meeting table. Russians try hard to provide a variety of refreshments when conducting business, and appreciate your reciprocating in kind.

- Russian hotels and restaurants may still have doormen who seem less than gracious. This is probably because doormen often double as security guards. Do not try to engage them in conversation.

- Russian restaurants have improved over the last decade. Menus generally reflect the available fare, and service is faster.

- Dinner generally begins around 7 P.M., because most offices close around 6 P.M.

- Quite often, Russians will state the time in a simple military format, so if you say "Meet me at 7 o'clock," they will assume that is

7:00 A.M. If you mean 7:00 P.M., specify nineteen o'clock, or nine-teen hundred. Just try to avoid sounding artificially militaristic; Russians do not say "zero seven hundred" for 7:00 A.M.

- Russians are very confident of their ability to drink heavily and still remain "clear." They may prefer to conduct business when you are drunk.
- It is a great honor to be invited to a Russian home. It may also be a great burden for the host. Russian tradition demands that you be served a lunch or dinner that far exceeds everyone's appetite and, sometimes, the financial capabilities of the hosts. For example, caviar might be served with huge spoons.
- It is good to know a few toasts. The most common is *Na zdorovye* (pronounced "Nah-zda-ROE-vee-ah"), which means "To your health."
- In a restaurant or nightclub, Russians may invite you to dance or to come over to their table. Accept graciously.

⊙ PROTOCOL

Greetings
- Russians only display affection in public during greetings. Relatives and good friends will engage in a noisy embrace and kiss each other on the cheeks.
- Except at formal or state occasions, Russians usually greet a stranger by shaking hands and stating their name, rather than uttering a polite phrase (such as "How do you do?"). Respond in the same way.

Titles/Forms of Address
- Russian names are listed in the same order as in the West, but the Russian middle name is a patronymic (a name derived from the first name of one's father). Thus, Fyodor Nikolaievich Medvedev's first name is Fyodor (a Russian version of Theodore), his last name is Medvedev, and his middle name means "son of Nikolai."
- Russian women add the letter a to the end of their surnames; Medvedev's wife would be Mrs. Medvedeva.

- Unless invited to do so, do not use first names. If a Russian has a professional title, use the title followed by the surname. If he or she has no title, use "Mr.," "Miss," "Mrs.," or "Ms.," plus the surname.
- Among themselves, Russians use a bewildering variety of diminutives and nicknames. They also address each other by first name and patronymic, which can be quite a mouthful. As you establish a relationship with them, you will be invited to call them by one of these. This is the time to invite them to call you by your first name.
- There are relatively few variations of first names and surnames in Russia. Some names (e.g., Ivan Ivanovich Ivanov) are so common that you will need additional information to identify the correct person. In official circles, Russians may use a person's birth date to differentiate between identically named individuals.

Gestures
- Russian is a language abundant in curses, and there are quite a number of obscene gestures as well. Both the American "okay" sign (thumb and forefinger touching in a circle) and any shaken-fist gesture will be interpreted as vulgar.
- Whistling is not taken as a sign of approval in a concert hall; it means you did not like the performance.
- The "thumbs-up" gesture indicates approval among Russians.
- You may encounter some superstitious behaviors if you are invited into a Russian's home. These include sitting for a minute before leaving a home, or knocking three times on wood to avoid bad luck.

Gifts
- Muscovites now have access to much of the same products as Manhattanites, and as a result it is more difficult to select a good gift for your Russian counterparts.
- Presents that represent your hometown or country are appropriate. Russians still identify cigarettes and rare Zippo lighters with the USA, so they may be appreciated. Currently popular electronic gadgets like digital cameras, MP3, DVD or CD players, high-quality pens, illustrated books of your homeland, or well-reviewed, sophisticated books are other good gifts.

- Take flowers, liquor, or a gourmet food item if invited to a Russian home.
- Feasting is also a part of religious holidays. Remember that the Russian Orthodox Church follows the Julian calendar, not the Gregorian calendar in official use throughout the Western world. Currently, the Julian calendar runs approximately thirteen days behind the Gregorian one.

Dress
- If you go to Russia during the winter, bring very warm clothes or buy Russian-style hats and gloves upon arrival. In addition, bring a pair of shoes or boots with skid-resistant soles.
- Russian buildings are usually well heated, so a layered approach is best.
- Business dress is conservative. Russians generally prefer European styles more than American. Business visitors should always appear in refined, well-cut clothes.
- While shorts are frowned upon for casualwear, you will note that Russians strip down to as little as possible on those rare days when it is sunny enough to sunbathe.

Cultural Note
Be cautious of using credit cards and ATM cards in Russia. Russia has many underemployed computer experts, some of which engage in such cybercrimes as capturing credit card numbers.

Slovak Republic

Slovakia
Local long form: Slovenska Republika
Local short form: Slovensko

Cultural Note

First and foremost, understand which country is represented by the name "Slovakia." Slovakia was the eastern half (more or less) of Czechoslovakia, which split apart peacefully on the first of January, 1993. Slovenia was one of the constituent republics within Yugoslavia, which seceded from Yugoslavia in 1991. The breakup of Yugoslavia was accompanied by the greatest violence Europe has seen since the Second World War, although Slovenia's secession from Yugoslavia was relatively bloodless.

▶ WHAT'S YOUR CULTURAL IQ?

1. Czechoslovakia split into two separate nations in 1993. TRUE or FALSE? At the time of the "Velvet Divorce," the independence movement did not have the support of the majority of the Slovak people.
   ANSWER: TRUE. But today most Slovaks are content with the breakup.

2. Slovaks like to claim the figurine known as the Venus of Monoravy as part of their artistic heritage. However, it dates from a time before the ancestors of the Slovaks arrived in Central Europe. TRUE or FALSE: The Venus of Monoravy dates back to the Roman Empire.
   ANSWER: FALSE. The Venus of Monoravy is of Paleolithic origin, predating both the Slovaks and the Romans by many thousands of years.

3. Match the following twentieth-century Slovakian artists with
   their primary art form:
   a. Dušan Jurkovic   1. Poetry
   b. Ivan Krasko   2. Cubist painting
   c. Ester Simerová-Martinceková   3. Architecture
   ANSWERS: a. 3; b. 1; c. 2

▶ TIPS ON DOING BUSINESS IN THE SLOVAK REPUBLIC

- When the Slovak and Czech Republics were merged into Czechoslovakia, the Slovaks often viewed Czech businesspeople as
  avaricious and untrustworthy. These sentiments are sometimes
  extended to all foreign businesspeople. Do not be surprised if you
  have to earn the trust of Slovaks.
- Whatever you drink in the Slovak Republic, don't drive afterward.
  The Slovaks have a zero-tolerance policy; it is illegal to drive with
  any percentage of alcohol in the blood. Your driver's license can
  be confiscated on the spot if even a trace of alcohol is found in
  your system.
- After a slow start, Slovakia has embraced free-market reforms. In fact,
  they have adopted business-friendly taxation faster than any other
  EU country. In 2003, Slovakia became the first EU nation to adopt a
  flat tax of 19 percent for all personal, corporate, and sales taxes.

▶ COUNTRY BACKGROUND

History

Czechoslovakia represented the westernmost migration of Slavic
tribes into Europe. During the fifth century A.D., these tribes arrived
in what would eventually become the Slovak and Czech Republics.
Two distinct Slavic groups emerged: the Czechs, who settled in the
west, and the Slovaks, who took the east.

By A.D. 900, the Slovak tribes were conquered by the Magyars
(Hungarians), who formed the short-lived Great Moravian empire.
The Slovaks spent the next 1,000 years under the control of the Hun-
garians and (eventually) their overlords, the Austrians.

The Austrians allowed the Hungarians to control Slovakia, which was deliberately kept agricultural and undeveloped. Ambitious Slovaks learned Magyar (the language of Hungary), but were granted no voice in their rule. The Czech lands were ruled directly by Vienna and developed differently, becoming highly industrialized.

After its defeat in World War I, the Austro-Hungarian Empire was broken up into smaller states. The Slovenes and the Czechs found themselves lumped together in the newly independent state of Czechoslovakia. The aggressive, educated, and more numerous Czechs quickly took charge, and the Slovenes felt excluded from their own government. The existence of other minorities within the Czechoslovakian borders, notably the ethnic Germans in the Sudetenland, also caused friction. Nevertheless, Czechoslovakia managed to remain a democracy until it was overrun by Nazi Germany in 1938–1939.

The Germans set up a puppet Slovakian state from 1939 to 1945. While nominally ruled by the Catholic Monsignor Jozef Tiso, it was very much under German control. Tiso's "parish republic" is important because it was the first state ruled by Slovaks for Slovaks, but it lacked civil liberties and oppressed minorities. Monsignor Tiso was executed as a war criminal in 1947. His place in history is ambiguous; most Czechs hate him, while many Slovaks have mixed feelings about him.

Liberated by the Red Army in 1945, Czechoslovakia became a Soviet satellite. Despite repressive measures, the Communist leadership in Prague was unable to keep protests from periodically erupting, notably in 1968 and 1977. The Warsaw Pact invasion that put down the 1968 "Prague Spring" embittered the Czechoslovaks against everything to do with the USSR, including the Russian language (the mandatory foreign language taught in schools). Finally, the tide of reform that washed over Eastern Europe in 1989 allowed the Czechoslovak people to elect a truly popular, non-Communist government. Dissident writer Václav Havel was elected the country's president.

In 1992, the country broke into two separate countries—the Czech and Slovak Republics. Few Czechs voted for separation. Only a minority of Slovaks actively supported independence, leading many to accuse nationalist leaders like Vladimir Meciar of fomenting nationalist sentiment in an effort to gain power.

As an independent state, the new Slovak Republic came into being on January 1, 1993. It joined NATO in 1999 and the European Union in 2004.

Type of Government

The Slovak Republic is a multiparty parliamentary democracy. The president is the chief of state—a largely ceremonial office. The prime minister is the head of the government. There are two legislative houses, an upper Senate and a lower Chamber of Deputies.

For current government data, check with the Embassy of the Slovak Republic at *www.slovakembassy-us.org*.

Language

The official language is Slovak, which is a West Slavic language related to Polish. Although the Slovaks and the Czechs have gone to great lengths to differentiate their languages, the Slovak and Czech languages are actually quite similar and are mutually intelligible.

While Slovak is considered a difficult language for English speakers to master, it is one of the easiest languages for speakers of Slavic languages to learn. Slovak is written in the Latin alphabet (with diacritical marks); its pronunciation includes several sounds that are not present in English.

The Slovak View

There is no official religion in the Slovak Republic. Religion was actively discouraged under the former Communist regime, but the Catholic Church has always remained influential.

Many Slovaks identify themselves as Roman Catholics, but most other religions are represented.

Avoidance of violence is an important part of Slovak philosophy. Slovaks are proud of the way they endured two wrenching changes without violence: the 1989 Velvet Revolution in which the Communist regime gave way to democracy, and the peaceful separation of Czechoslovakia into the separate Czech and Slovak Republics in 1993.

Egalitarianism is also a hallmark of Slovakian attitudes. Nevertheless, Slovakia has difficulties with its ethnic minorities.

Slovaks tend toward modesty and informality. Ostentation is seen only on old buildings from the days of the Austro-Hungarian Empire. However, some younger Slovaks are adopting a more opulent style, at least in matters of dress.

Slovakia, of course, is a new country, dating only from 1993. For the first five years of its existence, its nationalist government rejected market reforms and closer ties with Western Europe. After a change of government in 1998, Slovakia embraced the free market and joined both the EU and NATO. The populace is well educated, with a 99 percent literacy rate.

☑ Know Before You Go

Vehicular accidents are probably the greatest hazard to travelers to the Slovak Republic. Before independence, most of the good roads were built in the Czech part of Czechoslovakia. The Slovak Republic's road network is insufficient but is currently undergoing repair and expansion. In addition, Slovaks tend to be erratic drivers.

There is also a substantial amount of petty crime, mostly pickpocketing.

Tobacco smoke is also omnipresent. Slovaks even smoke in places meant primarily for children, such as ice cream parlors. This adds to the heavy pollution in many Slovak cities.

While bribery is not omnipresent, the Slovak police have a reputation for needlessly stopping foreign drivers, then accepting small bribes in lieu of a ticket.

⊙ CULTURAL ORIENTATION

Cognitive Styles: How Slovaks Organize and Process Information

Slovaks tend to be open to information on most issues. They are generally more analytic than associative, but they value relationships more than obedience to abstract rules of behavior.

Negotiation Strategies: What Slovaks Accept as Evidence

Typically, Slovaks find truth through a mixture of subjective feelings and objective facts. Their faith in the ideologies of humanitarianism and democracy influence the truth in most situations. However, Slovak history—especially the domination of Slovaks by outsiders—yields a strong strain of pessimism.

Value Systems: The Basis for Behavior

The amicable separation of Czechoslovakia into the Czech and Slovak Republic is an example of the humanitarian value systems of both cultures. The following three sections identify the Value Systems in the predominant culture—their methods of dividing right from wrong, good from evil, and so forth.

Locus of Decision-Making

The responsibility for decision-making rests on the shoulders of the individual. Individualism has always been encouraged, and individual achievement is more important than family in determining status. Slovaks feel that they have a right to a private life; their friends are few and specific to their needs. In general, Slovaks feel that the same values should apply to all members of their culture.

Sources of Anxiety Reduction

With the demise of Communist rule, the guarantee of full employment ended. This produces considerable day-to-day anxiety, and current surveys indicate that Slovaks are among the most insecure citizens in the European Union. Although the traditional role of the family as the basic educational and socialization unit has been weakened, the family unit is still recognized as a stabilizing force. The Roman Catholic Church seems to be regaining some influence on family life and social structure, and bringing more security for both the individual and the family.

Issues of Equality/Inequality

There is a moderately strong competition for status within the Slovak Republic. When individuals are recognized for their accomplishments, they gain prominence among equals. The desire for power may undercut the humanitarian need for equality. This drive for power can yield strong, hierarchical structures in government, business, and society.

The husband is the titular head of the home. However, since most women work outside the home, husbands take some responsibility for raising the children.

Although women have legal equality with men, sexual harassment is still widespread in the workplace. Also, older Slovak women often find difficulty getting or maintaining employment.

Cultural Note

Slovak women are well represented among administrative and managerial positions; the United Nations records that 60 percent of people in this category are female in the Slovak Republic. This percentage is high but not unusual in former Communist countries, where such jobs were neither prestigious nor highly lucrative. And, when all types of jobs are considered, fewer women are employed in the Slovak Republic than in most European Union countries.

▶ BUSINESS PRACTICES

Punctuality, Appointments, and Local Time

- Punctuality is important; be on time for business and social engagements.
- Slovaks, like most Europeans, write the day first, then the month, then the year (e.g. December 3, 2010, is written 3.12.10 or 3/12/10).
- For many years, Russian was the foreign language most frequently studied in schools. Since the Velvet Revolution of 1989, Western languages like English and German have become the most popular. English speakers should expect to hire a translator, especially if their destination is outside of Bratislava itself.
- Appointments should be made well in advance. Allow two weeks' notice for an appointment made by telephone or e-mail.

- Business letters may be written in English, although your counterpart will be favorably impressed if you take the trouble to translate the letter into Slovak.
- As the business day begins early and ends in mid-afternoon, expect to schedule your appointments between 9:00 A.M. and 12:00 noon or between 1:00 and 3:00 P.M.
- Most Slovaks receive four weeks of vacation per year. The traditional vacation time runs from mid-July to mid-August, so do not expect to be able to conduct business during this period.
- The Slovak Republic is one hour ahead of Greenwich Mean Time (G.M.T. + 1), or six hours ahead of U.S. Eastern Standard Time (E.S.T. + 6).

Negotiating
- Expect the decision-making process to operate at a fairly slow pace. Slovaks do not necessarily believe that "time is money."
- Many Slovaks have adopted the German propensity for slow, methodical planning. Every aspect of the deal you propose will be pored over by many executives. Do not anticipate being able to speed up this process.
- Some entrepreneurs will move more quickly. However, you should be cautious with partnerships, since you will probably be the one putting hard currency into the enterprise.
- Expect Slovaks to take a lot of time to establish a close business relationship. They have often been mistreated by foreigners, so do not be surprised if they are initially suspicious of you.
- Executives usually understand enough English to decipher a business card, so it is not necessary to have a card in English translated. However, it is preferable to have promotional materials and instruction manuals translated into Slovak.
- If your company has been around for many years, the date of its founding should be on your card. Education is highly respected, so include any degree above the bachelor's level as well.
- Slovaks typically converse for a while; do not expect to get down to business too quickly. Expect to be asked about your flight, your

accommodations, where you are from, your impressions of the country, and so forth.

- Your counterparts may not mind asking or being asked personal questions. You may reciprocate by inquiring about an executive's family. Part of establishing a relationship is expressing an interest in each other's family, although it may be a long time before you actually meet any of them.

- Slovaks tend to be well informed about politics and to have firm political opinions. They are also honest, and may freely offer their viewpoints. While they dislike what Communism has done to their country, they do not always approve of the West, or the EU either.

- Sports are a good topic for conversation; football (soccer), ice hockey, tennis, hiking, and cycling are popular sports. Music is a good topic as well.

- While the Slovaks drink less beer than the Czechs, fine beer is appreciated. A Slovak beer drinker will be happy to explain about good beer—and will no doubt explain that many foreign beers use hops grown in the Slovak Republic.

- Coffee is usually served during meetings. Taste it before you add sugar; it may already be sweetened. The coffee is Turkish, and may have grounds at the bottom.

Business Entertaining
- Historically, business meetings have been confined to offices. Business lunches were rare; the only meal one shared with a business associate was a celebratory dinner. However, this segregation was due in part to restrictive government regulations—fraternization with westerners was discouraged. Slovaks are now more accustomed to Western business practices, including business lunches.

- At a lunch, business may be discussed before and (sometimes) after the meal, but rarely during the meal itself. If you are invited out to a luncheon, you may offer to pay, but expect your host to decline your offer. Insist on paying only when you have made the invitation.

- Restaurants tend to be very busy. Always make a reservation. It may be easier to ask your counterpart to choose a restaurant; just be sure to explain that you intend to pay for the meal.
- Slovaks do not often entertain business associates in their homes. If you are invited into a home, consider it an honor. Do not be surprised if the living quarters are crowded. You may be asked to remove your shoes when you enter a private home.
- A host will invite you to eat additional portions. It is traditional to turn down the first invitation.
- When eating, always use utensils; very few items are eaten with the hands. Place your utensils together on one side of the plate when you have finished. If you just wish to pause between courses, cross your utensils on the plate.

Cultural Note

At formal Slovak introductions, the younger person is always introduced to the older person (or the lower-ranking person to the superior). The older person offers his or her hand first. Traditionally, Slovaks gave their last name first in such introductions, although they might not do so with a foreigner. If you are confused about which is the first name and which is the surname, be sure to ask.

▶ PROTOCOL

Greetings
- In both business and social situations, always shake hands, firmly but briefly, upon arriving and departing from any meeting. When introduced to a Slovak woman or an elderly person, wait to see if he or she extends a hand before offering to shake.
- When several people are being introduced, take turns shaking hands. It is impolite to reach over someone else's handshake.
- Never keep your left hand in your pocket while shaking hands with your right.
- In formal situations, it is better to be introduced by a third person than to introduce yourself. However, in informal situations, it is appropriate to introduce yourself.

Titles/Forms of Address

- The order of names is the same as in most of Europe: first name followed by a surname.
- Traditionally, only family members and close friends addressed each other by their first names. While young people use first names more frequently, most businesspeople you meet will still prefer to be called by their title or surname.
- When speaking to persons who do not have professional titles, use "Mr.," "Mrs.," or "Miss" and the surname:
  - *Mr. = Pán (pronounced "Pahn")*
  - *Mrs. (or Ms.) = Pani ("PAH-nee")*
  - *Miss = Slecna ("SLEH-chnah")*
- It is important to use professional titles. Attorneys, architects, engineers, and other professionals will expect you to address them as "Pán" or "Pani" plus their title. This goes for anyone with a Ph.D. as well.

Gestures

- To get someone's attention, raise your hand, palm facing out, with only the index finger extended. Avoid waving or beckoning.
- When sitting, cross one knee over the other, rather than resting your ankle on the other knee. Do not prop your feet on anything other than a footstool.
- The eldest or highest-ranking person enters a room first. If their age and status are the same, men enter before women.
- Do not talk to someone with your hands in your pockets or while chewing gum.

Gifts

- Under the Communist regime, frequent shortages made gift giving simple: you gave whatever was in short supply in Czechoslovakia. Now that consumer items are freely available (albeit somewhat expensive), gift giving is more challenging.
- By and large, businessmen do not give or expect to receive expensive gifts. A gift should be of good quality, but not exorbitant.

- Appropriate gifts include small electronics such as MP3 players or calculators, fine-quality pens, cigarette lighters, and imported wine or liquor, especially Scotch, bourbon or cognac.
- When invited to dinner at a Slovak home, send a bouquet of unwrapped flowers ahead for your hostess. The bouquet should have an uneven number of flowers, but not thirteen. Red roses are reserved for romantic situations, and calla lilies are for funerals.

Dress
- Slovak clothing is modest and unassuming; whether in business or casualwear. Ostentation is looked at askance, as are bright clothing and loud patterns.
- Generally, businessmen wear dark suits, ties, and white shirts. Businesswomen also dress conservatively, in dark suits, dresses, or sometimes, pantsuits.
- Follow the lead of your colleagues with regard to removing your jacket or tie in hot weather.
- There are many social events in the Slovak Republic, and Slovaks like to dress up for them. However, business wear can be appropriate for most formal social events: parties, dinners, and the theater.
- Casualwear is essentially the same as in the United States. Jeans are ubiquitous, but they should not be worn, torn, or dirty.

Spain

Kingdom of Spain
Local short form: Espana

Cultural Note

Spain suffered through a horrendous civil war from 1936 to 1939. Over 350,000 Spaniards were killed.

▶ WHAT'S YOUR CULTURAL IQ?

1. The year 1492 was highly significant for Spain. Which of the following events did not occur in that year?
   a. The Spanish recaptured all of the Iberian Peninsula from the North African Islamic invaders.
   b. Spanish Jews were required to convert to Catholicism or leave Spain.
   c. The Spanish and Portuguese thrones were effectively united.
   d. Columbus reached the Americas.
   ANSWER: c. This occurred earlier, in 1479. The countries remained technically separate but were ruled in concert until 1504.

2. The modern Spanish flag consists of two horizontal red stripes flanking a center yellow band. TRUE or FALSE: The design allegedly dates back to a French king wiping his bloodstained hands on a Spanish nobleman's yellow shield.
   ANSWER: TRUE. The story goes that the colors originated when the ninth-century King Charles I (also known as Charles the Bald) of France wiped his bloodstained hands on the plain yellow leather shield of the Count of Aragon.

3. TRUE or FALSE: The Prado, one of the most famous museums in the world, is located in Toledo.
ANSWER: FALSE. The Prado is in Madrid. Another famous site, the Alhambra, is in Toledo.

▶ TIPS ON DOING BUSINESS IN SPAIN

- Do not try to get too friendly too soon with your Spanish associates, and never underestimate a person based upon a job title.
- As is common in countries where personal relationships are of primary importance, job titles do not reflect the true importance or power of individual executives.
- Spanish businesses tend to be very hierarchical. Departments may be compartmentalized to the extent that personnel are not very familiar with what other divisions are doing. Their part of the decision-making process is to pass their recommendations on to the supervisor.

▶ COUNTRY BACKGROUND

History

Iberians, Celts, and Basques settled Spain. Then, conquering Carthaginians, Romans, Visigoths, and Moors subsequently influenced its development. The seizure of Granada in the fifteenth century by Christians was the culmination of their reconquest of the Iberian Peninsula over the Moors. This united Spain for the first time under a Christian king and marked the beginning of Spanish nationalism. Spain began its acquisition of a colonial empire in 1492.

Over the next few centuries, Spain gained a global network of possessions, then gradually lost them all. The first losses were those non-Iberian possessions inherited by the royal house of Spain: the Netherlands and parts of Italy and Germany. Then came the loss of much of North, Central, and South America. Finally, defeat in the Spanish-American War of 1898 resulted in the loss of Cuba, the Philippines, and Puerto Rico, ending Spain's global ambitions. Spain retained a few African colonies until recent times.

The Spanish civil war lasted from 1936 to 1939 and caused the deaths of more than 350,000 Spaniards. At the end of the war, Francisco Franco became dictator of Spain, and he retained control for nearly four decades.

Franco's long rule was marked by centralization and repression of regional ambitions. One of his most implacable opponents was the underground organization Euskadi Ta Askatasuna (which means "Basque Homeland and Freedom"). ETA is dedicated to achieving independence for the Basque region, by any means necessary. Formed in 1959, ETA first resorted to violence in 1961, when it attempted to derail a train. Their terrorist attacks—usually bombings—continue to this day, although they can no longer claim the support of a majority of Basques.

Franco remained in power until his death in 1975. To ensure political stability, Franco had already designated Prince Juan Carlos as the future king of Spain in 1969.

King Juan Carlos ascended to the throne of Spain in 1975, and soon had to put down an attempted military coup. He rapidly and independently mustered the support of many other parts of the military, allowing Spain to remain under civilian rule. In 1977, Spain held its first democratic elections in four decades. Spain has enjoyed democratic elections ever since, although there was an aborted attempt at a military coup in 1981.

Spain joined NATO in 1982 and the European Economic Community (now known as the European Union) in 1986.

In 1992—the five-hundredth anniversary of Columbus's first voyage—the Summer Olympic Games were held in Barcelona and Expo 92 was held in Seville. Both events were considered successes.

Just before the national elections in March 2004, radical Islamic terrorists bombed rush-hour trains in Madrid. Over 200 people were killed. The incident (and the government's clumsy reaction to it) was enough to upset the election. Aznar was voted out, and José Luis Rodriguez Zapatero of the Socialist Party became prime minister.

Zapatero soon fulfilled his campaign promise to withdraw all Spanish troops from Iraq. This was accomplished by May of 2004.

Type of Government

The Kingdom of Spain is a parliamentary monarchy. The current constitution was written in 1978 and made Spain a constitutional monarchy. The king is the chief of state. Legislative power resides in the Cortes (parliament), consisting of two chambers: the Congress of Deputies and the Senate. Deputies and senators are elected by universal suffrage and serve for four years. The executive branch consists of a prime minister (who is the head of the government), his deputy, and ministers, all of whom are responsible to the Cortes.

Spain is organized into multiple Autonomous Communities; each is granted considerable local control.

Spain continues to request the return of Gibraltar, which has been under British control since 1704.

In May of 2003, Spain lost sixty-two Spanish peacekeepers when their plane crashed in Turkey. They were returning from duty in Afghanistan.

For current government data, check with the Embassy of Spain at *www.spainemb.org.*

Language

Spanish, or Castilian, is the official language nationwide (it is also referred to as español, or castellano). There are other official regional languages: the Basques of the north, the Galicians of the northwest, and the Catalans of the extreme northeast all speak their own languages.

Dialects include Andalusian, Murcian, Aragonese, Navarrese, and a Canary Islands Spanish. Spanish is classified as a member of the Indo-European linguistic group: it is a Romance tongue. Worldwide, Spanish is one of the most commonly spoken languages, with an estimated 350 million speakers.

The Spanish View

Although Spain is an overwhelmingly Catholic country, Spain has no official religion. Approximately 94 percent of Spaniards practice Catholicism to some extent. Spaniards are known to have a deep religious sensibility—they appreciate the stability and structure of the

Catholic Church, and may have a profound mystical connection to their faith.

Every Spaniard, religious or not, is familiar with the basic precepts of Catholicism.

Spaniards observe many Catholic holidays and rituals. Besides the elaborate Semana Santa (Holy Week) processionals during the week that precedes Easter in many cities, there is a famous pilgrimage to Santiago de Compostela. Santiago is Spanish for "St. James," and the apostle's tomb is believed to be located under the church. During the Middle Ages, the relics made Santiago de Compostela the most important city of pilgrimage after Jerusalem and Rome. The saint's relics are still credited with miracles.

Many Spaniards are highly independent, but rely heavily on the support of their families. Work will rarely be a Spaniard's first or second priority in life.

☑ Know Before You Go

The explosions on commuter trains in Madrid killed over 200 people in March of 2004. Responsibility for the terrorist bombings was initially placed upon the Basque separatist group Eta, but subsequently the investigation pointed to Al Qaeda.

However, political tension continues in the northern Basque region, and Eta is suspected in other bomb blasts. Foreign executives are not at any particular risk.

Driving can be hazardous in Spain. Traffic is unpredictable, and drivers can be very aggressive.

There is a problem with air pollution, and smoking is still extremely common.

⊚ CULTURAL ORIENTATION

Cognitive Styles: How Spaniards Organize and Process Information

The culture of Spain was released with the fashioning of a working democracy. Spaniards are open to information on all issues but do not change their attitudes easily. Most information is processed associatively and subjectively. Spaniards' personal involvement with issues makes it difficult for them to use more abstract rules and laws to solve their problems.

Negotiation Strategies: What Spaniards Accept as Evidence

One's subjective feelings on an issue are the ultimate source of truth. However, faith in the ideologies of the church or nationalism may help to formulate this truth. Objective facts may be used to prove a point, but they are rarely the sole source of evidence.

Value Systems: The Basis for Behavior

The philosophy that all people are equal because each person is unique is a fundamental Spanish principle. Therefore, one must get to know each person as an individual. The following three sections identify the Value Systems in the predominant culture—their methods of dividing right from wrong, good from evil, and so forth.

Locus of Decision-Making

Individuals shoulder responsibility for their own decisions, but the best interests of the family or group are always kept in mind. Self-identity is obtained from the family, and one's position in society. Relationships (both kinships and friendships) are generally as important as one's expertise in obtaining a job. The elite at the top of the social scale are a privileged minority with substantial control over economic resources.

Sources of Anxiety Reduction

Although the Catholic Church has lost most of its direct influence, the more educated a person is, the more likely he or she is to be a practicing Catholic. The Church's teachings are basic to most of the population and are a source of structure, stability, and security. The extended family is being replaced by the nuclear family as a source of security. There is a strong belief in nationalism.

Issues of Equality/Inequality

Society is differentiated along class, occupational, and professional lines, with an expanding middle class and a decreasing proportion of rural poor. Changes in the system were made by revolutions or military coups in the past, but now the democratic form of government seems to be well in place. Machismo is still very strong. However, women figure more prominently in education, politics, and the work force. Women have complete equality with men before the law.

▶ BUSINESS PRACTICES

Punctuality, Appointments, and Local Time

- While you should be on time for all business appointments, Spaniards are not always punctual. Be prepared to wait, and never take offense at your Spanish associates' late arrival.
- Social events rarely begin at the scheduled time. Try to ask what time you are really expected to arrive; it is likely to be from fifteen to thirty minutes after the scheduled time.
- Spaniards, like many Europeans, write the day first, then the month, then the year (e.g. December 3, 2010, is written 3.12.10 or 3/12/10).
- Always make business appointments well in advance, and confirm them by phone and/or e-mail just before your arrival.
- The work week is generally forty hours in Spain, but hours of operation may vary.
- If a holiday falls on a Thursday or Tuesday, many people take a four-day weekend. Most Spaniards have thirty days paid vacation per year and usually take them in July or August. Also avoid scheduling appointments around Easter or Christmas.
- Some Spaniards like to go home for lunch, so do not be surprised if your invitation is politely declined.
- Conducting business over lunch can be problematic; wait for your Spanish counterpart to begin the discussion. It will probably be at the very end of the meal—over coffee.
- Do not schedule breakfast meetings before 8:30 A.M.
- Spain is one hour ahead of Greenwich Mean Time (G.M.T. + 1), or six hours ahead of U.S. Eastern Standard Time (E.S.T. + 6).

Negotiating

- Personal contacts are essential for business success in Spain. Select your Spanish representatives with great care, because once a representative is associated with you, it is very difficult to switch to another person.

- To the Spanish, information is considered a valuable commodity. For this reason, they may not be anxious to share useful facts with you, no matter how encouraging they may seem.
- Be warm and personal during your negotiations yet retain your dignity, courtesy, and diplomacy. Your Spanish counterparts may initially seem restrained and indirect, but this is normal until your relationship has been established.
- Do not expect to discuss business at the start of any meeting.
- Politics, sports, and travel are good topics of conversation. Avoid discussions of religion.
- Bullfighting is considered an art, and should not be judged on any but Spanish terms; derogatory remarks about bullfighting are inappropriate.
- The Spanish give advice to one another and to foreigners freely; don't be offended by this.
- Have business cards printed with English on one side and Spanish on the other. Present your card with the Spanish side facing your Spanish colleague.
- Expect protracted negotiations, and be prepared to renegotiate topics that already seemed to have been resolved.

Cultural Note

Spaniards are known for their pride and personal sense of honor. However, international visitors are sometimes surprised that business acumen and expertise are not always highly regarded in Spain. (As with the upper class English, to call someone "clever" in Spain is a veiled insult.) Spaniards often take more pride in personal characteristics than in business skills.

Business Entertaining

- Always invite Spanish clients to excellent restaurants; many Spaniards are highly conversant about gourmet food and vintage wines.
- If a prospect or client accepts your invitation to lunch, remember to keep the discussion on a social level at least until coffee is served following the meal.

- At around 5:00 or 6:00 P.M., many Spaniards go out for hors d'oeuvres, called "tapas." These tapas are eaten at a series of bars or cafés (also called tabernas or mesónes) and can vary from salted almonds and olives to octopus and potato omelets. Spaniards will walk from bar to bar, eating tapas, drinking sherry, and visiting friends for an hour or two.
- Dinner is not served before 8:00 P.M., and often not until 10:00 P.M.
- You will probably not be invited to a Spanish home, as this type of socializing is reserved for intimate friends. You might, however be invited out to dinner.
- If an invitation to a Spanish home is extended, you may decline at first, and accept it only when pressed; first invitations are often offered out of politeness. If the invitation is repeated, you may accept.
- In the continental style of eating, the fork is held in the left hand and the knife in the right, and they are never switched. Push food onto the fork with the knife. When you are finished, place knife and fork side by side on the plate; if they are crossed or on opposite sides of the plate, you will be offered more food. Hands should be kept above the table. Pay compliments to your host (and to the waiters in a restaurant).
- If you have been invited out, reciprocate at a later date, being careful not to mention "repaying" your hosts.
- Be aware that many restaurants close for a month of vacation.

▶ PROTOCOL

Greetings
- A handshake is a normal greeting.
- You will note that among close friends, Spanish men will add a pat on the back or a hug to the handshake.
- Women may lightly embrace and touch cheeks while kissing the air. A professional woman may also greet a Spanish man who is a close colleague in this way.
- Be ready to repeat the process when you depart.

Cultural Note

In Spain, the use of the familiar (tú) and formal (Usted) forms of address are different from their usage in Latin America. For example, Spaniards generally speak to domestic employees in the formal (Usted) manner; they feel this confers dignity and shows respect for the person.

Titles/Forms of Address
- First names are appropriate among friends and young people. Although things are changing in Spain, it is better to err on the side of formality at work. Wait for your Spanish counterpart to initiate the use of first names or the use of the familiar form of address (tú) as opposed to the formal form (Usted).
- First (and possibly middle) names are generally followed by compound family names (or surnames): one from the father, which would be listed first, followed by one from the mother. The father's surname is commonly used when addressing someone—for example, Señor José Antonio Martínez de García would be addressed as Señor Martínez, and Señorita Pilar María Nuñez de Cela would be addressed as Señorita Nuñez.

  If the two people in the above example married, the woman would traditionally add her husband's surname and go by: Señora Pilar María Nuñez Cela de Martínez. Most people would refer to her as Señora de Martínez or, less formally, Señora Martínez.
- As women become increasingly independent, they may retain their maiden names or use any combination thereof. Most people you meet should be addressed with a title and their surname.
- As a general rule, use only one surname when speaking to a person, but use both surnames when writing.
- It is important to address individuals by any titles they may have, followed by their surnames. For example, teachers prefer the title *Profesor*, and engineers go by *Ingeniero*.

Gestures
- There are many gestures used in daily Spanish conversation. Their significance may vary from region to region, so observe local behaviors, and ask if you are unsure.

- To beckon another person, turn the palm down and wave the fingers or whole hand.
- Snapping the hand downward is used to emphasize a point.
- The "okay" gesture (making a circle of the first finger and thumb) is rude.
- Hands are a form of communication unto themselves in Spain. Motions are often made near the face, and they reflect the emotional aspects of a conversation.

Gifts

- Generally, if you are given a gift, you should open it immediately.
- If you are invited for a meal at a Spanish home, it is appropriate to bring chocolates, pastries, or flowers (but not dahlias or chrysanthemums, which are associated with death).
- Don't give thirteen flowers—it is considered bad luck.
- Business gifts are usually not given at a first meeting.
- If you give a business gift, choose it carefully; it should not be a vehicle for your company logo.
- Local crafts or illustrated books from your region are appropriate; university or sports team shirts and caps are good gifts for children.
- The latest electronic gadgets, fine writing implements, lighters, quality crystal, etc., can all be appropriate.
- Gifts should always be name-brand items of high quality, and they should be beautifully wrapped.

Dress

- The Spanish are highly aware of dress. They like to project a refined image, and they will scrutinize clothing in order to ascertain a person's social position or business success.
- Always select well-made conservative attire. Name brands will be noticed. Dress in subdued colors.
- Men tend to dress conservatively, while women are expected to be stylish.

Sweden

Kingdom of Sweden
Local short form: Sverige
Local long form: Konungariket Sverige

> **Cultural Note**
> Swedes were some of the first Europeans to own a cell phone, use the Internet, and invest in technical gadgets. This has led to a large number of technology firms coming to Sweden, despite the country's high taxes.

▶ WHAT'S YOUR CULTURAL IQ?

1. TRUE or FALSE: The Swedish firm Stora Kopparberg is the oldest known company in the world.
   ANSWER: TRUE. Stora Kopparberg began as a medieval copper mine, and its earliest records are more than 700 years old. The copper has long since run out, but its successor firm, Stora-Great, is still around as a forest products firm.

2. Swedish director Ingmar Bergman made some of the most important movies of all time. Which of the following was not directed by Bergman?
   a. *Cries and Whispers*
   b. *Fanny and Alexander*
   c. *My Life as a Dog*
   d. *The Seventh Seal*
   e. *Wild Strawberries*
   ANSWER: c. This film about a twelve-year-old boy in 1950s Sweden was directed by Lasse Hallström.

3. Which of the following is characteristic of Swedish business methods?

   a. Careful, meticulous planning
   b. Insisting on quality
   c. Considering a verbal agreement and a handshake binding
   d. Being punctual
   e. All of the above

ANSWER: e. Violation of any of these norms by foreign executives may dissuade Swedish firms from doing business with them.

▶ TIPS ON DOING BUSINESS IN SWEDEN

- Swedes traditionally find outward displays of emotion to be distasteful. While this trait is common to all Scandinavians, it is especially pronounced in Sweden. Sales techniques that use hype or high enthusiasm are generally not as successful in Sweden.

- Swedish executives have a reputation as good negotiators who can remain polite even while driving a hard bargain. They also consider quality to be one of the most important issues.

- Among themselves, Swedes prefer to make decisions via a consensus. However, they can be so subtle about it that foreigners never even know that the process is taking place. Instead of a formal vote, Swedes can establish a consensus through eye contact, slight nods, and murmurs.

▶ COUNTRY BACKGROUND

History

The Vikings (also called "Norsemen") were feared for their raids throughout northern Europe from the eighth to eleventh century. These Vikings eventually became the Swedes, the Norwegians, and the Danes.

Christianity was introduced to Sweden by Saint Ansgar in A.D 829.

Political power was concentrated first in Denmark, which came to rule much of Scandinavia. In 1389, the Union of Kalmar formally united Sweden with Denmark and Norway under Margaret I. Sweden left this union in 1448.

Denmark conquered Sweden in 1520. Many prominent Swedes were slain by the Danes in this "Stockholm Bloodbath." Denmark's rule did not last long; Sweden broke away from Denmark in 1523 and became a rival power under Gustav I. He later established Lutheranism as the state religion.

By 1660, expansionist Sweden had reached its greatest extent, gaining control of the Danish territories around Göteborg and Malmö, as well as parts of Norway.

Peter the Great of Russia defeated Swedish forces at the Battle of Poltava in 1709. Swedish power in Europe declined after this point.

In 1809, Sweden lost Finland to Russia during the Napoleonic Wars. Sweden and Denmark fought on opposite sides during this time. To punish Denmark for supporting Napoleon, the postwar Congress of Vienna took Norway from Denmark and gave it to Sweden in 1814.

Sweden had become an aristocratic nation of landed noblemen, and had little in common with the fishermen, sailors, and merchants of Norway. Friction developed. Fortunately for the Norwegians, their rugged, rocky nation could not be divided up into the vast farming estates preferred by the Swedes. Norway finally broke away from Sweden in 1905 and was recognized as an independent nation.

Sweden remained neutral in both World Wars. In 1946, Sweden joined the United Nations, but retained its policy of neutrality.

During the 1960s, Sweden enjoyed strong economic growth and became one of the world's most prosperous nations.

Prime Minister Olaf Palme was assassinated in Stockholm in 1986, shocking the nation.

Faced with soaring costs and high unemployment during the 1990s, Sweden implemented tax reforms and reductions to its comprehensive welfare system.

Sweden became a member of the European Union in 1995, but as of September 2003, Swedish voters continued to turn down entry into the euro system.

Type of Government

The Kingdom of Sweden is a parliamentary state under a constitutional monarchy. Sweden's current constitution was adopted in 1975. In the executive branch, the Cabinet (which consists of the prime minister and the advising ministers) is responsible to Parliament. The Parliament has one house, the Riksdag. Its members are elected by universal suffrage and serve for three years.

The king is the chief of state, while the prime minister is the head of the government.

Sweden has a free-enterprise economy, while maintaining an extensive social welfare system. State benefits include child care, health care, and extensive pension plans. Taxation is very high.

Sweden historically maintained neutrality and felt that membership in the European Union would not be consistent with this policy. However, the end of the Cold War put Sweden's entire foreign policy into question. Sweden did join the European Union in 1995, but declined to join NATO.

For current government data, check with the Embassy of Sweden at *www.swedenabroad.se.*

Language

The official language of Sweden is Swedish; it is closely related to Danish and Norwegian.

The Swedish View

Sweden once had an official church, the Church of Sweden (a form of Lutheranism). While Sweden has complete religious freedom, until 1996, all Swedish citizens were automatically registered from birth as members of the Church of Sweden. This automatic registration has been dropped, and today, baptism is required for church membership. Furthermore, the official status of the Church of Sweden was revoked in the year 2000. Since then, the Church has been fully independent (although it continues to receive some government subsidies). Many Swedes attend church on holidays.

Other Christian denominations are also represented in Sweden. There are small Jewish and Muslim populations.

One-eighth of the population is foreign-born, and absorbing these foreign influences is a major concern for Swedes. Certain incidents, such as the tragedy in which a Kurdish father killed his own daughter because she adopted Swedish customs, are becoming more common and generating alarm.

Sweden's egalitarianism is considered a cornerstone of Swedish society. Although authority is respected, positions of authority do not grant one special privileges. And Swedes believe that hierarchy can and should be bypassed when necessary.

Neutrality has been Sweden's foreign policy for over 190 years. This enabled Sweden to stay out of both World Wars. However, Sweden does send personnel out on international peacekeeping missions.

Despite their neutral status, Swedes often consider themselves the conscience of the world. They feel free to comment on real or perceived injustices occurring anywhere, worldwide.

In the past, Swedes looked upon lifetime employment as a right. This ended with economic dislocations in the 1990s. Younger Swedes do not have the same loyalty to their employers that their parents had, nor do they expect to be employed by the same company their entire lives.

Cultural Note

A bridge linking Sweden and Denmark opened in the summer of 2002. Swedes can now easily drive into the rest of Europe. This, along with membership in the European Union, has gone a long way to ameliorate Swedes' traditional feelings of isolation.

☑ Know Before You Go

The primary hazard to visitors comes from the weather. Sweden's winter is cold, dark, and snowy.

Aside from that, Sweden is a very safe country. The closest thing to a hazard a foreigner is likely to encounter in Sweden is bafflement at the impenetrable Swedish sense of humor. (Swedes tell jokes with a straight face, which has led many foreigners to believe that Swedes have no sense of humor.)

⊳ CULTURAL ORIENTATION

Cognitive Styles: How Swedes Organize and Process Information

The Swedes are a proud people. Their education teaches them to think conceptually and analytically. Swedes tend to look toward universal rules or laws to solve their problems.

Negotiation Strategies: What Swedes Accept as Evidence

Truth is supported by objective facts. Subjective feelings are considered suspect. Belief in the beneficence and desirability of the social welfare state is itself an ideology.

Like most Scandinavians, Swedes tend to accept data on face value. They extend trust to others until the source proves unreliable. However, the cosmopolitan Swedes are not naive.

Value Systems: The Basis for Behavior

The Swedes have a humanitarian culture. Top priority is given to the quality of life and to the environment.

The following three sections identify the Value Systems in the predominant culture—their methods of dividing right from wrong, good from evil, and so forth.

Locus of Decision-Making

Although decisions are made by group consensus, Swedes have a strong self-orientation and respect individual initiative and achievement. An individual's ability is considered more important than his or her station in life.

Swedes are very good at compartmentalization. They feel that they have a right to a private life totally apart from their careers. These lives are rarely discussed with business colleagues, but they can nevertheless affect business decisions.

Sources of Anxiety Reduction

Sweden has been rated as having a low level of uncertainty avoidance, which would indicate that Swedes are very tolerant of divergent opinions.

Sweden's comprehensive social welfare system is a great source of anxiety reduction. Swedes also tend to have strong nuclear families, which give stability and structure to their lives.

Issues of Equality/Inequality

Sweden has created a middle-class society that strives to minimize social differences, so there is very little evidence of poverty or wealth. The largely homogeneous population inhibits the development of largely divisive ethnic issues. Protected by their social welfare state, Swedes often feel a deep need to find a challenge in life, since most necessities are taken care of. Some ambitious Swedes seek their fortunes abroad, away from their country's high taxation rates.

Some sociologists believe that Sweden has the lowest masculinity index of any country in Europe. This reflects an extremely low degree of gender discrimination. Certainly, Swedes live in an androgynous society, with no limits to the roles women may fill. Men and women share the responsibilities of child care.

⊚ BUSINESS PRACTICES

Punctuality, Appointments, and Local Time

- The Swedes respect punctuality. Be on time for all business and social appointments.
- Not only do Swedes expect meetings to start on time, they expect them to end at the appointed time as well. If your meeting runs overtime without good reason, they are likely to question your time management skills.
- Appointments should be made two weeks in advance.
- The residents of Sweden, like most of their European neighbors, write the day first, then the month, then the year (e.g. December 3, 2010, is written 3.12.10 or 3/12/10).

- The minimum vacation in Sweden is five weeks per year (this has been legislated!). Most Swedes take off the entire month of July—so try to avoid scheduling any business trips during that time.
- During the Christmas holidays (from December 22 to January 6), many Swedish businesspeople are unavailable.
- Sweden is one hour ahead of Greenwich Mean Time (G.M.T. + 1), or six hours ahead of U.S. Eastern Standard Time (E.S.T. + 6).

Negotiating
- Although your first meeting with Swedes will be very low-key and seemingly informal, you are being evaluated. The Swedes will be well prepared, and will expect you to be the same.
- Small talk is generally kept to a minimum at the start of business.
- Most Swedes consider humor inappropriate in a business setting. Swedes tend to be serious in general, and may appear downright stuffy during business hours.
- Swedes rarely express strong emotions in public, and certainly not in a business environment. They will react negatively to a foreigner who displays strong "feelings." Even "I'm so happy to be here!" might put off the Swedes if it is stated too enthusiastically. The more remote the phrasing, the better; try "It is a pleasure to be here."
- Similarly, appearing reserved or even slightly shy can leave a positive impression with your Swedish hosts.
- Among themselves, Swedes prefer to make decisions via consensus. However, they can be so subtle about it that foreigners never even know such a process is taking place. Instead of a formal vote, Swedes can establish a consensus through nonverbal communication.
- Many Swedish businesspeople are fluent in English, particularly in large cities.
- While Swedes can be quite blunt, they also avoid confrontation. If a discussion begins to become heated, don't be offended if the Swedes cut it off abruptly.
- Avoid conducting private conversations in public areas.

- Do not ask personal questions or be offended if Swedes do not inquire about your family, your hobbies, and so forth.
- Swedes accept silence with ease. Do not rush to fill in pauses in the conversation.
- Swedes are very proud of each of their local regions. Be careful not to praise one locale over another.
- Scandinavians appreciate knowledge of the differences among the people of Finland, Norway, Sweden, and Denmark.
- The Swedes have an intense appreciation of nature.
- Relaxation is important to the Swedes. This includes breaks in their work schedule. Don't try to rush a Swede who is taking a long coffee break or an even longer lunch break, even if you are inconvenienced by it.

Business Entertaining
- Business lunches and dinners are quite popular. Make reservations in advance. Formal restaurants are recommended for business meals.
- Business breakfasts are becoming more common.
- Invite spouses to business dinners, but not to lunches.
- It is not uncommon for businesswomen to pick up the check in Sweden, especially if they are on an expense account.
- The Swedes generally do not socialize with coworkers after working hours, although they do consider their colleagues to be good friends.
- Swedes often remove their shoes when they enter their homes. There may be a place for your shoes to be stored in your host's hallway during your visit.
- Toasts, although uncommon among young people, are more formal in Sweden than elsewhere in northern Europe. Allow your host and your seniors to toast you before you propose a toast to them.
- Skoal is the Swedish word for "cheers." Wait until your host has said skoal before touching your drink.
- If you are seated left of the host as the guest of honor, you may be expected to make a speech.

- The smörgåsbord is a buffet (hot and cold) served year-round, and especially during Christmas and Easter. The cold foods are generally eaten first, then guests progress to the hot dishes.

⊙ PROTOCOL

Greetings
- The handshake is the standard greeting. Swedes also shake hands upon departure. Handshakes should be accompanied by direct eye contact.
- The handshake between men is short and firm. Handshakes between women—or between men and women—are less firm.
- Good friends (especially among the young) who see each other often may not bother to shake hands. Sometimes they will exchange kisses on the cheek.
- Older, upper-class Swedes may be very formal. Be sure to shake their hands when greeting and when leaving. Older Swedes may avoid the pronoun "you," instead referring to people in the third person (e.g., when greeting Mr. Jarl, they will say "How is Mr. Jarl today?"). This is a rare but endearing custom.
- Swedes generally prefer to be introduced by a third person.

Titles/Forms of Address
- The order of names in Sweden is the same as in most of Europe: first name followed by surname.
- Young people are most likely to go to a first-name basis quickly, and the egalitarian Swedes often use first-names in the workplace.
- Older Swedes generally still expect to be addressed by their surnames.
- Persons with professional titles should be addressed by that title (Doctor, Engineer, Professor, and so forth) followed by a surname. In truth, Swedes are not as obsessed with titles.
- It is important to say hello and goodbye to employees in stores and restaurants.

Gestures
- The Swedes are a restrained people and do not use many gestures. When dealing with them, you should avoid gesticulating or talking with your hands.
- Swedes are also a relatively quiet people. Keep your voice calm and well modulated.
- In general, Swedes do not like physical contact with anyone except close friends. Do not touch, backslap, embrace, or put your arm around a Swede.
- Direct eye contact is expected. Look a Swede in the eye when speaking with him or her.
- A toss of the head means "come here."
- While Swedes have a reputation for sexual openness, do not mistake a Swedish woman's forwardness for a sexual invitation. Swedish women often speak to strangers, especially foreigners, when they want to practice the foreigner's language.

Gifts
- In general, gift giving is not a part of doing business in Sweden. Sweden's anticorruption legislation makes gift giving problematical; a gift must not be interpreted as a bribe.
- For a foreigner, a practical rule of thumb is to have a gift ready for your Swedish business associates, but not to give the gift unless you get a gift from the Swedish contact.
- Despite recent tax abatements, liquor is still expensive in Sweden, so it is a highly appreciated gift. Fine liquor or wine from your home country makes a good business present.
- If you are invited into a Swedish home, you should bring a gift for your hostess. Appropriate gifts include flowers, liquor, wine, cake, or candy. If there are children in the home, you may also bring a small gift for them.
- Swedes often remove the paper, or wrapping, from bouquets before they present them to the hostess.

Dress

- Conservative dress is appropriate. For business appointments, men should wear suits and ties, while women should wear suits or dresses.
- During the snowy winter, many Swedes wear boots to work and change into regular shoes when they arrive.
- Swedes are usually fashionably well dressed in public. Even when jeans are worn, they should be neat and clean.
- Public ostentation is avoided in Sweden. Try not to dress in clothing that attracts too much attention.
- You can't always distinguish the boss by his or her clothes in Sweden. Swedish egalitarianism allows high-ranking executives to wear clothes similar to those of their employees.

Switzerland

Swiss Confederation
French long form: Confederation Suisse
German long form: Schweizerische Eidgenossenschaft
Italian long form: Confédérazione Svizzera

Cultural Note

Switzerland has three official languages: French, Italian, and German, plus a fourth "protected" language called "Romansch." In addition to one or more of these languages, businesspeople generally speak English as well.

▶ WHAT'S YOUR CULTURAL IQ?

---

1. The flag of Switzerland is always easy to recognize, even among a host of flags. Why?
   a. It is the same as the flag of the Red Cross.
   b. By law, it must be larger than any other European flag.
   c. It is square.
   d. It is circular.
   ANSWER: c. Most flags are rectangular, but the Swiss flag is square. The Red Cross flag is a red cross on white, the reverse of the Swiss white cross on red.

2. Neutral Switzerland managed to avoid both World Wars. TRUE or FALSE? Switzerland has been peaceful for over 500 years.
   ANSWER: FALSE. Like most of Europe, Switzerland suffered from warfare. The last foreign incursion was from Napoleon in 1798. When Napoleon pulled his troops out in 1802, it prompted a short civil war.

3. Which of the following people were not born in Switzerland?
   a. Louis Chevrolet, founder of the U.S. Chevrolet Motor Company
   b. Albert Einstein, physicist and winner of the Nobel Prize for physics
   c. Alberto Giacometti, world-renowned sculptor
   d. Karl Jung, pioneering psychoanalyst

   ANSWER: b. Although Einstein was educated at the University of Zurich and taught at the University of Berne, he was born in Germany.

▶ TIPS ON DOING BUSINESS IN SWITZERLAND

- Switzerland remains one of the world's most expensive nations (in terms of consumer goods). Cartels wield great influence over prices, and consumers pay the price. The Economist's "Big Mac Index" often lists Switzerland as having the most expensive burger in the world.

- An influential contact is vital to success in Switzerland. All Swiss males serve in the military, where they also form friendships and networks. Businesses tend to be run by old-boy networks of men who were friends in the Swiss Army.

- Age and seniority are important in Switzerland. Young executives, sent alone to major appointments, may not be taken seriously. Expect to defer to the elderly. Also, if your company has a long lineage, the year it was established should appear on your business card and/or letterhead.

Cultural Note

The Swiss tend to judge a person by appearances. No matter how competent you are, if you are underdressed or ill groomed, the Swiss will not trust you.

The Swiss put great importance upon footwear. Wear good dress shoes and keep them shined.

▶ COUNTRY BACKGROUND

History

Archaeological evidence shows that Switzerland has been occupied for thousands of years. The Romans pacified and colonized an area they called "Helvetia" that more or less corresponds to modern Switzerland. In A.D. 260, the Alemanni invaded, destroying the local economy. The Romans kept nominal control of the region until they withdrew around A.D. 400.

Some 200 years later, most of northwestern Europe was conquered by the Franks. The Franks spread Christianity throughout their empire.

On the death of the Carolingian emperor, the Frankish empire was traditionally divided between his surviving sons. In 870, that dividing line went right through the middle of northern Switzerland. Chaos ensued, and peace was not restored until 1050.

In 1291, three Swiss cantons signed the Perpetual Covenant to defend against foreign domination. This Swiss Confederation achieved independence from the Holy Roman Empire in 1648.

During the Reformation, Switzerland did not escape religious violence. For example, Protestant reformer Huldreich Zwingli was slain in 1531. Switzerland eventually established Catholic cantons and Protestant cantons, and both religions coexist in Switzerland today.

Switzerland's borders were fixed in 1815 by the Congress of Vienna, which also guaranteed Switzerland's neutrality. Several Catholic cantons tried to secede from the Swiss Confederation in 1847, but a new Swiss Constitution in 1848 gave each canton enough control over its local affairs that the nation held together.

The International Red Cross was founded in Geneva in 1863.

Switzerland remained neutral in the First World War. Following the war, the League of Nations was established in Geneva in 1920. This league was powerless to prevent the outbreak of another world war.

With the rise of Nazi Germany, Switzerland accepted a substantial number of refugees fleeing Nazi persecution. Switzerland managed to remain neutral during the Second World War. At the time, their continued independence was attributed to the Swiss Army. Only later was it revealed how much Switzerland had to accommodate Nazi Germany in order to remain free.

During the postwar period, Switzerland joined the European Free Trade Association. In 1963, Switzerland joined the Council of Europe. They continued to resist joining international organizations that might violate their policy of neutrality—including the European Union.

During the late 1990s, revelations about Swiss compliance with Nazi Germany became public. Swiss banks refunded large sums of money to the heirs of depositors who were killed by the Nazis.

Type of Government

The Swiss Confederation is a federal state of twenty-eight sovereign cantons. The president is head of both the state and the government. There are two legislative houses: the Council of States and the National Council.

Switzerland has a policy of permanent neutrality.

Switzerland did not enter into either world war; indeed, it has not been involved in a war since Napoleon invaded in 1798. Yet national defense is taken seriously, and all men must serve in the military.

For current government data, check with the Embassy of Switzerland at *www.swissemb.org*.

Language

Linguistically, Switzerland is complex. There are three official languages: French, German, and Italian. Around Lake Geneva (in the southwest), French is spoken. Italian is spoken by about 10 percent of the population of the country, concentrated in the Ticino region. German is spoken in many parts of Switzerland. A fourth language, Romansch, is a Romance language spoken by only 1 percent of the population. The Swiss take the preservation of traditional languages and cultures quite seriously.

In the cities, or in work environments, finding someone who speaks English does not pose a problem.

Most Swiss are multilingual, and the majority of businesspeople include English as one of their languages.

Cultural Note

Switzerland is a small, highly developed, multilingual market located at the crossroads of Europe. Its population of approximately 7.5 million people (2004 estimates) is diversified, well educated, and affluent. It has a strong and stable economy, low inflation, relatively low unemployment, and a highly qualified work force—all factors which contribute to making the Swiss Confederation a desirable market environment. Per capita income is the highest in Europe and spending power for foreign goods and services is commensurately high.

The Swiss View

Switzerland's four cultures—German, French, Italian, and Romansch—encompass a variety of religious traditions. Roman Catholics, at 46 percent, constitute the majority, with various Protestant denominations making up 40 percent. Others include Muslims, Jews, Buddhists, and Mormons.

Switzerland was at the center of the Protestant Reformation. Reformer Ulrich Zwingli (1484–1531) lived in Zurich; Jean Calvin (1509–1564) was French but was exiled to Geneva. Years of warfare between Protestants and Catholics devastated Switzerland. As a result, the Swiss today consider religion to be a private concern. Religion is rarely discussed in public. The doomsday cult known as the Order of the Solar Temple came to international prominence when fifty-three members were found dead in October of 1994, the victims of murder and mass suicide. The Swiss were aghast at these events, which served to drive religion even further out of public discourse. Nevertheless, the Swiss consider themselves privately devoted to religious principals.

The Swiss believe that they have developed a fair and beneficent society, and exert strong social pressures on their citizens to conform to Swiss patterns of behavior.

Divided by language and religion, the Swiss find unity in their devotion to their families, their work, and their country. The Swiss are patriotic and deeply involved in their country's politics. Their political system, which involves strong local government, allows each citizen's vote to have great effect on their everyday lives. Referendums are frequent.

Even the Swiss Constitution can be challenged by a system called the People's Initiatives.

The Swiss are intensely concerned about the environment. They recycle most consumer products, and are second only to Germany in environmental restrictions.

The Swiss have, to date, refused to join either the United Nations or the European Union. (However, Switzerland is a member of many UN agencies, such as the World Health Organization.)

Long a banking center, Switzerland's reputation was tarnished by its acceptance of assets from the Nazis in World War II, as well as its refusal to return funds to the heirs of persons executed by the Nazis. Under threat of a U.S. boycott initiated by the World Jewish Congress, Swiss banks agreed in 1998 to disburse $1.25 trillion in funds, most of it to the heirs of Jewish victims of Nazi atrocities.

As a prosperous, neutral nation, Switzerland remains a magnet for refugees. Thousands of would-be-refugees are turned back at the borders, but many manage to enter the country, legally or otherwise. During the Kosovo crisis of 1998 to 1999, Switzerland sheltered some 40,000 refugees.

☑ Know Before You Go

Violent crime is very rare in Switzerland.

The Swiss tend to divide foreigners into "those who bring" and "those who take." The former are visitors from wealthy countries, who have money to bring (and will leave some of it in Switzerland). The latter are refugees, who must take from the Swiss welfare system. While Switzerland has the highest rate per capita of political refugees in Europe, there is resentment against "those who take."

Because the Swiss are so law-abiding, the police in Switzerland are able to keep a low profile. However, they can be heavy-handed with foreigners. Be sure you can produce your passport at all times. If you and a traffic officer do not share a common language, you may have to accompany the officer to a police station.

The Swiss are very law-abiding, so graft and corruption are uncommon. However, some things that are illegal in other countries are legal under Swiss law. For example, price fixing may occur in Switzerland, but is illegal in many other nations, like the United States.

▶ CULTURAL ORIENTATION

Cognitive Styles: How the Swiss Organize and Process Information

Swiss culture has historically been very ethnocentric and circumspect toward outside influence; however, the younger generation is becoming more open. The German and French segments of Switzerland process information conceptually and analytically; the rest tend to think associatively. The former will use universal rules to solve problems, while the latter tend to become personally involved in each situation.

Negotiation Strategies: What the Swiss Accept as Evidence

The German and French segments rely on objective facts to determine the truth, while those of Italian heritage generally use subjective feelings. In both cases, faith in the ideologies of nationalism and utopian ideals may influence the truth.

Value Systems: The Basis for Behavior

The culture of Switzerland is made up of four subcultures with differing value systems: German, French, Italian, and 1 percent of the indigenous population who speak Romansch. The following three sections identify the Value Systems in these predominant cultures—their methods of dividing right from wrong, good from evil, and so forth.

Locus of Decision-Making

The individual is the decision-maker. Although he or she may defer to the interest of the family, the company, or the state, he or she is still responsible. Decision-making is a slow and involved process in which a relationship must be developed between the negotiators.

Ethnocentric values may shape the decision. In families, there is joint decision-making between parents and older children.

Sources of Anxiety Reduction

The four languages and two religions are all very important to the Swiss, but they have come to terms with all cleavages and do not find them to be sufficient cause for civil unrest. They may acquire this ability to live together in the Swiss military, where all of the groups are brought together in a well-integrated force. The nuclear family is the basic social unit, and there is a very high feeling of ethnocentrism—a belief that languages and religions mix and work together as Swiss.

Issues of Equality/Inequality

Although there is a history of disagreement among the groups, the central government has been able to negotiate acceptable conditions for all. Equal rights for men are guaranteed by law, and those who feel discriminated against use the law to work out their problems. A Swiss motto is "Unity, yes; uniformity, no." The Swiss are competitive, responsible, tolerant, materialistic, proud, and private. There are still some classic role differences between the sexes, and discrimination against women still exists in some cantons.

▶ BUSINESS PRACTICES

Punctuality, Appointments, and Local Time

- The Swiss reputation for promptness is deserved. Always be punctual. This applies to both business and social events.
- The Swiss, like most Europeans, write the day first, then the month, then the year (e.g., December 3, 2010, is written 3.12.10 or 3/12/10).
- Introductions are necessary to conduct business in Switzerland. Cold-calling a potential customer will rarely be productive. Switzerland is a small country and everybody knows everybody else in each industry. If no one is willing to recommend you, the assumption is that you are not worth knowing.

- Most people take their vacations in July and August. It is not advisable to try to schedule important appointments during that time.
- Each canton celebrates its own holidays. The Swiss National Day is the first of August. For further official holidays in Switzerland, visit *www.kissboworshakehands.com.*
- Switzerland is one hour ahead of Greenwich Mean Time (G.M.T. + 1), or six hours ahead of U.S. Eastern Standard Time (E.S.T. + 6).

Negotiating

- Business is a serious and sober undertaking. Humor has little purpose in negotiations.
- Expect deliberations to proceed slowly. High-pressure tactics inevitably fail; there is no way to speed up decisions.
- Generally, the Swiss take a very long time to establish personal relationships. Be patient. A good relationship will help immensely down the road.
- German Swiss tend to get right down to business. The French and Italians will expect some small talk first.
- The Swiss are usually willing to negotiate anything except price. Once a price has been established, the Swiss tend to stick to it—even if it costs them the deal.
- If you use an interpreter, speak slowly and clearly. Avoid idioms. Frequently confirm that what you have said has been understood.
- Ideally, you should translate one side of your business card into the language of your Swiss client. If you aren't sure what language to pick, choose German. However, many businesspeople speak English, so you can have English on your card as a default.
- If your firm is an old one, put the year it was established on your Web site, letterhead, and business cards. The Swiss respect longevity in business.
- Good topics of conversation are sports, positive aspects of Switzerland, travel, and food.
- The Swiss attribute their independence to their military preparedness, which includes universal military conscription. Opinions on

this subject are passionately held. Bringing up the topic can result in an argument.

- It is not appropriate to talk about dieting, especially while eating. Avoid personal questions and talk about work.
- Keep your wrists on the table at meals. Never put your hands in your lap.
- The elderly are respected in Switzerland. On public transportation, younger people may relinquish their seat to the elderly.
- When entering a Swiss shop, say "Hello" to the clerk.
- It is not unusual for passersby to admonish strangers for "improper behavior" in the street. This is more common in German areas.

Business Entertaining
- Business lunches and dinners are popular, but business breakfasts are somewhat uncommon.
- Business lunches are often quite informal, sometimes taking place in the company cafeteria.
- Business dinners are the time to impress your client with a meal at a fine restaurant. The Swiss eat dinner as early as 6:30 P.M. You will have a hard time finding a good Swiss restaurant open after 11 P.M.
- The Swiss rarely invite business associates into their homes.
- If you are invited into a Swiss home, expect the evening to end early. Most Swiss are an early-to-bed, early-to-rise sort. Do not phone anyone after 9 P.M.
- Toasting is a formal process. After your host has proposed a toast, look directly at him or her and respond verbally ("To your health" covers most occasions, but try to say it in the local language), then clink glasses with everyone within reach—preferably the whole table; then you may drink.

Cultural Note
The Swiss frown upon ostentation and obvious displays of wealth. It is acceptable to spend a large amount on possessions—as long as the items do not look flashy or showy. Many Swiss buy pricey items which, to the uninitiated, look as if they might be modestly priced.

⊚ PROTOCOL

Greetings
- The standard greeting is the handshake. Even children are encouraged to shake hands.
- Always rise to be introduced to someone. Wait to be introduced by a third person.
- In the German areas of Switzerland, women sometimes embrace, but men do not.
- In the French and Italian areas, both men and women may embrace. The French also kiss each other twice on the cheek.

Titles/Forms of Address
- The order of names is the same as in the United States: first name followed by surname.
- Only children immediately address each other by their first names. Always address Swiss adults by their title or "Mr.," "Mrs.," or "Miss," plus their surname.

Gestures
- The German-speaking Swiss rarely display strong emotions in public. In fact, most Swiss never reveal what they are thinking—at least not initially.
- By and large, gestures are kept to a minimum. Avoid frequent or wild gesticulations.
- French-speaking and Italian-speaking Swiss tend to be more willing to be emotional in public.
- It is impolite to talk with your hands in your pockets.
- Gum chewing in public is inappropriate.
- Do not sit with one ankle resting on the other knee.
- Backslapping is not appreciated.

Gifts
- Gift giving is not normally part of business in Switzerland.
- If you are invited to a Swiss home, always bring a gift. Wine, flowers, or chocolates (boutique-quality Swiss chocolate, never

Belgian!) are good gifts. A foodstuff from your home country would also be appreciated.

- A gift with a significant connection to your home region will be remembered (for example, local folk art, liquor produced in your region, or a book about your home city).
- Keep company logos small.
- If you give flowers, remember that red roses are reserved for lovers.
- Interpreters or guides appreciate personalized gifts rather than a tip.

Dress

- Conservative dress is expected of foreign businesspeople. Be sure to wear well-shined dress shoes.
- Swiss bankers are well known for their formal attire. However, in some industries, the Swiss dress more casually.
- The Swiss appreciate discretion regarding wealth. Do not wear ostentatious jewelry—except for expensive Swiss watches.

Cultural Note

The Swiss attribute much of their success to their work ethic. They work hard (and play hard). Punctuality is required and planning is done in advance. Everything is kept clean (this also applies to the country as a whole). Perhaps the only negative is that the Swiss are not usually good at improvising.

Turkey

Republic of Turkey
Local short form: Turkiye
Local long form: Turkiye Cumhuriyeti

Cultural Note

Turkey occupies one of the most strategic locations in the world. Turkey controls access to the Black Sea. Russia's only warm-water ports lie on the Black Sea; Bulgaria, Romania, Ukraine, and Georgia also depend upon their Black Sea ports. Access out of the Black Sea into the Mediterranean is via the straits of the Bosporus and the Dardanelles, both of which lie entirely in Turkish territory. Furthermore, as the only member of NATO in direct proximity to Russia, Iran, and Iraq, Turkey's strategic importance cannot be underestimated.

▶ WHAT'S YOUR CULTURAL IQ?

1. Many of the places and events noted in Greek mythology did not occur in Greece. Which of the following were located in Turkey?
   a. The Temple of Artemis (one of the Seven Wonders of the Ancient World)
   b. King Midas (whose touch turned everything into gold)
   c. The Trojan Horse
   d. All of the above
   ANSWER: d. The Temple of Artemis was in Ephesus, Midas was king of Lydia, and the ancient city of Troy are all in modern Turkey.

2. Many persons and places associated with early Christianity were also in Turkey. TRUE or FALSE? Saint Nicholas (the inspiration for Santa Claus) lived in Turkey.
   ANSWER: TRUE. Nicholas was a fourth-century bishop of Myra, which is now the Turkish city of Demre. He was also born in the Turkish port of Patara.

3. Asia Minor—which more or less corresponds to modern Turkey—has been home to many civilizations. Place the following in the correct order, from oldest to youngest:
   a. The Republic of Turkey
   b. The Byzantine Empire
   c. The Ottoman Empire
   d. The Seljuk Empire
   ANSWER: b, d, c, a. "Ottoman" is a Western corruption of the Turkish name of Osman I (1281–1324), who was the most aggressive of the Seljuk Turkish leaders.

▶ TIPS ON DOING BUSINESS IN TURKEY

- Age is highly respected in Turkey. Elders are introduced first, served first, and are allowed to go through a doorway first. In a family-owned business, the decision-maker is probably an elder, even if some other member of the family does most of the negotiating.
- All meetings will begin with extensive small talk. Expect to be asked about your journey, your lodgings, and how you like Turkey. (Be sure to have good things to say about Turkey. Turks can say negative things about Turkey, but foreigners may not.)
- Although the majority of Turks are Muslim, the government and the military are determined to keep Turkey a secular state. While Muslim theocracies like Iran and Saudi Arabia insist that women cover their hair in public, the Turkish government has actually prohibited women from wearing head coverings in some situations, such as universities. Most women in Turkey do not live under harsh religious restrictions. In fact, Turkish women are well represented in business.

▶ COUNTRY BACKGROUND

History

The Republic of Turkey is the successor to a series of empires that have existed on the Anatolian peninsula since the dawn of recorded history.

The Byzantine Empire ruled out of what is now Istanbul for over 1,100 years, until the Turks conquered it in 1453. In some ways, the Ottoman Empire represented a continuation of the Byzantines. (True, the Ottoman religion was Islamic rather than Christian, but the Byzantine Empire survived a change in religion: it began as the pagan Eastern Roman Empire.)

The current state emerged from the dissolution of the Ottoman Empire after its defeat in the First World War. The history of modern Turkey is inseparable from the biography of one man: Kemal Atatürk. A war hero, Mustafa Kemal (later known as Kemal Atatürk), held the ethnically Turkish areas of the empire together. Despite invading armies, fundamentalist opposition, and the total absence of a democratic tradition, he turned the core of a crumbling Islamic empire into a secular republic. The current Republic of Turkey dates to 1923.

Turkey managed to remain neutral in World War II. Choosing to ally itself with the West in the Cold War, Turkey sent an infantry contingent to fight in Korea in 1950 and joined NATO in 1952. Political turmoil following the introduction of multiparty elections sometimes resulted in the Turkish military involving itself in government. But throughout it all, Turkey has maintained a more stable, pro-Western government than most countries with Islamic majorities.

The 1990 invasion of Kuwait by Iraq put enormous strains upon Turkey. Turkey was a major trading partner of neighboring Iraq, but it supported both the embargo against Iraq and the multinational coalition that liberated Kuwait in 1991. Although Turkish troops did not serve in the liberation, the use of Turkish air bases was considered vital. Turkey experienced economic problems from both the embargo and high inflation during the Gulf crisis, although these were partially offset by $4 billion in grants and credits from Turkey's grateful allies.

In June 1992, Turkey initiated the Black Sea Economic Cooperation Treaty. Signed by Turkey, Greece, Bulgaria, Romania, and several ex-Soviet republics, the treaty was designed to enhance trade within the region.

Turkey suffered massive earthquakes in 1999. Turkey's traditional enemy, Greece, sent aid, which helped to relieve tensions between the two nations.

Like fellow NATO states France and Germany, Turkey declined to participate in the 2003 invasion and occupation of Iraq.

Type of Government

The Republic of Turkey is a multiparty democracy. The president is the chief of state. The presidency was traditionally a largely ceremonial office, but the late President Turgut Ozal (who was also a former prime minister) turned it into a forum for directing Turkey's international affairs. The prime minister is the head of the government.

There is one legislative house, the Grand National Assembly.

The occupation of Iraq by the United States and allied forces put Turkey in a difficult position. Turkey supported the first Gulf War, but has declined involvement in the second one.

Turkey is also concerned about conflict in various regions of the former USSR, especially between Armenia and Azerbaijan (centered on the autonomous region of Nagorno-Karabakh). The Muslim Azeris are considered friends of Turkey, while there is historic animosity between the Turks and the Christian Armenians. The border between Turkey and Armenia is currently closed.

For current government data, check with the Embassy of Turkey at *www.turkishembassy.org.*

Language

Turkish is the official language. It is a member of the Ural-Altaic linguistic group—totally unlike any Indo-European language (such as English, German, or the Romance tongues). Turkish used to be written in Arabic script, but in 1928, the Latin alphabet was officially adopted. This made education much simpler, and today the literacy rate has increased to over 70 percent.

Many businesspeople speak a foreign language, usually English, German, or French. Executives often receive degrees from colleges outside of Turkey.

The Turkish View

Turkey has no official religion, although 90 percent of the Turkish population is Sunni Muslim, mostly of a non-orthodox sect called Alevi. The remaining 10 percent are primarily other Muslim sects, along with some Christians and Jews.

Since its founding in 1923, the Turkish Republic has been a secular state with no official religion. While there is considerable pressure to change this, other forces—including Turkey's powerful military—are determined to keep Turkey officially secular.

Every Turkish citizen, religious or not, is familiar with the basic precepts of Islam. The word Islam literally means "submission" (to the will of Allah). Consequently, success and misfortune are attributed to the will of Allah. Destiny is not under the control of man.

Most Turkish children are trained to be self-reliant, to care for others, and to be satisfied with their lot in life.

Cultural Note

There are many superstitions in Turkey. Of importance to businesspeople is the avoidance of the numbers 13 and 100. The number 13 is considered unlucky. The number 100 is not unlucky but unpleasant: "100" (*yüz numara* in Turkish) is a slang term for "toilet." Avoid renting a room or building with these numbers in the address, and try not to package items in lots of these numbers.

☑ Know Before You Go

The greatest hazard to visitors in Turkey comes from the chaotic vehicular traffic. Pedestrians, drivers, and passengers alike are at risk. Traffic is also made unpredictable by the variety of vehicles, from taxis to buses to minibuses (called a dolmus). Only bicycles are missing: Turks view bicycles as fit only for children.

Although terrorist incidents—usually car bombings—do occasionally occur in Turkey, foreign businesspeople are not usually affected.

In addition to heavy air pollution in the cities, tobacco is everywhere in Turkey. No-smoking zones are virtually nonexistent. If you are allergic to tobacco smoke, you will have a difficult time.

▶ CULTURAL ORIENTATION

Cognitive Styles: How Turks Organize and Process Information

Historically, Turks are generally closed to outside information. This is ameliorated somewhat by Turkey's position as a bridge between East and West. Turks are trained to process information subjectively and associatively. Turkey is a secularized Islamic nation, and one's personal involvement is more important than rules or laws.

Negotiation Strategies: What Turks Accept as Evidence

On any question, the answer comes from a combination of immediate feelings and faith in the ideologies of Islam. Among Turks, truth seldom comes solely from the accumulation of objective facts.

Value Systems: The Basis for Behavior

Turkey's territory lies in both Europe and Asia, and its value systems are an amalgam of East and West. The following three sections identify the Value Systems in the predominant culture—their methods of dividing right from wrong, good from evil, and so forth.

Locus of Decision-Making

The male leader is usually the decision-maker, but he always considers the family group upon which the decision is binding. Private life is overwhelmed by family, friends, and organizations, and these guide one's opinions. A relationship between participants must be established before any formal negotiations can take place. Identity is based on the social system, and education is the primary vehicle for moving up the social ladder.

Sources of Anxiety Reduction

Turks have been charted to have a fairly high index of uncertainty avoidance. They generally use laws and morality to give structure to their worldview.

In addition to the family, a Turk's identity derives from his or her role in the social structure. There is a deeply ingrained work ethic, but time is not a major source of anxiety. Pride in one's country, society, and family bolsters one's self-image and self-esteem. Emotions are shown, assertiveness is expected, and risks are taken to develop self-reliance.

Issues of Equality/Inequality

There is a definite social hierarchy, with some bias against classes, ethnic groups (especially the Kurds), and religions. The privileged elite control the country. There is not a lot of trust in people outside of the family and intimate friends. (Curiously, most ethnic Turks see the military as the nation's most trusted institution, despite the military's intervention in the political process.) The old dominate the young, and men often try to dominate women even though they have equal rights by law.

Historically, men and women had separate social subsocieties and did not mix in public. Today this is rapidly changing. Compared to most of its Arab neighbors, Turkey has more gender equality. However, although no jobs are barred to women, they still make up a minority of the full-time work force.

⊚ BUSINESS PRACTICES

Punctuality, Appointments, and Local Time

- You are expected to be punctual for all business appointments.
- Traffic jams are frequent in both Istanbul and Ankara, so allow yourself plenty of travel time.
- Arrange appointments well in advance. A personal introduction (or at least a letter of introduction) will facilitate your acceptance.
- Turks have an unusual way of writing the date. They usually write the day first, then the month, then the day of the week, and finally the year. That is, December 3, 2010, is written as 3.12.Thursday.10 (periods are used rather than commas). Sometimes the day of the week is eliminated.
- Turkish businesspeople who work internationally are usually able to communicate in one or more foreign languages. English is commonly understood, as are German and French. Given advance notice, your Turkish colleagues should be able to conduct

business in English; they probably have an English-speaking person on their staff. Business letters may also be in English. However, Turks will appreciate the effort if you learn at least a few phrases in Turkish.

- Do not expect to get right down to business at your appointment. The small talk that precedes business is important to Turkish executives—they want to get to know you.
- Although Friday is the Muslim holy day, offices are usually still open. Sunday is the government-mandated "day of rest."
- Business appointments can rarely be made during the months of June, July, and August; most Turkish businesspeople take extended vacations during that time.
- Obviously, you cannot expect to conduct business on a Turkish holiday. Be aware that many people will begin the holiday around noon the day before.
- November 10 is a secular holiday remembering the death of the founder of modern Turkey, Kemal Atatürk, in 1938. It is an insult not to observe the moment of silence at 9:05 A.M., the time of Atatürk's death.
- Turkey is on Eastern European Time, which is two hours ahead of Greenwich Mean Time (G.M.T. + 2)—except between April and September, when Turkish clocks are advanced one hour. It is seven hours ahead of U.S. Eastern Standard Time, (E.S.T. + 7).

Negotiating

- The pace of negotiation is much slower in Turkey than it is in the West. Patience is exceedingly important; negotiations may take place over innumerable cups of tea or coffee. Meetings start slowly, with many inquiries as to your background, your education, and so on. Some of this may seem irrelevant to the purpose of your visit, but it is a serious breach of etiquette to cut this information-gathering process short.
- Negotiations are predicated upon the trust you have built with your new associates. Most business is conducted based upon personal relationships.

- In a family-owned business, the decision-maker may be quite elderly. Remember that elders are always respected in Turkey.

Business Entertaining

- By and large, most business entertaining will take place in restaurants. This is not a drawback, as Turkish cuisine is one of the finest in the world. However, you may not get the chance to act as host; Turkish hospitality is legendary, and your colleagues may insist upon doing (and paying for) all of the entertaining. When your colleagues invite you to a restaurant, you will not be allowed to pay for even part of the meal.

- Only when you issue an invitation to a meal will you be allowed to pick up the tab—and even then, you may have to fight off your colleagues' efforts to grab the check.

- In general, restaurants in the international hotels are bland and uninteresting compared to the average Turkish restaurant. However, Western-style alcoholic drinks are more readily available in such hotels.

- Turks use the same eating utensils used in Europe and the Americas. The fork is held in the left hand and the knife in the right; the knife is used for cutting and to push food onto the fork.

- Service in Turkish restaurants is very quick. Except in the international hotel restaurants, Turks do not usually order the entire meal at once. Instead they order the courses one at a time, deciding what to eat next only after finishing the last course.

- Turks usually smoke between courses.

- Good topics of conversations include Turkey's long history (avoiding the conflicts), sightseeing, cultural achievements, and sports. The most popular spectator sport is football (soccer). Wrestling is a traditional Turkish sport that remains very popular. Oddly, although Turks love horses, they have no tradition of organized horseracing.

- Always ask a Turkish father about his family; few subjects give a Turk more pride.

- Bad topics of conversation usually have to do with ethnic conflicts—with the Greeks, the Kurds, and especially with the Armenians.

⊚ PROTOCOL

Greetings
- Shake hands firmly when greeting or being introduced to a Turkish man. It is not customary to shake hands again upon departure.
- Male visitors should wait to see if a Turkish woman extends her hand before offering to shake. (Observant Muslims avoid physical contact with members of the opposite sex.)
- Turks may greet a close friend of either sex with a two-handed handshake and/or a kiss on both cheeks.
- Elders are respected in Turkey; if you are seated, rise to greet them when they enter a room. When being introduced to a group of men, shake hands with each one, starting with the eldest.

Cultural Note
The traditional Turkish greetings are *Merhaba* (MEHR-hah-bah; Hello) and *Nasilsiniz?* (NAHS-sulh-suh-nuhz; How are you?). The response to the latter is *"Iyiyim, teshekur ederim"* (ee-YEE-yihm, tesh-ek-KEWR eh-dehr-eem; I'm fine, thank you!). Turks will appreciate any effort you make to speak their language.

Titles/Forms of Address
- The easiest and most respectful way to address a Turkish professional is by his occupational title alone. Simply say "Doctor" (Doktor) or "Attorney" (Avukat). If the professional is a woman, add the word Bayan after the title (e.g., Mrs./Miss Attorney is Avukat Bayan).
- When your Turkish colleague does not have a title, the situation becomes more complicated. Realize that most Turks did not have surnames until they were made mandatory by the 1934 Law of Surnames. The order of names is the same as in the United States: first name followed by the surname.

- The traditional mode of address was to use a Turk's first name, followed by bey (for men) or hanim (for women). Use this form with older people unless instructed otherwise.
- Most of the Turks you will do business with use the modern form of address. The modern way is to use the surname, preceded by Bay (for men) or Bayam (for women). For example, Cengiz Dagci, a male novelist, would traditionally be addressed as Cengiz bey. The modern form of address is Bay Dagci (note the difference in spelling: Bey vs. Bay). Nezihe Meric, a female author, would traditionally be addressed as Nezihe hanim. The modern form of address is Bayam Meric.

Gestures
- It is safest to keep both feet flat on the ground when sitting. Displaying the soles of your shoes (or feet) to someone is insulting. Keep this in mind when changing from outdoor shoes into indoor slippers in a Turkish home.
- It is considered discourteous for women to cross their legs while facing another person.
- It is rude to cross your arms while facing someone.
- Keep your hands out of your pockets while speaking.
- Avoid blowing your nose in public, especially in a restaurant. If you must, turn away from others and blow as quietly as possible.
- Do not kiss, hug, or even hold hands with someone of the opposite sex in public.
- While Turks indicate "yes" by nodding their heads up and down (the same way as in North America), the gestures for "no" are different. Two ways to indicate "no" are as follows:

1. Raising the eyebrows is a subtle way to indicate "no." This may be accompanied by the sound "tsk."

2. A broader way to indicate "no" is to accompany the eyebrow-arching with a backward tilting of the head and lowering of the eyelids (rather like someone trying to peer through the lower half of a pair of bifocals).

- The North American gesture for "no" (shaking the head from side to side) is a Turkish gesture for "I don't understand." If you inadvertently make this gesture in response to a question, a Turk may assume that you did not comprehend.
- Describing a desired length by holding the palms apart in midair (in the manner of a fisherman describing "the one that got away") will not be understood in Turkey. The Turks approximate length by extending one arm and placing the palm of the other hand on the arm; the length indicated is measured from the fingertips of the extended arm up to the side of the hand.
- To attract attention, Turks wave (palm out) with an up-and-down motion, rather than from side to side.
- The Turkish "follow me" gesture is done with the entire curled hand moved in a downward "scooping" motion, not by curling an upraised index finger. It is considered rude to point your finger directly at someone.

Gifts
- If you know that your colleague drinks, a fine whiskey or liqueur is appropriate.
- If you are invited to a Turkish home—and an invitation may come more quickly from someone you meet socially than from a business colleague—a gift will be expected. Unless the gift needs immediate attention (such as foods that need to be refrigerated, or flowers that need to be placed in water) your gift will probably not be opened in your presence.
- Turks generally give presents in two ways: by leaving them or by presenting them apologetically. Often, a visitor simply leaves a wrapped gift near the door. The host will notice it but no verbal acknowledgement needs to be made by either party. Alternately, the gift may be presented while uttering a phrase such as "this gift is not worthy of you." Even then, the host might not open it immediately.
- Again, wine or liquor is appropriate if you are sure your hosts drink alcohol. Other suitable gifts are candy, pastries, or other treats. Fine glassware is also appropriate.

- Flowers are a good gift for a host, but tradition demands that the bouquet contain an odd number of flowers.
- If your invitation is for an extended stay (rather than a meal), further gifts are advisable. Items such as CDs, iPods, MP3 players, or other electronic gadgets are good. Be sure to bring gifts for the children, such as candy (especially chocolate) or small toys.
- Orthodox Islam prohibits alcohol and depictions of the human body (including photographs and drawings). Ascertain whether your hosts adhere to these strictures before giving such gifts.

Cultural Note

When entering a Turkish home, it is customary to remove your shoes and change into a pair of slippers. The homeowner provides the slippers. Sometimes, a Turkish host may tell you that you do not need to remove your shoes when you enter. This does not mean you should not do so; the host may simply be trying to save you from embarrassment in case your socks are dirty or worn.

- Turkish hospitality demands that a guest be given the finest the household has to offer. You will be asked to sit in the best chair; you will be given the choicest cut at a meal. And if you use the bathroom, someone may offer you the finest guest towel in the house, stored away just for that occasion.

Dress

- Business dress is conservative: dark suits for men; suits and heels for women. However, Turkey is very hot in the summer, yet jackets and ties are rarely removed, even on the hottest days.
- Women's clothing may be comfortable but should remain modest; even in severe heat, necklines may not be low and skirts may not be short.
- Formal dress is required to attend the balls held at New Year's and on the Turkish national holiday (October 29). Men may need tuxedos; women may wear long gowns.
- Casual dress should also be modest. Shorts are appropriate only at seaside resorts. Jeans are acceptable for both men and women, but they should not be torn or frayed.

- Always wear clean socks in good repair. You will need to remove your shoes if you enter a mosque or if you are invited into a Turkish home.

Cultural Note

Should you enter a mosque, your clothing should be modest. Expect to leave your shoes at the door—one does not walk on mosque carpets in shoes. If you wish, you may rent slippers from an attendant at the mosque for a small fee. Pants are usually acceptable for women, but they are expected to cover their heads, shoulders, and arms. If your clothing is judged unacceptable, an attendant may offer you the loan of a long robe. A small donation to the mosque is always appreciated. Avoid visiting during prayer times or on Fridays (the Muslim holy day).

Ukraine

Local short form: Ukrayina
Former: Ukrainian National Republic, Ukrainian State,
Ukrainian Soviet Socialist Republic

Cultural Note

The name Ukraine *means "borderland," and Ukraine has often constituted the border of several empires. This also resulted in the use of the definite article before Ukraine. English speakers said "the Ukraine" just as they said "the Bronx" or "the Netherlands." Current usage omits the article; the country is now just "Ukraine" or "Republic of Ukraine."*

⊚ WHAT'S YOUR CULTURAL IQ?

1. TRUE or FALSE: The Cossacks are a legendary ancestral archetype to Christian Ukrainians, just as the Vikings are to the Scandinavians or cowboys are in the United States.
   ANSWER: TRUE. But they are not fondly remembered by Poles or Jewish Ukrainians, who were the victims of innumerable Cossack raids.

2. Which of the following cities was the capital of the first great civilization of Eastern Slavs?
   a. Kiev
   b. Moscow
   c. St. Petersburg
   ANSWER: a. Between the tenth and thirteenth centuries, Kievan Rus was the first great Eastern Slav city. A Russian proverb calls Moscow the heart of Russia, St. Petersburg its head, and Kiev its mother.

3. Match the following Ukrainian names with their identities:

   a. Taras Bulba   1. National poet; revived Ukrainian language

   b. Bogdan Chmielnicki   2. Mythic Cossack leader; Nikolai Gogol short story

   c. T. D. Lysenko   3. Cossack leader who incited revolt and pogroms

   d. Taras Shevchenko   4. Soviet agronomist; he persecuted scientists

ANSWERS: a. 2; b. 3; c. 4; d. 1

▶ TIPS ON DOING BUSINESS IN UKRAINE

- Ukraine has proven to be a difficult country in which to conduct business, due to corruption and constantly changing laws. In one case, a European firm tried to buy a building and turn it into a restaurant. After giving gifts to numerous officials, they had all the required permits; then the land commission of the local State Property Fund ruled that the original permits were invalid. These commissioners wanted to be bribed as well.

- Under communism, all faiths except the Russian Orthodox Church were repressed. Many houses of worship belonging to the Greek Catholic (a.k.a. Uniate) Church were seized and given to Russian Orthodox congregations. Government repression of indigenous religions ceased in 1989. Since then, many followers of the Greek Catholic Church have tried to reclaim their old churches from the Orthodox. This has led to hostility and occasional violence. If you are either Catholic or Orthodox, it might be wise to be reticent about your religion until you learn the beliefs of your Ukrainian associates.

- Ukraine has its share of cybercrime, concentrated in the theft of credit card and bank account information. The U.S. Federal Bureau of Investigation believed that the most skilled computer hackers in the world are concentrated in Ukraine and Russia.

▶ COUNTRY BACKGROUND

History

Slavic peoples populated Ukraine at least 2,000 years before Christ. Kiev, the capital, dates to about the eighth century A.D.—some four hundred years before Moscow. One of the oldest and most important of Slavic cities, Kiev is often considered the "mother" city of Ukraine, of the Russian Empire, and of the Slavic Orthodox churches.

Christianity came to Ukraine (and from there spread to Russia) when Prince Vladimir of Kiev was converted to Orthodoxy by Byzantine missionaries from Constantinople in A.D. 988.

Ukraine's flat, fertile expanses historically made it difficult to defend. The Mongols sacked Kiev in 1240, and from this point on, Moscow became the dominant Slav city. (Orthodox Russians see a progression of "holy cities of Orthodoxy," from Constantinople to Kiev to Moscow.)

Ukraine has been a prize coveted by many warring peoples. The Mongols were eventually driven back eastward, but other rulers took their place. The Lithuanians conquered Ukraine around 1392. When Lithuania and Poland merged in 1569, Polish influence became dominant. Under Polish rule, Ukrainian farmers were forced into serfdom.

Those who resisted began to band together and became known as Cossacks. They lived a harsh existence in frontier areas, and gave only nominal allegiance to the Polish king.

In the 1600s, Polish Jesuits began to impose Catholicism on the Ukrainians by force. This rallied the Orthodox Cossacks, and in 1648, the Cossacks drove the Poles out of part of Ukraine.

Fearing that their independent state was too weak to stand alone, the Cossacks requested that Moscow rule them in 1654. Moscow tightened its grip on the Ukrainians decade after decade, reducing the Cossacks' power and completing the process of enserfment.

In 1871, the first of the modern-day pogroms against Jews occurred in Odessa. After the assassination of Czar Alexander II in 1881, pogroms became more frequent and were unofficially sanctioned by the Czarist government.

In the First World War, the subsequent Russo-Polish War, and the Russian Civil War, armies under several flags decimated Ukraine. In 1918, Ukraine experienced its first, brief period of independence, but it was soon absorbed into the new Soviet Union.

Between the World Wars, Stalin decided to enforce collectivization upon Ukraine. Thousands of peasants who resisted were slain. The result was widespread famine. Millions of Ukrainians starved to death in what was called the "bread basket of Europe."

Ukraine suffered again in the Second World War. Axis armies from Nazi Germany and Romania advanced far into Ukraine. Although some Ukrainians saw the Germans as liberating them from the USSR, Nazi atrocities soon turned most Ukrainians against the Axis. Many Ukrainians were slain. More than 2 million Ukrainian Jews were killed: some shot in their homes, some gassed in concentration camps.

From the start of the First World War to the end of the Second World War, more than 5 million Ukrainians lost their lives—one in every six Ukrainians. This is a greater proportion than any other nation involved in the World Wars.

The breakup of the USSR in 1991 granted Ukraine its independence once more. Since independence, Ukraine has struggled to establish a democratic and capitalist society. The "Orange Revolution" of 2004 was a significant, peaceful event that resulted in a rerun of the election, and consequently, the swearing in of Viktor Yushchenko as president in January of 2005. (President Yushchenko had been poisoned with dioxins prior to the election and accused the former governmental authorities of the act.) The current government is seeking membership in the European Union and NATO.

Cultural Note

Although the true Cossacks were absorbed into the Ukrainian population long ago, the name "Cossack" has frequently been revived. Various groups called themselves Cossacks during the Russian Civil War. Today, some Ukrainian nationalist groups invoke the Cossack image.

Type of Government

Ukraine is a multiparty republic with a single legislative house, called the Supreme Council. The head of government is the prime minister. The president is the chief of state.

For current government data, check with the Embassy of Ukraine at *http://ukraineinfo.us.*

Language

The official language of Ukraine is Ukrainian. There are several dialects. Until recently, Ukrainians were taught Russian in school, so people may switch from Ukrainian to Russian in the same sentence. Many technical terms in Ukrainian have been borrowed from Russian.

Ukrainian is similar, but not identical, to Russian. Modern Ukrainian has Polish linguistic influences that are absent in Russian. Today, Ukrainian and Russian are about as close as Dutch and German. Although the languages are different, native speakers can manage some communication. (However, foreigners who learn Russian usually report that they cannot understand Ukrainian without study.)

The Ukrainian View

There is no official religion in Ukraine, but over 27 percent of the population identify themselves as Ukrainian Orthodox, with a Moscow patriarchate; and over 20 percent say they are Ukrainian Orthodox with a Kiev patriarchate.

About 13 percent of the population belong to the Greek Catholic or Uniat Church, a church that follows Byzantine Orthodox rituals but accepts the authority of the Roman Catholic pope.

Immediately after the breakup of the USSR, Ukraine wanted to join both the European Union and NATO, but both moves were strongly opposed by Russia. However, President Leonid Kuchma revised Ukraine's military doctrine in June of 2004, and the new doctrine states that Ukraine does not view any nation as its military adversary.

Historically, Ukraine was usually ruled by either Poland or Russia. Poland's control, or suzerainty, ended before the Second World War, long enough ago that most Ukrainians have no animosity toward Poland. On the other hand, ethnic Ukrainians may have strong feelings about Russia. For many, it is a love-hate relationship: Ukraine was under Moscow's brutal rule, but Ukraine was also the most favored of Russia's possessions. For some former Communist Ukrainians, life was better under the USSR.

Under communism, a coal miner in the Ukraine was paid more than a chemical researcher. Today, salaries echo Western patterns: unskilled labor is paid less than jobs that require college degrees. Ukrainian youth now want to postpone marriage and children in favor of education and careers, so it is expected that the birth rate in Ukraine will continue to decline.

☑ Know Before You Go

As of 1997, Ukraine requires all visitors to obtain mandatory health insurance from the state. The cost varies depending upon the anticipated length of stay, but is generally modest. This insurance only covers medical care inside Ukraine. It does not cover the cost of medical evacuation.

Most travelers to Ukraine encounter no problems, despite a higher rate of street crime than in most Western European countries. Ukraine does have organized crime and computer hackers, but the majority of travelers are not affected by them.

The U.S. State Department has periodically recommended that visitors to Ukraine refrain from using bank or credit cards because of identity theft.

If you travel to Ukraine with young children, bring extra proof of your parenthood. Ukrainians are sensitive about foreigners (especially North Americans) coming to Ukraine to adopt Ukrainian children. They have initiated procedures at entry and exit points designed to prevent illegal adoptions.

There is still residual radiation from the Chernobyl nuclear accident in Ukraine. However, this is a problem throughout the region. Some studies assert that most of the Chernobyl radiation was blown into Belarus. And, recently, dozens of radioactive hot spots were found around Moscow itself, from badly stored nuclear waste and decades-old experiments.

▶ CULTURAL ORIENTATION

Cognitive Styles: How Ukrainians Organize and Process Information

Ukrainians have traditionally maintained freedom of discussion and have been open to outside information. At the same time, they hold to their beliefs strongly and are quick to confront. Ukrainians have excelled in the sciences, and higher education teaches abstractive and conceptual thought. However, their emotions bind them to the associative and the particular.

Negotiation Strategies: What Ukrainians Accept as Evidence

Ukrainians usually rely on the accumulation of objective facts. However, their ability to reason analytically and objectively is often influenced by subjective feelings.

Value Systems: The Basis for Behavior

The Ukrainian culture is one of contrasting value systems—Ukrainians are deeply idealistic, but just as deeply attached to the personal and subjective. The following three sections identify the Value Systems in the predominant culture—their methods of dividing right from wrong, good from evil, and so forth.

Locus of Decision-Making

To Ukrainians, the individual is the primary unit for decision-making. He or she may be so independent that it is difficult to reach a consensus. Ukrainians tend to repudiate all forms of communal life that call for strict obedience. Decisions are not fixed on objective reality, but on idealistic viewpoints containing many elements. Ukrainians tend to confront reality with emotion, make decisions on the spur of the moment, and intermix theoretical and practical issues.

Sources of Anxiety Reduction

With the Communist Party no longer in control, religion is regaining its importance as the focal point for external structure and stability. Ukrainians are deeply religious but not fundamentalist;

they look for ways to comprehend the essence of a creed rather than being fixated on dogma. Strong family ties help to ease the feelings of uncertainty. However, since feelings generally take precedence over reason, a person may go from deep love to great hatred or from great enthusiasm to deep despair in a short time. Thus, the system may not seem to be in a stable condition.

Issues of Equality/Inequality

Ukrainians possess strong moral courage. They have a desire for harmony and an inclination to compromise and tolerate differences. Poetic by nature, they associate love not with eroticism but with a more philosophical, maternal love. There is a genuine softness of character that is expressed in politeness and high regard for the female sex. Women are considered the moral leaders of the nation.

▶ BUSINESS PRACTICES

Punctuality, Appointments, and Local Time

- Always be punctual, but do not be surprised if Ukrainians are not. It is not unusual for Ukrainians to be an hour late to an appointment.
- Punctuality was not considered essential under the Soviet system, since employment was guaranteed and no one could be fired for tardiness. Although this has changed, punctuality is still the exception rather than the rule.
- Even today, patience, not punctuality, is considered a virtue in Ukraine.
- Allow plenty of time for each appointment. Not only may they start late, but they may run two to three times longer than originally planned.
- The residents of Ukraine, like most Europeans, write the day first, then the month, then the year. (For example, December 3, 2010, is written 3.12.10 or 3/12/10.) For some reason, a number of U.S. travelers have incorrectly read the date on their Ukrainian visas and have encountered difficulty entering or exiting the country.

- Obtaining an appointment can be a laborious process. Be patient and persistent. Once you have booked the appointment, make every effort to keep it.
- Ukraine is in the westernmost time zone of the CIS, three hours ahead of Greenwich Mean Time (G.M.T. + 3). This is eight hours ahead of U.S. Eastern Standard Time (E.S.T. + 8).

Negotiating
- Be factual and include technical details.
- Until you have a signed agreement, do not get overconfident about the deal at hand. Never expect that you can renegotiate later, either; the existing contract may be as advantageous as you will ever get.
- Never accept the first "no" as an answer. "No" is a quick and automatic response. Remain pleasant, try to establish a personal rapport, and ask again in a different way.
- "Final offers" are never final during initial negotiations. Be prepared to wait; the offer may be made more attractive if you can just hold out.
- Ukrainians may make dire proclamations that the deal is off during negotiations. Be prepared to play hardball.
- Haste always puts you at a disadvantage. If you give the impression that you cannot wait out your counterpart, you will inevitably lose.
- North Americans view negotiation as an exercise in compromise. However, the traditional Ukrainian view is that compromise equals weakness. If they can avoid compromising, they will. To yield on even an insignificant matter is something to be avoided.
- Ukrainian negotiators tend to speak with one voice. Foreign negotiators need to be in agreement among themselves and present a unified front.
- Ukrainians are fairly status conscious. They will probably have several people at any negotiation. They prefer you to have an executive whose rank is equivalent to that of their top negotiator at the discussions. A lone foreign executive in a room with a team of Ukrainians will have a difficult time.

- Include a clause requiring the joint venture partners to submit to arbitration in a neutral country if they can't come to an agreement. Sweden is the most popular choice for third-country arbitration.
- Ukrainian regulations represent the biggest liability to a successful joint venture. Since these regulations are in constant flux (reforms are being made all the time), don't count on your partner to have a full grasp of the legal issues involved. Get your own expert on Ukrainian law. Don't be surprised if the way you did something yesterday isn't permitted tomorrow; many laws are nebulous, and their interpretation is subject to change.
- Traits that many Ukrainians and North Americans have in common include a respect for nature and the outdoors, a fascination with technology and gadgets, and a tendency toward building things "big." All of these make good topics for conversation.
- Receiving a positive response from Ukrainians usually requires groundwork. Before making a decision, the bureaucrat should know who you are, what you want, what your project is, and which other bureaucrats have agreed to it so far. This information is best communicated through a third person, but e-mail or a letter will sometimes serve.

Cultural Note

While Ukrainians will criticize many aspects of life in Ukraine, they feel that only they have the right to do so. They quickly become defensive in the face of any criticism by a foreigner.

Business Entertaining

- In relation to other countries, dinner tends to be eaten early, around 6:00 P.M.
- Business success in Ukraine hinges upon establishing a personal rapport with your Ukrainian partners. Much of this will develop out of social events.
- Ukrainian restaurants historically had poor service and menus that did not reflect the dishes that were actually available. Today, Ukraine has restaurants which meet any international standards.

- Traditional Ukrainian restaurants had large tables set for many people. In such an establishment, if your party consisted of just two or three, you may have had to share a table with other people. Now, you will be able to reserve a table, or room, for your party.
- Two bottles will be on the table: one has water, the other has vodka. The vodka will not have a resealable lid—once it is opened, Ukrainians expect your party to drink it all.
- Ukrainians do most of their entertaining of foreigners in restaurants. Consider it an honor to be invited into a Ukrainian home.
- Ukrainians do not feel obligated to phone before dropping by a friend's house. Once you have established true friendship, a Ukrainian may stop by at any time—even late at night if a light is visible in your window.
- Guests are always offered food and drink (usually alcohol).
- Expect to do a lot of drinking.
- In a restaurant or nightclub, Ukrainians may invite you to dance or to come over to their table.
- Good topics of conversation include sports and music.

▶ PROTOCOL

Greetings
- Ukraine is home to several ethnic groups, notably Ukrainians, ethnic Russians, Belarussians, Moldavians, and Poles. While each group has its own cultural traditions, their similarities are greater than their differences.
- Throughout Ukraine, men shake hands with other men upon meeting and leaving.
- Allow women to take the initiative on handshaking.
- Although ethnic Ukrainians are generally less inhibited than Russians, both cultures can be rather dour and sedate in public. Smiles are reserved for close friends.
- Only during greetings do Ukrainians and Russians display affection in public. Relatives and good friends will engage in a noisy embrace and kiss each other on the cheeks.

- Ukrainians and Russians often greet a stranger by shaking hands and stating their name, rather than uttering a polite phrase (such as "How do you do?"). Respond in the same way.

Titles/Forms of Address

- Ukrainian and Russian names are listed in the same order as in the West, but the middle name is a patronymic (a name derived from the first name of one's father). Thus, Fyodor Nikolaievich Medvedev's first name is Fyodor (a Slavic version of Theodore), his last name is Medvedev, and his middle name means "son of Nikolai."

- Ukrainian and Russian women traditionally add the letter a on the end of their surnames; Medvedev's wife would be Mrs. Medvedeva.

- The variety of Russian names (both first and last) is quite limited. Ethnic Ukrainian names have somewhat more variety; surnames ending in -enko are characteristically Ukrainian. Even so, it can be difficult to track down a person in Ukraine by a name alone. Additional data, such as birth date and place of birth, is often necessary.

- Unless invited to do so, do not use first names. Call Ukrainians and Russians by their surname preceded by "Mr.," "Miss," "Mrs.," or "Ms." If they have a professional title (e.g., Doctor), use their title followed by their surname.

- It is considered quite respectable to address friends, even elders, by their first names and patronymics, although many foreigners find this to be quite a mouthful. Do not be surprised to be asked about your father's first name, and to have that name scrambled into an unrecognizable patronymic.

- Among themselves, Ukrainians and Russians use a bewildering variety of diminutives and nicknames. As you establish a relationship with them, you may be invited to call them by a nickname or just their first name. Be sure to return the favor.

Gestures

- Ukrainians and Russians stand about one arm's length away from each other when conversing.
- The "thumbs-up" gesture indicates approval.
- The "fig" gesture—a clenched fist with the thumb protruding between the knuckles of the index and middle fingers—means "nothing" or "you will get nothing" in Ukraine. It is definitely not considered obscene, as it is in the Mediterranean. Indeed, a Ukrainian parent may use this gesture to his or her own child to indicate that the child cannot have something.
- When going to your seat in a Ukrainian theater, it is very impolite to squeeze in front of seated patrons with your back to them. Always face seated people as you move past them.

Gifts

- Good gift ideas include cigarette lighters, watches, currently popular electronics (like iPods) and thermos-type products (Ukrainians like to take food and drink with them on trips).
- If you are invited to a Ukrainian home, try to bring flowers, liquor, or a gourmet food item.
- Hard liquors that are easily available in Ukraine are vodka, champagne, cognac, and a Ukrainian honey-based cordial.

Dress

- While parts of Ukraine are quite cold in the winter, the country is generally warmer than Russia. In fact, the Ukrainian Crimea, which can be comfortable even in winter, was the major vacation area for all of the USSR.
- If you go to Ukraine during the winter, bring warm clothes or buy Russian-style hats and gloves upon arrival. In addition, bring a pair of shoes or boots with skid-resistant soles.
- Ukrainian buildings are usually well heated, so a layered approach is best in clothing, allowing you to take off clothes to be comfortable while inside.
- Business dress is conservative. Ukrainian clothing styles are not generally driven by the latest fashions in the West.

United Kingdom

*United Kingdom of Great Britain
and Northern Ireland*
Abbreviation: UK

Cultural Note

England is only one part of the entity known as "the United Kingdom of Great Britain and Northern Ireland." Most of the United Kingdom's international business is conducted through England. Nevertheless, it is useful to know the following nomenclature:

- Britain refers to the island on which England, Wales, and Scotland are located. Although the English are in the habit of referring to all natives of Britain as "Brits," this term is not appreciated by many Welsh, Irish, and Scots.

- Northern Ireland shares the island of Eire with the Republic of Ireland. It is both incorrect and insulting to call someone from Eire a "Brit."

- Each of the four constituent parts of the United Kingdom (England, Wales, Scotland, and Northern Ireland) has a distinct history, culture, and ancestral language. There are also separatist pressures pulling each of these regions apart, and you must be sensitive to the individual ethnic heritage of your associates.

▶ WHAT'S YOUR CULTURAL IQ?

1. The Magna Carta is remembered as the first document delineating the rights of the English. TRUE or FALSE: King John I only signed the Magna Carta under duress.
   ANSWER: TRUE. In fact, John repudiated the agreement just months later. But he was then dethroned by the nobles, who forced successive monarchs to respect the document.

2. After King Charles I was executed in 1649, Oliver Cromwell led England for nearly a decade. Which of the following did not occur under Cromwell's busy rule?
   a. Scotland was brutally suppressed.

293

   b. Ireland was brutally suppressed.
   c. The Spanish Armada was defeated as it was about to invade England.
   d. England went to war against the Netherlands.

   ANSWER: c. The famous defeat of the Spanish Armada occurred in 1558, long before Cromwell became Lord Protector. However, the English fleet did battle a Spanish fleet during Cromwell's reign.

3. Sir Winston Churchill (1874–1965) inspired the allies with his oratory during WWII. In which of the following wars was he not actively involved?
   a. The Crimean War
   b. The Boer War
   c. WWI
   d. WWII
   e. The Korean War

   ANSWER: a. Young Sir Winston was a war correspondent during the Boer War, and was in the government—either in Parliament or as prime minister, during all or part of World Wars I, II, and the Korean War. He wasn't born until after the Crimean War of 1854–56.

▶ TIPS ON DOING BUSINESS IN THE UNITED KINGDOM

- The United Kingdom does not consider itself part of Europe—although it appreciates the economics of the European Union. Its first overture to join the European Economic Community in 1961 was vetoed by President Charles de Gaulle of France. The United Kingdom subsequently joined in 1973, but it still debates whether or not to adopt the euro.
- Rapid change is not embraced wholeheartedly by most English. Traditional ways are valued, and the class system still has an impact on lifestyles.
- Perhaps the biggest change relates to wealth; today, members of the aristocracy are not necessarily the wealthiest people in England. Successful entrepreneurs come from all backgrounds, and many younger citizens are focused on future opportunities—rather than the past glories of the British Empire.

Cultural Note

The English are tremendous sports fans. Football (soccer) is a national obsession, and millions of pounds are waged on important games. Other popular sports include horseracing, rugby, cricket, and golf.

▶ COUNTRY BACKGROUND

History

Britain was first brought into contact with the world when it was invaded by Rome in the first century B.C. Rome ruled much of the region until the fifth century A.D. Various tribes from Europe and Scandinavia—the Angles, Saxons, and Jutes—invaded after the Romans departed.

In 1066, the Normans invaded from France. This event, the Battle of Hastings, was the last successful invasion of Britain. The Normans transformed the region, making it a feudal kingdom.

Britain was frequently at war with continental powers over the next several centuries. Because it is an island, Britain had a tremendous defensive advantage. They realized they needed a strong navy to protect themselves, and this navy made the British Empire possible.

Great Britain was the strongest of the European powers in the nineteenth century, with many territories abroad. The Industrial Revolution first arose on British soil.

In 1926, the United Kingdom granted autonomy to New Zealand, Australia, and Canada; later in this century, it granted independence to India, Egypt, and its African colonies.

The First and Second World Wars caused great hardship for the United Kingdom; the First World War marked the end of the Victorian way of life. The Second World War ushered in the dismantling of the British Empire. After the war, many sectors of the British economy were nationalized. Britain did not fully recover from the destruction of WW II until the 1960s.

During the 1980s, Conservative prime minister Margaret Thatcher privatized many services, undoing some of the postwar nationalization policies.

In 1997, Tony Blair was elected prime minister, and the Labour Party assumed power in government once again. He was re-elected in 2001, and strongly supported the U.S. campaign against terrorism. Controversy surrounded him as he joined the United States of America in launching attacks against Iraq without UN approval.

Great Britain's devolution of powers has continued over the last decade. The Scottish Parliament in Edinburgh opened in 1999, as did the National Assembly for Wales in Cardiff.

Type of Government

England is a constitutional monarchy. Its constitution is unwritten, and consists partly of statutes and partly of common law and practice. In its equivalent to the U.S. government's executive branch, the monarch is the chief of state, while the prime minister is the head of government. In practice, it is the Cabinet (selected from Parliament by the prime minister) that has power, rather than the monarch. The prime minister is the leader of the majority party in the House of Commons. The Parliament consists of the House of Commons and the House of Lords, with the Commons having more real power. The Commons is elected by universal suffrage every five years, although the prime minister may ask the monarch to dissolve Parliament and call for new elections at any time. Unlike the U.S. Supreme Court, the English judiciary cannot review the constitutionality of legislation.

For current government data, check with the Embassy at *www .britainusa.com.*

Language

In all its varieties, dialects, and accents, "the Queen's English" has had an immense influence on the languages of the world. While there is a "Standard Oxbridge" or "BBC English accent" that most foreigners recognize, there are a multitude of dialects as well. Just ten minutes outside of London, pronunciations begin to change.

In the United Kingdom overall, Welsh is spoken by about 26 percent of the population of Wales, and a Scottish form of Gaelic is used by approximately 60,000 people in Scotland.

The British View

England has an official religion—the Anglican Church, or Church of England. Most English belong to this church, which was founded when King Henry VIII decided to split from the Roman Catholic Church during his reign. The Church no longer has political power. Other religions represented in England are Roman Catholicism, Islam, Methodism, Hinduism, Sikhism, and Judaism. Religion is considered to be a very private subject. Scotland also has an official religion, the Church of Scotland. However, Wales and Northern Ireland do not have official religions.

Britain boasts some of the finest educational institutions in the world. A large portion of tax revenue is spent on the educational system. Schooling is free and compulsory from age five to age sixteen. Literacy is 99 percent, and school attendance is almost 100 percent. There are more than forty universities in the United Kingdom, and many professional schools.

The stoic English "stiff upper lip" has changed in the last few decades. In some circles, the concept of personal responsibility for one's actions has morphed into a predilection for blaming someone else for life's problems, and seeking damages. The tabloids are calling it a "compensation culture"—and lawsuits for everything from personal injury to tenuous negligence claims are becoming more common. On the other hand, some believe that the change from the long-suffering English consumer to a more assertive comparison shopper is a positive development.

☑ Know Before You Go

The weather in England is generally less than balmy. More than half of the days are overcast, and it is subject to winter windstorms and floods. When a true warm spell occurs, the English suffer, because air-conditioning units are not ubiquitous. (However, more and more businesses now have air conditioning.)

Be aware there may be difficulties in rail transportation.

England has some territorial disputes—one with Spain over Gibraltar, another with Argentina over the Falkland Islands (Islas Malvinas), and several more.

▶ CULTURAL ORIENTATION

Cognitive Styles: How the English Organize and Process Information

(Note: we have included the predominant ethnic population for the United Kingdom in this section. Please be aware there is variation within other cultures of the United Kingdom.)

The English are somewhat closed to outside information on many issues. They will participate in debate but are not easily moved from their perspective. They are quite analytical and process information in an abstractive manner. They will appeal to laws or rules rather than looking at problems in a subjective manner. There is a conceptual sense of fairness—unwritten, as is the constitution—but no less vital. Company policy is followed regardless of who is doing the negotiating.

Negotiation Strategies: What the English Accept as Evidence

Objective facts are the only valid source of truth. Little credence is given to the feelings one has about an issue. Faith in few if any ideologies will influence decisions. They are the masters of understatement.

Value Systems: The Basis for Behavior

The usefulness of a monarchy is being questioned more seriously because of the expense of financing it. The following three sections identify the Value Systems in the predominant culture—their methods of dividing right from wrong, good from evil, and so forth.

Locus of Decision-Making

The English are highly individualistic, taking responsibility for their decisions, but always within the framework of the family, group, or organization. Individual initiative and achievement are emphasized, resulting in strong individual leadership. They do not find it difficult to say "no"; however, the English "no" is often communicated in a polite and somewhat subtle manner. The individual has a right to his or her private life, and this should not be discussed in business negotiations. Friendships are few and specific to their needs.

Sources of Anxiety Reduction

There are established rules for everything, and this gives a sense of stability to life. Well-entrenched external structures (law, government, organizations) help to insulate them from life. The English are very time oriented, and they are anxious about deadlines and results. However, many do not display their anxiety; traditionally emotions are not shown in public.

Habits are changing, though. The stalwart, emotionless "stiff upper lip" is seen less among the younger generation. And these habits are relative. By the standards of the optimistic entrepreneurs of the United States, the English are slow to take risks. But by the standards of the severe, conservative Slavs, the English are foolhardy risk-takers. In fact, the English take risks at about the same rate as many Europeans.

Issues of Equality/Inequality

There is an inherent trust in the roles people play (but not necessarily in the people) within the social or business system, and a strong feeling of the interdependency of these roles. There are necessarily inequalities in these roles, but the people are supposed to be guaranteed equality under the law. There is some bias against ethnic groups. There is a high need for success, and decisions are made slowly and deliberately. Women have a great deal of equality in both pay and power.

▶ BUSINESS PRACTICES

Punctuality, Appointments, and Local Time

- Always be punctual. In London, traffic can make this difficult, so allow plenty of time to get to your appointments.
- Schedule your visits at least a few days ahead of time, and then confirm your appointment upon your arrival in the United Kingdom.

- There is no designated national holiday in England; however, there are several weeks of official holidays in the United Kingdom—(including several bank holidays).
- The English are on Greenwich Mean Time, (obviously, since the Prime Meridian runs right through Greenwich), which is five hours ahead of U.S. Eastern Standard Time (E.S.T. + 5).

Cultural Note
An oral agreement is considered binding, followed by written confirmation; only major agreements will require legal procedures.

Be discreet when you suggest contacting an attorney (called a "solicitor" in the United Kingdom).

Negotiating
- The best way to make contact with senior executives is through a third party.
- It is not appropriate to have this same third party intervene later if problems arise.
- The hierarchy in business is as follows: the managing director (CEO in the United States), the director (corporate vice president to U.S. executives), the divisional officers, the deputy directors, and, finally, the managers.
- Sometimes a secretary will introduce you to the executive; otherwise, introduce yourself.
- Businesspeople are normally more interested in short-term results than in the long-term future.
- Change is not necessarily a good thing to the British.
- The British do not often reveal excitement or other emotions; try to keep yours restrained as well. They also traditionally underplay dangerous situations.
- Similarly, they refrain from extravagant claims about products or plans.
- Some British executives stereotype U.S. businesspeople as condescending; to be safe, make every effort to avoid this impression.
- Avoid the hard sell.

- Do not rush the British toward a decision.
- Allow the British executive to suggest that the meeting has finished, then do not prolong your exit.
- Exchanging business cards is common, because of the necessity of e-mail addresses, cell phone numbers, etc.
- While U.S. executives are known for being direct, the British are even more so. Don't be offended if there's no hedging about whether your suggestion is good or not.
- It is wise to send your senior executives to the United Kingdom, as they may be received with more respect, and are usually more restrained in conduct.
- The British do not consider themselves European. This is vital when discussing issues regarding the European Union.
- Do not ask the typical U.S. conversation starter "What do you do?" because the British feel it is too personal. Avoid other personal questions as well, even "What part of the United Kingdom are you from?"
- In general, try to avoid interrogating your British contacts. They feel that excessive questions are intrusive.
- Avoid controversial topics such as politics or religion, and do not discuss comparative work ethics.
- Speak in complete sentences. Many U.S. executives have a habit of starting a sentence and then allowing it to trail off without ever completing the thought. This is a good way to provoke . . . (annoying, isn't it?).
- While the British are often self-critical, visitors should avoid joining in any criticisms—simply listen. Similarly, if they share their complaints with you, do not participate.
- The British apologize often, for even small inconveniences. They also have a habit of adding a question to the end of a sentence; for example: "It's a lovely day, don't you think?"

Business Entertaining
- Business breakfasts in hotels are becoming more common, and are changing to a more Continental style—from the very large traditional breakfasts of eggs, bacon, sausage, kippers, etc.

- Lunch is generally between noon and 2:00 P.M.
- A business lunch will often be conducted in a pub and will be a light meal.
- Legislation to ban smoking in English pubs and private clubs was passed in 2006. A similar vote passed in Scotland, Northern Ireland, and the Republic of Ireland. This means that the traditional thick layer of smoke in pubs will be one more English tradition left by the wayside.
- With senior executives, lunch will be eaten in the best restaurants or in the executive dining room.
- Dinner is generally from 7:00 to 11:00 P.M. in most restaurants.
- When you go out after hours, do not bring up the subject of work unless your British associates do—otherwise, you will be considered a bore.
- Most business entertaining is done in restaurants and pubs rather than at home.
- If you do smoke, always offer the cigarettes around to others before taking one for yourself.
- It is not polite to toast those who are older or more senior than you.
- If you are the guest, you must initiate your departure, as your hosts will not indicate that they wish the evening to come to an end.
- Do not invite a business associate out until you know him or her fairly well (or after twenty years, whichever comes first).
- When inviting the English out, it is best to include people of the same background and professional level in the invitation.
- When you are the host, be sure to offer the seat of honor to the most senior person. He or she may decline, offering it to you as host; accept it graciously.
- The English hold their forks in their left hands and their knives in the right.
- When passing items around the table, pass them to the left.
- Always keep your hands above the table (but no elbows on the table!).
- The knife above your plate is used for butter.

- When dining out, it is not considered polite to inquire about the food you see around you.
- Likewise, you should not ask to sample the dishes of others.
- In general, maintain very proper manners.
- Animals are usually a good topic of conversation.
- Do not make jokes about the royal family.
- It is not good form to discuss one's genealogy.
- The English are only beginning to be concerned about diet and health; don't press your views on this matter. However, vegetarianism is popular, especially among women.

▶ PROTOCOL

Greetings
- A handshake is standard for business occasions and when visiting a home.
- Women do not always shake hands.
- When introduced, say "How do you do?" instead of "Nice to meet you." The question is rhetorical.

Titles/Forms of Address
- Business titles are not used in conversation.
- Find out the honorary titles of anyone you will be in contact with, and use them no matter how familiar you are with the person.
- Doctors, clergy, and so forth are addressed by title plus last name; however, surgeons are addressed as "Mr.," "Mrs.," or "Miss."
- Rather than "sir," you should use the title of the person you are addressing (i.e., "Yes, Minister," and not "Yes, sir").
- The use of first names is becoming more common. However, you should follow the initiative of your host.
- Avoid repeating the other person's name often during the conversation. This is generally viewed as an inane sales technique.

Gestures
- It is considered impolite to talk with your hands in your pockets.
- The British often do not look at the other person while they talk.

- In business, a light handshake is standard.
- When visiting a home, a handshake is proper; however, a handshake is not always correct at social occasions. Observe what others do.
- Don't point with your fingers, but instead indicate something with your head.
- Sitting with your ankle resting on your knee may be seen as impolite.
- If you give the "victory" sign (a V with two fingers), do so with the palm facing outward. If you reverse the sign, the deal is over.
- Tapping your nose means confidentiality, or a secret.
- It is inappropriate to touch others in public; even backslapping or putting an arm around the shoulders of another can make the English uncomfortable.
- In addition, the English maintain a wide physical space between conversation partners.
- Avoid excessive hand gestures when speaking.
- Men may give their seats to women on crowded public transportation.

Gifts
- Gifts are not part of doing business in England.
- Rather than giving gifts, it is preferable to invite your hosts out for a meal or a show.
- In a pub, never miss your turn to "shout for a round" (buy everyone a drink) in your party.
- When you are invited to an English home, you may bring flowers (not white lilies, which signify death), liquor or champagne, and chocolates. Send a brief, handwritten thank-you note promptly afterward, preferably by mail or e-mail—not by messenger.
- When bringing flowers, consult with the florist about the appropriate type and number.
- Be cautious in making purchases, as there is usually no refund or exchange policy.

Dress

- Conservative dress is very important.
- Men in executive positions still generally wear laced shoes, not loafers.
- Men's shirts should not have pockets; if they do, the pockets should be empty.
- Men should not wear striped ties; the British "regimentals" are striped, and yours may look like an imitation.
- Men's clothes should be of excellent quality, but they do not necessarily have to look new. Well-broken-in clothes are acceptable.
- Avoid plaid trousers, or any loud attire.
- Women should also dress conservatively.
- Avoid draping your camera around your neck, and ask permission if you intend on taking a picture. If it is digital (even a cell phone), show them the picture immediately afterward, and delete it if they so desire.

Why Learn a Foreign Language?

Throughout Europe, Asia, and much of the world, business travelers are frequently multilingual. Their study of foreign languages begins in primary school, and often continues far into adulthood. Why do they study so hard to learn an unfamiliar tongue?

U.S. executives generally assume that foreigners learn English because it is the universal language of business. English has commonly predominated in business transactions for years, but that does not explain why German, Japanese, and Finnish executives expend substantial time and effort to learn Spanish, Mandarin, or Tamil.

The reason these business travelers study is to expand their trade in areas of the world such as Europe, Latin America, Asia, and the Indian subcontinent. And they understand that, in much of the world, business is built upon relationships. Speaking with prospects in their own language demonstrates a great deal of respect for that culture—it establishes a level of credibility for that executive, it builds trust, and it bridges the cultural gap.

Furthermore, many international executives are exceedingly self-reliant. They do not like depending upon interpreters. They resent missing out on various aspects of conversations, and they want clients to look at them—not the interpreters. So, frequent flyers from France, Austria, and Korea dedicate years to learning languages. And their clients respond.

Learning a country's language—and its regional dialects, accents, and vocabulary—gives one a deeper understanding of its culture. For example, when several French businessmen who had spoken perfect "British English" for twenty years were given new assignments in the Midwestern region of the United States, they started taking customized courses in "American-style English." Why? Because their Midwestern bosses thought that their English was "too Euro." Their "American English" training included television shows that reflected current U.S. cultural styles—like *The Apprentice*. It also taught them how to communicate in sound bites, write in bullet format, and pepper their communications with sports analogies. Just like their American bosses.

But what if you do not have a background in languages, and want to begin learning the most widely spoken language on earth—Mandarin? Numerous multinationals now realize they will require employees who are fluent in Mandarin, and they are initiating programs to build their own multilingual work forces.

Bettina Anagnostopoulos, Manager of Language Projects at Cartus (*www.cartus.com*), has been involved in this process for years. Recently she helped design a "Seven Level Mandarin" program at a corporate university in California. The training is not just for "high potentials" who are being considered for assignments in China, but also for non-traveling virtual team members, business travelers, and others who may be offered Asian assignments in the future. The program includes various courses, from "Beginner Chinese for Heritage Learners" (these are employees with Chinese parents, or those who grew up in China), to "Advanced Business Chinese," which includes accent modification for Chinese-Americans who need to adjust their pronunciation and inflections in order to communicate effectively with native Chinese. One interesting aspect of the "sustained training" that Cartus recommends is that it must be stimulating enough to motivate learners beyond their second or third year. The program integrates "Cultural Mentors" (or coaches) with language teachers, electronic training, videos, music, podcasts, and other personalized learning methods.

Of course, the best option for absorbing a language is still a formal educational program, starting at a young age. The United States is slowly catching on to the importance of teaching Chinese in public schools, and hopefully will soon follow programs like one beginning in Seattle, Washington, which has a twelve-year curriculum in Mandarin.

Besides formal educational programs and corporate training resources, you can find scores of language and translation options on the Web. A search on "foreign phrases" or "foreign language learning" will generate any number of products. As a start, try the British Broadcasting Corporation's Web site for languages at *www.bbc.co.uk/languages*. Other links for foreign language programs and translation systems are available at *www.kissboworshakehands.com*.

Considering the kinetics of world demographics, English may not be the sole language of business in the decades to come. Be ahead of the curve, and buon viaggio!

"Una persona que habla dos lenguas vale dos personas."
Translation: A person who speaks two languages is worth two people.
—SPANISH PROVERB

Appendix B

Contacts and Resources

Because of the dynamic nature of travel warnings, customs requirements, and so on, this section directs you to several large Web sites that provide broad-based, helpful data for international travelers. While every country has its own respective requirements, the U.S. Web sites included here are a reasonable start for international business contacts, travel advisories, medical information, passports, etc.

Government Sites

Make it a practice to contact your country's embassy when you travel, as it can prove helpful in emergency situations. Many embassies now allow registration of your information online.

Embassies can arrange appointments with local business and government officials; provide counsel on local trade regulations, laws, and customs; and identify importers, buyers, agents, etc. They may also provide economic, political, technological, and labor data. There are many lists of embassies on the Web, such as *http://usembassy .state.gov*. Other helpful government sites include:

www.state.gov/travel
Provides:
- Travel warnings, consular information sheets, and public announcements
- Passports and visas for U.S. citizens
- Country background notes
- Foreign consular offices in the United States
- Key officers at U.S. foreign service posts

www.customs.ustreas.gov
Produces a database that can be queried by topic, (e.g., travel requirements, importing procedures, etc.), or an individual's status (e.g., importer, traveler, carrier, etc.).

www.cia.gov
The U.S. Central Intelligence Agency produces several documents of note for global travelers. These include:

- The World Factbook (at *www.cia.gov/cia/publications/factbook*)
- An online directory called "The Chiefs of State and Cabinet Members of Foreign Governments," available at *www.cia.gov/cia/publications/chiefs/index.html*. This directory is updated weekly and includes many governments of the world, including some with which the United States of America has no diplomatic exchanges, and which are not officially recognized.

Corruption and Bribery

www.transparency.org
Transparency International, a worldwide nongovernmental organization, reports on corruption and bribery around the world. They issue an annual "Corruption Perceptions Index," which relates to perceptions of the degree of corruption as seen by businesspeople, academics, and risk analysts. In the "2005 Corruption Perceptions Index," the five least corrupt countries out of 158 were Iceland (number 1), Finland, New Zealand, Denmark, and Singapore. The five most highly corrupt were Haiti, Myanmar, Turkmenistan, Bangladesh, and Chad (number 158).

Medical Information

www.cdc.gov/travel
The Centers for Disease Control provides an abundance of medical resources for international travelers. It includes everything from health information and vaccinations required for specific destinations, to advice on traveling with children and pets.

Of course, you will want to be thoroughly prepared for your trip, so schedule physical and dental examinations well before leaving. Remember that some vaccinations must be given over a period of time. Also take current medical documentation with you, and list any chronic conditions and current prescription drugs (including dosages). In order to avoid problems at customs, carry all medications in their original containers. Also, take an extra set of glasses, contacts, or prescriptions. In your bags, include the name, address, and phone number of someone to be contacted in case of an emergency.

Prepare a basic medical travel kit, which might include aspirin, a topical antibiotic, bandages, a disinfectant, 0.5 percent hydrocortisone cream (for bites or sunburn), sunblock, a thermometer, and diarrhea medication. Pack the kit in your carry-on luggage.

Also confirm that you have sufficient travel medical insurance. There are two main types of travel insurance: 1) policies that make direct payments for medical care and provide assistance, and 2) policies that reimburse you for emergency expenses. (With the latter option, you might have to pay the doctor or hospital immediately—in local currency—and file a claim once you return home.)

While we do not endorse any specific organizations, the Bureau of Consular Affairs maintains an extensive list of Travel Insurance Companies, as well as Air Ambulance, Med-Evac companies, and Executive Medical Services. A list of these firms is available at *http://travel.state.gov/travel/tips/health/health_1185.html.*

INDEX